Assessment for Social Justice

Also available from Bloomsbury

Assessment for Social Justice

Perspectives and Practices within Higher Education

Jan McArthur

BLOOMSBURY ACADEMIC
LONDON • NEW YORK • OXFORD • NEW DELHI • SYDNEY

BLOOMSBURY ACADEMIC
Bloomsbury Publishing Plc
50 Bedford Square, London, WC1B 3DP, UK

BLOOMSBURY, BLOOMSBURY ACADEMIC and the Diana logo are trademarks of
Bloomsbury Publishing Plc

First published in Great Britain 2018

ISBN: HB: 978-1-4742-3606-5
ePDF: 978-1-4742-3605-8
ePub: 978-1-4742-3607-2

Typeset by Newgen KnowledgeWorks Pvt. Ltd., Chennai, India
Printed and bound in Great Britain

To find out more about our authors and books visit www.bloomsbury.com
and sign up for our newsletters.

Contents

Acknowledgements

I could not have written this without the inspiration and support of my colleagues in the Department of Educational Research at Lancaster University, UK. In particular, I need to thank Paul Ashwin, Sue Cranmer, Ann-Marie Houghton, Carolyn Jackson, Rebecca Marsden, Murray Saunders, Paul Trowler, Jo Warin and, finally, Steve Dempster who sadly passed away during the final stages of writing this book, and who was an academic inspiration and a wonderful friend. The first time I used the expression *assessment for social justice* was during the job interview for the post I currently hold – so it has a special significance for me and evokes the happy professional life I enjoy in this extraordinary department. Special thanks go to my friend and colleague Mark Huxham from Edinburgh Napier University. His name features many times in this text as he has inspired my thinking and walked with me exploring issues of social justice, assessment and feedback. I also remain grateful for the influence of Dai Hounsell and Jenny Hounsell, who shaped and nurtured my initial interest in assessment. I owe a special debt of gratitude to Gwyneth Hughes of the UCL Institute of Education who provided extremely useful feedback on an earlier draft of this book. Many thanks to Ally, Camilla and Maria Giovanna at Bloomsbury for help and ongoing support. I could not have written this book without the tremendous support of my husband, Clive Warsop. His insightful comments rescued my thoughts at many times when I thought I would never see my way clear. Special thanks too to my sons Ben and Christopher who put up with me, especially during the final stages of writing. Their support, encouragement and patience while I was rather distracted from everyday life are greatly appreciated. Final thanks to my amazing parents Don and Alison McArthur, for I could not have written this book without their support. Some of the research underpinning sections of this book was made possible by a research grant from the Faculty of Arts and Social Sciences, Lancaster University – for which I am very grateful. Finally, I am grateful to Taylor and Francis for permission to reproduce sections from my journal article, Assessment for social justice: The role of assessment in achieving social justice, *Assessment & Evaluation in Higher Education*, 41(7), 2016, pp. 967–81. This forms a large part of Chapter 2 and smaller sections in Chapter 5 and Chapter 6. Full details are available from the journal website at: http://www.tandfonline.com.

Introduction

Assessment for Social Justice

This is a book about social justice and the nature and purposes of higher education. It takes assessment as its explicit focus because I believe that assessment is key to what we currently do in higher education, and to what we should do differently. This book reflects my own commitment to higher education serving the purposes of greater social justice within society as a whole. It is written within the tradition of critical theory and critical pedagogy. The former raises our awareness of unseen and potentially damaging social forces and demands a commitment to change and greater social justice. The latter combines such a commitment with our understanding of education: education and society become understood as intimately interrelated and, again, the explicit purpose of education is understood as contributing to social justice. In a previous book (McArthur, 2013) I used this critical pedagogy perspective to focus on the nature of knowledge with which we engage in higher education. I argued for active involvement with complex and dynamic forms of knowledge in order to pursue greater social justice within and through higher education. In many ways, this book is a logical extension because assessment is so much at the heart of how we engage with knowledge in higher education. Thus I do not intend this to be a book simply about assessment. Assessment is the focus to the extent that it plays a pivotal role in what we do within higher education and how we realize our goals.

In this book I will explore assessment and social justice from two interrelated perspectives. First, the extent to which assessment policies and practices within higher education may be considered socially just. Second, the extent to which such policies and practices contribute to student learning in such a way as to promote socially just dispositions, engagement with knowledge and other practices in students' ongoing social and professional lives. Clearly, both of these perspectives are themselves formed by many facets. In considering whether assessment is socially just within higher education, I am suggesting something beyond simply whether assessment is considered fair to the student. For example, of equal importance is the extent to which policy and practice is fair to the academic and administrative staff who play a crucial role in its undertaking. Is it justifiable to have assessment regimes that induce high levels of stress and overwork among academics? The socially just nature of assessment thus requires consideration of many dimensions and factors. The extent to which these are interrelated is another facet of this book.

The title of this book alludes to the way in which I have first approached the exploration of the many issues connecting social justice and assessment in higher education. A clear influence has been the scholarship on *assessment for learning*, or learning-orientated assessment, which has led to welcome changes in the ways in which the nature and role of assessment has been conceptualized, explored and realized. A revolution of sorts was led by a range of scholars who inspired us to rethink the role and nature of assessment in higher education. These included Sadler (1987, 1989), Hounsell (2003, 2007), Boud & Falchikov (2006, 2007b) and Knight (1995, 2002, 2006). To begin with, these writers simply gave assessment a prominence and significance that had been lacking too long in much of the mainstream literature. Higher education research had long been complicit, often through simple neglect, in assessment's relegation to 'that bit at the end'. Assumptions that assessment simply checked up on or made a judgement about the learning achieved by students were not just accepted, they were not even acknowledged sufficiently to then be challenged. These authors all contributed to a major change within the research literature and academic discourses. The literature on assessment for learning supports the idea of assessment as key not simply to what students learn, but also to how they go about learning. Rather than vilifying students for being concerned with 'what was on the exam', this interest became recognized as perfectly reasonable. The notion that students should study for a term and then find an exam full of tricks and surprises was unveiled as pedagogically questionable and ethically unsound.

The growing influence of ideas around assessment for learning has occurred, however, at the same time as other trends that are arguably pulling us in other directions. Most notable here is the rise of an audit culture and increasingly complex moderation and quality assurance processes. The practical implications of these trends means that the spaces required for genuinely formative forms of assessment and for feedback loops, which give students the chances to apply what they have learned through assessment, are diminished. It is arguably harder to realize the full learning potential of assessment when it becomes more and more regimented and constrained within narrow timelines. A further paradox here is that while assessment is the 'core business' of universities in many ways, assessment practices have been able to remain 'ineffectual, limited, irrelevant and blatantly unfair' (Flint & Johnson, 2011, p. 12). A major theme of this book is that simply adding more quality processes or quality assurance checks does not address the underlying problems with assessment in our universities, and certainly does not begin to touch on the social justice issues to be considered here.

Of course, much depends on how one conceptualizes social justice, and so that too is an important theme of this book. Critical theory leads to an understanding of social justice nested in the lived realities of people's lives, and takes particularly seriously issues of power, domination and distortion. It involves both critique of current social arrangements and a looking forward to a more just society. In particular, in this book I use the work of third generation critical theorist Axel Honneth, because he focuses our attention on the interplay between individual experience and the social world: the two are always understood as interdependent. As Honneth argues,

> What is just, is that which allows the individual member of our society to realize his or her own life's objectives, in cooperation with others, and with the greatest possible autonomy.
>
> (Honneth, 2010b, p. 13)

Thus the fates of the individual are always entwined with fellow members of society. In contrast, I will suggest that the prevailing view of social justice informing assessment and education, to the extent that any is informing them, reflects a more procedural type, with the emphasis on having the right systems in place. In such an approach, the just outcome is assumed to follow from good procedures rather than the emphasis being on the lived reality of that outcome. Typical of this procedural approach is the following extract from the UK quality assurance agency *Quality Code for Assessment* (QAA, 2016), giving one of their indicators of 'sound practice':

> Higher education providers operate effective policies, regulations and processes which ensure that the academic standard for each award of credit or a qualification is rigorously set and maintained at the appropriate level, and that student performance is equitably judged against this standard.
>
> (p. 9)

This is clearly a perfectly reasonable statement to make; however, it also demonstrates the difference between a focus on procedures and one on lived realities. There are, therefore, important differences between the ways in which I deal with assessment in this book and the treatment it gets in such official documentation. The greater focus on lived realities rather than procedures is fundamental. I am interested in the experiences students take away from their assessment tasks, and the ways they go on to use the knowledge with which they engage. What are students able to do, and to contribute to society, as a result of their assessment experiences? How do they think about and value their own contributions to wider society? I am interested in how students feel about themselves and their social world, and the type of citizens they go on to become and the social contributions they make. If assessment is recognized to shape students' learning, then we must also understand how assessment shapes our students.

Pledges to social justice, along with well-being and civic responsibility, feature in the mission statements of most universities and in many government policy statements. However, such statements are made hand in hand with others that continue to reflect the increased marketization of higher education. On the surface, such policy documents end up containing parallel discourses: one of marketization and another of social justice. The links between the two, arguably somewhat tenuous, are made by inference and implication. Claims to social justice often appear to be made not in their own right, but as forms of legitimation for the prevailing marketization ethos. A clear example of this is the recent UK green paper on teaching within higher education which even includes social mobility in the report title and claims that 'universities are playing their part as powerful engines of social mobility'(DBIS, 2015, p. 8). However, this is the same green paper that is effectively seeking to lift the gap on student fees from the already high levels of £9000 per annum.

Claims to social justice can be far from radical or committed to genuine change, but actually work as little more than further support for the injustices of the present social arrangements. Here the influence of Adorno's critical theory (e.g. 1973, 1991, 2005a, 2005b) is clear in my approach. In particular I take seriously his warnings about the pervasiveness and strength of the status quo and mainstream thought. The status quo is propped up by unreflective assumptions about what is just, fair or right. I will argue that this can be seen in common assessment practices today: assumptions about what is the right way to undertake assessment are frequently treated as natural or obvious truths. Change is regarded as risky or strange, hence the status quo is further reinforced. Thus for anyone committed to real social change in pursuit of greater social justice, a strong and thoughtful conceptual basis for such work is essential. For, as Adorno also reveals, it is not about theory or practice but the two are intertwined, and the battle for social justice needs to be played on the conceptual field as well as in the classroom.

Explicit engagement with social justice and assessment is surprisingly rare among the higher education literature. This is not to suggest that other writers on assessment are not concerned with social justice issues. But it is telling that this interest is more often than not something to be inferred rather than explicitly discussed. I suggest that this, in turn, adds to the sense that so much of our assessment ideas are still underpinned by taken-for-granted practices. While justice may not be explicitly discussed in much of the assessment literature, issues of fairness and equity receive considerable attention. Indeed, it may be that sometimes fairness is used as a proxy for social justice. There is a tendency, however, to assume that what counts as 'fairness' is obvious and uncontested: frequently this focuses on treating students the same or having clear rules in place. A particular problem is the lack of a more critical understanding of the relationships that frame and shape the assessment experiences of students and academics. There are many barriers to good assessment practice which result from power differentials, distorted understandings, lack of trust and fear of uncertain futures.

The genesis of assessment for social justice is the simple idea that if assessment is a key driver of what and how students learn *and* if we are committed to greater social justice within and through higher education, then assessment must surely play a fundamental role in such social justice aspirations. However, a second strand rests on a belief that by engaging with the notion of assessment for social justice we can transcend some of the problems that have affected the implementation of assessment for learning more broadly within the academy. We need to understand the ways and reasons why students may experience their time at university, including their assessment experiences, as unjust. We also need to consider in greater depth and breadth the relationship between what happens within the university and what happens in wider society. Such a relationship is complex and multifaceted in ways that notions such as employability or graduate attributes simply fail to capture adequately.

Assessment in higher education has in some ways become a confused area of enquiry and practice. On the one hand, notions of assessment for learning, or learning-orientated assessment, have become prominent and led to welcome changes in assessment policy and practice. Across our universities there are some terrific examples of innovative assessment and feedback practices. The myriad potential implications of how we assess have never been more scrutinized, fuelled by the odd alliance of assessment scholarship and the ever-growing audit agenda in higher education. But on the other hand, assessment practices appear resistant to fundamental change. Despite the growing body of literature on assessment and learning, we must be careful not to conflate the extensive research and literature with what is happening in actual practice. Assessment has proven a sticky practice, reluctant to change, immune to innovation. To be sure, assessment for learning has led to some welcome changes and improvements in approaches to teaching and learning in higher education. And yet, within many higher education institutions, assessment practice can appear relatively unchanged. Exams are often still considered the norm, bell curve graphs implying normative judgements are still produced with ridiculous pride at exam boards and many students still regard assessment as a trial or trick gleefully imposed by academics trying to 'catch them out'. In the United Kingdom, the National Student Survey (NSS) has consistently shown assessment and feedback to be the areas of least satisfaction among students (Bols, 2012; HEFCE, 2010). The need for substantial change is expressed clearly and decisively by Boud and Associates (2010):

> Universities face substantial change in a rapidly evolving global context. The challenges of meeting new expectations about academic standards in the next decade and beyond mean that assessment will need to be rethought and renewed.
>
> (p. 1)

Some caution, however, about change is also understandable and, indeed, wise. Changing assessment can be risky because it has such an impact on students' future lives (Boud & Falchikov, 2007a). However, as the same authors go on to argue,

> This has meant that there has been very slow movement in the development of new assessment ideas and changes in practice. We face a system of assessment that has been subject to slow incremental change, to compromise and to inertia. We are afraid to change the system because of the risks, but we also avoid looking at it because doing so might entail major effort.
>
> (p. 3)

Too often, solutions to perceived problems in assessment and feedback have rested on introducing more policies or systems to address this. Instead, I argue, we should take the time to go deeper into understanding the multidimensional nature of our relationships with students – and their relationships with us and with each other – in order to establish foundations for better assessment practices. The aim of this book is to explicitly use lenses of social justice to reconsider assessment from the broad level of policy to the details of everyday practice. Included under the umbrella term of assessment for social justice is also the issue of feedback, because such feedback is crucial to realizing the aims of learning through assessment and has clear ramifications for social justice.

This book aims to provide a multifaceted philosophical lens with which to view and rethink our current assessment and feedback practices and the existing literature. But that is not to say that this book does not have practical relevance – and I have sought to include examples of everyday practices that can help move towards greater social justice. Indeed, it is in the spirit of critical theory to challenge any dichotomization of the philosophical and the practical. I acknowledge that those who want to use this book to reconsider assessment practices in higher education will need to do some work with it. My focus is on general principles and ideals, underpinned with examples – but there is a required act of interpretation and contextualization to take this and apply it in your own realm. I hope the book serves to raise questions from perhaps previously unconsidered perspectives. It contains no definitive answers, but does offer a lens which may inspire and enable academics to argue for change in your own contexts and practices. An important part of doing so is also to arm us as academics committed to social justice with a different vocabulary and different set of core values than those contained in prevailing managerialist and audit-driven quality regimes. We cannot argue for change in the language of the status quo. But here I would also say that we need to challenge our own practices and habits within higher education. How have we allowed such a reductionist view of the purposes of higher education to dominate? Why has such a powerfully well-educated workforce seemed so unable – or unwilling – to resist policy cultures that position higher education in narrow economic terms and assessment in a purely competitive skills-based agenda? How do we as academics regain, protect and nurture agency over our own professional practice, including the extent to which it meaningfully contributes to greater social justice?

One of the threads in this book is an understanding of the processes of change using social practice theory to try to overcome the dominance of institutional systems over individual agency. But for any of this to be achievable, we must be prepared to experience the discomfort, pain and peril that come with challenging mainstream practices. Assessment for social justice is not simply a nice idea, pleasing to those of us with good intentions in our hearts. It is also a dangerous idea. It involves the risk of not remaining passive in the face of institutional policies that lose sight of the real experiences of student learning and assessment or social conventions that have reduced higher education to a narrow, technocratic purpose. Thus when I entreat readers to use this book to reflect upon and question their own practices, this necessitates a commitment to dissent, and even subversion, in the face of a dominant culture of managerialism. I do not underestimate how difficult this is to do, particularly where we have an increasingly casualized academic workforce. Such agitation for change is clearly far more precarious when one's employment rights are partial and tenuous. But to do nothing and to stand by as the academic role is distorted and diminished hardly seems an option either. If we do not make the arguments for more emancipatory practices, then no one else is going to do it for us.

My aim is twofold. First, to provide a theoretically rigorous understanding of the reasons why assessment should be understood in terms of social justice and what might be involved in doing so. In so doing, a vocabulary for thinking beyond the status quo can be nurtured and shared. Second, if more of us are having such conversations and putting forth alternative positions in our exam boards, department and institutional meetings as well as more informal talks with colleagues and students, then the fragile process of radical change can be advanced.

Structure of this book

This book is in two main parts. In the first part, I establish the theoretical foundations upon which my alternative view of assessment and social justice is based. Some of this theoretical material is complex, though I have sought to make it accessible to readers from different backgrounds. Even so, you may find the theoretical terrain challenging, but I would urge the reader to persevere as it is through negotiating this work that the robust foundations for assessment for social justice are laid.

In Chapter 1 I outline a selection of the research on assessment that demonstrates why assessment is a social justice issue. Such literature may not always explicitly deal with social justice, but nonetheless we can infer such issues from the analysis of assessment and its impact on students' current and future lives.

In Chapter 2 I consider the implications for assessment of different theories of social justice. In so doing, I provide a brief overview to three different approaches to social justice: John Rawls's work in the social contract tradition; the capabilities approach and critical theory. I seek to demonstrate that what may count as 'just' assessment policy or practice depends very much on the understanding of social justice we have, explicitly or implicitly. In particular, I contrast the proceduralism of the social contract tradition with the emphasis on people's lived realities and the outcomes of social justice, as represented by both the capabilities approach and critical theory. Such theories focus on everyday practices as the unit of analysis, and are thus well placed to illuminate where changes in practices can lead to the broader social justice aims. Many of the issues raised here are developed further in Part 2 of this book.

In Chapter 3 I focus in greater depth on the particular conceptualization of social justice that informs the rest of this book. Here I explore further the work of third-generation critical theorist Axel Honneth and his notion of social justice as mutual recognition. Honneth conceptualizes mutual recognition in terms of three *relationships to self* that can be nurtured through different social contexts. It is only through the realization of all three of these relationships that a person can enjoy genuinely autonomous selfhood, free of the distortions of instrumental rationality. These relationships are also based on mutuality, hence the recognition of others is entwined in our capacity for self-realization. Honneth enables a close and intricate understanding of the relationship between individuals and their social world.

Chapter 4 completes the first part of the book, introducing social practice theories and considering how they can be related to Honneth's conception of social justice. If theories of social justice cast light on what is flawed in current arrangements and illuminate the way ahead towards a more just society, then social practice theories enable our understanding of how to move from one to the other: they offer a robust conceptualization of change, which is perhaps missing from social justice theory on its own. I argue that assessment needs to be understood as a social practice, and consider the implications of this. Here I draw particularly on Schatzki's (1996, 2002) practice theory. I put forward my case for this, perhaps unusual, approach in bringing these two rather different theoretical works together.

Part 2 of the book builds on the conceptual foundations of Part 1 to offer my alternative vision for assessment and social justice. Conventional texts on 'good' assessment practices often argue that assessments should meet the criteria of being SMART: specific, measureable, achievable, relevant and timely. My own approach has some resonance with the holistic assessment for learning approach outlined by Sambell, McDowell and Montgomery (2013), which they describe as 'almost like a philosophy ... an overall approach to assessment, rather than a set of techniques which can be "dropped in"' (p. 5). However, where these authors place a high priority on sharing practical techniques for better assessment, my focus is more on the way we approach our shared practices with students, and with the nature of the knowledge being assessed. I would hope that this book would be seen as complementary to such existing literature. In Part 2, I consider the general understandings on which our assessment practices should occur – and particularly the cultural qualities of these practices and their outcomes. This is not to say that the elements of SMART are not useful in some ways, but they are a fairly technocratic approach to assessment, and the realization of our social justice commitments requires a more philosophical perspective. Therefore I propose the following five concepts that should be part of our assessment practices in order to realize assessment for social justice: trust, honesty, responsibility, forgiveness and responsiveness. I position these five concepts in terms of Schatzki's idea of 'general understandings', which thereby offer radical promise as they help shape the nature of assessment practices. These ideas clearly do not offer a 'how to' list of tasks for assessment, but they could be used, in a critical way, in conjunction with more practical advice. What these traits offer is a sense of the foundations needed if we are to make claims about assessment and social justice from the perspective of Honneth's critical theory. My aim is to challenge many of our tacit assumptions and recurrent practices that, upon closer exploration, stand as barriers to greater social justice within and through assessment. I will also argue, however, that they stand as barriers to better assessment practices, and certainly the realization of genuine assessment for learning.

Chapter 5 begins the second part of the book by considering the ways in which our assessment practices should feature *trust*. My argument is quite simply that we cannot work towards assessment for social justice without practices of trust. In particular I consider how an instrumentalized form of distrust has become established in our assessment processes and practices, and I consider two examples of an institutionalized lack of trust: the growth of the plagiarism industry and the debates over anonymous marking.

Chapter 6 considers *honesty*, a concept closely aligned with the previous chapter's discussion of trust. Here I use two examples of areas where greater honesty is needed, and indeed argue how this could enhance our assessment practices from a social justice perspective. Thus I first consider the conditions under which academics mark – the workload and time pressures and what these mean for the lived reality of marking students' work. I argue that there are strong social justice implications for students and academics arising from the extreme stress under which a lot of marking currently occurs. We must be more honest about the lived reality of how academics often have to assess work. Second, I consider the precision with which we can attribute grades. I suggest that we mislead students if we employ systems that suggest a high degree of precision and reliability. Moreover, such schemes encourage a fetishization of 'the mark' when our true focus should be on what students are able to do with the knowledge they engage with.

Chapter 7 argues that assessment must enable students to take genuine *responsibility* within their assessment practices. I consider assessment regulations and the extent to which these are enabling or restrictive of students' capacities to be actively involved in their assessment experiences. I also consider the tacit knowledge involved in understanding assessment expectations and marking criteria, and the ways in which students may develop such knowledge through genuine participation in assessment practices.

In Chapter 8 the focus is on *forgiveness*: assessment policies and practices that leave scope for the mistakes and iterative processes essential to the learning of complex knowledge. I consider the powerful social construction of our understandings of failure, and consider how these can impair learning through assessment. I argue that students must develop a capacity for clear-sighted evaluation of their own work, in order to permit ongoing learning to take place.

Chapter 9 champions the importance of *responsiveness* in our assessment practices. I consider the social justice, and learning, implications of rigidly predetermining what students will learn, and contrast this with a more iterative approach. Thus I argue that assessment responsiveness should be sensitive to what students learn, rather than forcing them into predetermined moulds. I also consider responsiveness in terms of the relationship between assessment practices and the wider social world. What are the implications of ensuring that assessment is always outward looking? I challenge simplistic ways of connecting assessment to the world of work, where the latter is understood through the perspective of narrow, economic interests, rather than society as a whole.

Finally, Chapter 10 concludes by looking forward to the possibilities of assessment for social justice as well as the implications of trying to sustain current practices and policies. How long can we continue to mislead students about how assessment really occurs? How long can we continue to promote assessment for learning and yet devise systems that create such a workload and such stress that learning is the last thing that either academics or students are able to think about? How long can we argue that assessment matters, and yet pull up from comprehensively re-examining the foundations of current practice?

In Chapters 5–9 I build up an understanding of assessment practices that I propose as the foundation for assessment for social justice. But I do so in the spirit of dialogue – as a starting point for those of us committed to greater social justice within and through higher education, and who appreciate the role assessment should play towards this. I write at a time in which assessment in higher education raises many contradictions and tensions. Leathwood (2005) observes a 'somewhat contradictory trend' emerging between 'the demand for ever more reliability and comparability of assessment outcomes' and concern to 'foster student learning' through assessment (p. 312). Similarly, Shay (2008) observes the paradox in higher education assessment literature between an ongoing sense of crisis in terms of the roles and nature of assessment practices and the now established claims that assessment can play a key role in shaping student learning. In one sense I envisage this book to sit on the interface between assessment literature and critical pedagogy literature. To assessment literature it offers a new lens with which to consider assessment issues, sometimes challenging and sometimes complementary. To critical pedagogy literature it brings the importance of assessment as an integral part of learning and teaching interactions. My hope is that it has something worthwhile to offer both traditions.

My use of Honneth's conceptualization of social justice involves a reinterpretation of his overarching work into this particular context of assessment. I do so with some caution but believe the process of using theory in this way is legitimate and important. It is, after all, the use of theory that makes it so valuable and important. As Giddens (1984) argues,

> If ideas are important and illuminating, what matters much more than their origin is to be able to sharpen them so as to demonstrate their usefulness, even if within a framework which might be quite different from that which helped to engender them.
>
> (p. xxii)

In this spirit I have tried to use Honneth's work with respect for the integrity of the original ideas, and I hope to be sufficiently clear when the analysis moves between Honneth's original work and my reapplication of it. Honneth warns that we live in times of 'moral bewilderment and perplexity':

> We no longer have to deal merely with an increased lack of clarity in our social circumstances but, as a result of an acceleration of discrepancies and opposing trends, we are now in a situation that shows all the symptoms of political–moral disorientation.
>
> (Honneth, 2010b, p. 6)

In such circumstances we may intuitively feel that easy solutions are inadequate to the challenges we face, but not have the necessary confidence to seek out more complex, and less certain, pathways. My aim in this book is to be neither too naïve nor overly world-weary about the possibilities for change. I want to encourage us as academic colleagues, managers and policymakers to, in Proust's (2006) words, 'look with new eyes' at assessment and to see the very real possibilities – and need – for doing things differently. Greater social justice is possible, within and through higher education, and it is high time that assessment was recognized and embraced for the key role it can play towards this goal.

Part One

Conceptual Foundations

1

Assessment as a Social Justice Issue

Introduction

In this chapter I explore the ways in which social justice issues are reflected in current literature on higher education assessment. I will focus on two different, but clearly interrelated, approaches to linking assessment and social justice. I begin by considering the relationship between fairness and assessment. Fairness is a recurring theme within the assessment literature. Indeed it is reasonable to infer that for many writers (and students and academics as well), fairness and justice are closely related. But the ways in which we conceptualize fairness can vary. Most striking is the difference between straightforward, technocratic understandings of fairness as simply due process and more complex explorations reflecting varied perspectives and multifarious issues of power. The power dimension of assessment is laid bare when we consider the impact assessment can have on students' lives. Thus in the second part of this chapter I look at the literature which considers what assessment means to students' current and future lives and their place in society. Assessment can shape or shatter a person's sense of self-worth and their ongoing place in society. Does assessment foster healthy self-esteem or denigrate and diminish people's sense of worth? Does it 'fairly' set all deserving students up for successful careers and membership of society? The answers to these questions are complex and involved. My aim in this chapter is to lay the foundations for answering them through the rest of the book by first understanding how these are explored in current literature.

Assessment and fairness

In many ways fairness is a byword for good assessment in the eyes of students, academics and policymakers. In particular, the issue of fairness is often at the forefront of students' minds when they consider assessment (Sambell, McDowell & Brown, 1997). As Flint and Johnson (2011) observe, 'considerations of "fairness" are inextricably linked to university assessment practices' (p. 3). While it is very difficult to imagine anything other than unilateral agreement over the virtues of fairness, it does not follow that there is agreement as to what constitutes such fairness within the assessment context. What counts as fairness may differ considerably and may not even be explicitly analysed. This is no less the case because fairness is so often a matter of *perception* rather than any 'objective' measure (Flint & Johnson, 2011). But being a matter of perception does not diminish the importance of fairness to students' experiences. Indeed, Entwistle (1991) argues that student perceptions of their learning environment, which, I suggest, includes judgements of fairness, can be as critical to how students learn as the actual environment itself.

Searching for literature that explores deeply the connections between assessment and fairness, the results provide slimmer pickings than anticipated. The implicit importance clearly accorded fairness in assessment processes is simply not reflected in the explicit engagement with this as a complex and contested concept. Indeed, I suggest it is problematic how little attention is given to unpicking and examining assumptions about fairness within our university contexts. Further, I imagine some authors will wonder why their work is not discussed here, as the links between it and fairness in the assessment context are, to them, abundantly clear. But this reinforces my point – that notions of fairness are often taken for granted and are frequently implicit.

Within some sections of the literature, and in policy documents, fairness is presented in an unproblematic way, suggestive of fairly technocratic assumptions. The theme of fairness through procedure is strong: fair procedures, fairly applied, lead to just assessment. Yorke (2008) suggests that in traditional, technical approaches to assessment, fairness rests simply on the question of whether the 'chosen approach disadvantages particular groups of students' (p. 20). This is the interpretation of fairness apparent in much of the official higher education documentation, such as quality assurance requirements. It is an understanding steeped in the assumptions of the 'audit culture', with its heightened emphasis on procedure and bureaucracy such that these processes 'take on the contours of a distinct cultural practice' (Strathern, 2000, p. 2). Challenging and changing this cultural practice is a key theme of this book, which I shall develop further in later chapters.

This technocratic approach defines what Boud (2007) has termed the dominant discourse of assessment, one reified in assessment and quality assurance policies and frameworks. The focus is on the end product and the importance of maintaining standards, rules and procedures. But such an end product is itself defined rather narrowly, with an emphasis on the 'right mark' rather than on students' actual engagement with complex knowledge and on the implications of this for their future lives. That the rules and procedures are themselves fair is a fundamental assumption; the only question remaining as to whether fairness is achieved or not lies in following those procedures. It is particularly worrying when such viewpoints are connected to notions of 'empowerment' and other worthy principles, but actually involve considerable direction, and even coercion (Shore & Wright, 2000):

> The self-directed, self-managed individual is encouraged to identify with the university and the goals of higher education policy: challenging the terms of reference is not an option.
>
> (Shore & Wright, 2000, p. 62)

Boud (2007) refers to the ways in which this approach 'constructs learners as passive subjects'. Assessment is a process *done* to them, rather than understood as a complex web of social practices. They are little but cogs in the wheels of the assessment system:

> Students are seen to have no role other than to subject themselves to the assessment acts of others, to be measured and classified. They conform to the rules and procedures of others to satisfy the needs of an assessment bureaucracy: they present themselves at set times for examinations over which they have little or no influence and they complete assignments which are, by and large, determined with little or no input from those being assessed.
>
> (p. 17)

Fundamental to a technocratic, procedural approach to fairness is the idea of 'academic standards', which must be clear and apparent to all, thus easily followed and protected. Here again, the assumptions are that academic standards are fixed and easily understood and applied. However, as Bloxham (2012) observes,

> Academic standards are the cornerstone of university education, a fundamental basis for universities' credibility in the world ... Yet academic standards are poorly researched and understood, particularly in their everyday use by academics, managers and those involved in quality assurance.
>
> (p. 185)

Sadler (2011) argues that while academics may feel they hold to academic standards, these can 'be somewhat fuzzy and subject to drift over time' (p. 97). While Yorke (2008) describes the notion of academic standards as an 'elusive concept' (p. 83). Indeed, the concepts of academic standards and fairness have much in common in terms of how they are handled – both being implicitly ubiquitous in the assessment literature and in policy, yet seldom clearly *and complexly* defined. Simply understanding fairness as treating all students the same, as is frequently implied, suggests the easy application of definite rules and procedures in an array of situations. But as Davis (2009) observes,

> Applications of 'fairness' to educational assessment reveal a rich minefield of conceptual and normative obscurities and inconsistencies.
>
> (p. 387)

Davis further warns against 'predetermined theories of fairness and justice':

> I do not think that all is well, normatively speaking, with current policies and practices. As far as I am concerned, real world attempts to secure fairness in assessment procedures may involve confusion, inconsistency and lack proper justification. Yet current practices comprise vital data for exploration, and must be examined on their merits rather than being marginalised in the interests of predetermined theories of fairness and justice.
>
> (p. 373)

Committed as he is to being 'constantly on the lookout for unwarranted certainties', Davis argues that 'no wholly coherent and consistent approach' to fairness and assessment is possible (p. 373). Thus, he alleges that

> confident verdicts about what is and what is not fair often depend on other ethical and political assumptions that are hard to justify and are in tension with each other.
>
> (p. 387)

Narrow, technical-rationalist understandings of fairness are inconsistent with the aims of assessment for social justice. Such approaches are imbued with a myopic lack of appreciation of the various currents of power which influence, shape and potentially distort the contexts and relationships in which assessment takes place. More interesting and helpful are critical conceptualizations of fairness, attuned to the conflicted and messy nature of the concept. Fairness in assessment is multifaceted – it does not refer to just one part, process or outcome. Most importantly, fairness is a concept interpreted and engaged with in complex social situations, in which nuances of context and power are critically important. A more critical understanding of fairness and assessment, in contrast to the technocratic approach, regards the existing social framework as problematic and views the possibilities of fairness as fraught and complex.

Leathwood (2005) argues that assessment must 'be understood in its social, political and historical context' (p. 308). Focusing on the practices of exam boards, Stowell (2004) argues that 'the taken-for-granted cultures and practices which determine the operation of assessment boards' (p. 496) can actually lead to unfair outcomes for students, including unintended biases. Indeed, she argues, 'Impartial processes do not guarantee just outcomes.' (p. 497). Further, Stowell argues,

> Procedural approaches to equal opportunity, in focusing on decision making, essentially leave unchallenged the processes of higher education themselves. The structures, cultures and processes of academe are assumed to be neutral in their impact on chances of success.
>
> (p. 506)

Similarly, Bloxham (2009) suggests that false assumptions are made about what forms of reliability and accuracy can be achieved in marking, and that such assumptions underlie many current procedures. Many current moderation processes are based on a belief that more processes result in a higher degree of marking accuracy. Bloxham suggests that there is little research evidence to support this; indeed, the reality may be quite the opposite (I return to this issue in Chapter 6).

At the heart of taking a more critical approach to assessment and fairness is a fuller appreciation of the student perspective, and indeed the active role of students in assessment practices. Carless (2015) argues that we can identify a shift from traditional notions of fairness – treating students exactly the same – connected with psychometric perspectives, to a more inclusive sense of 'providing all students with an opportunity to show their best performance' (p. 18). A further useful contribution to this gap is the work of Flint and Johnson (2011). Focusing on the student perspective – and noting that student perceptions of fairness can vary considerably from those of academics – these authors propose five different forms of fairness (although note the use of fairness and justice seemingly interchangeably). These five forms of fairness are,

- distributive justice – the fair allocation of assessment rewards
- procedural fairness – clear and transparent assessment criteria
- interpersonal justice – the quality of interactions between students and teachers
- informational justice – clear explanation of how a decision is made and
- retributive justice – an opportunity to 'put things right' in the case of perceived unfair treatment.

(p. 5)

Thus we can observe in assessment a parallel movement to the major shift that occurred in our understanding of teaching and learning, from a focus on what the teacher does to what the student is doing. The same shift is arguably evident within the assessment literature, and particularly in terms of our understanding of fairness. This is demonstrated in Carless's (2009) argument for an inclusive and active role for students – his stress upon their participation when judging matters of fairness. This issue will be developed further in Chapter 7 where I explore how we can make student engagement with the rules, practices and expectations of assessment more inclusive and authentic.

In practice many academics may still misunderstand the student perspective when it comes to fairness and assessment. They may wrongly assume that students confuse fairness with tasks that are easy. Sambell et al. (1997) make this point clearly:

> Lecturers have a tendency to dismiss students' complaints about a lack of fairness, perhaps believing that they are asking for assessment systems which are in some sense easy or undemanding. In fact, the students we interviewed consistently used the concept of fairness to describe assessment systems which are, from their point of view, genuinely valid measurements of what they deem to be meaningful and worthwhile learning.

(p. 365)

Flint and Johnson (2011) argue that students regard assessment as fair if it meets four criteria:

> It is conducted on a 'level playing field' where none of the competing students has an advantage at the outset of the assessment activity. In practice, this means that work is marked on its merits, there is consistency in marking, and there is consistency of information about assessment arrangements.
>
> Students receive feedback that justifies or explains a grade, including suggestions about how to improve the grade.

Students are given a variety of relevant assessment tasks to demonstrate their capability. Perceptions of relevance are strongly tied to what students think is valued in the workplace.

Students are taught by competent, skilled and caring staff who are approachable, display empathy, engage with students and assist them with their work.

(pp. 9–10)

Sambell et al. (1997) demonstrate that student perceptions of fairness are more multifaceted than many academics may assume, and more complex than technocratic understandings suggest:

The issue of fairness, from the student perspective, is a fundamental aspect of assessment, the crucial importance of which is often overlooked or oversimplified from the staff perspective. To students, the concept of fairness frequently embraces more than simply the possibility (or not) of cheating: it is an extremely complex and sophisticated concept which students use to articulate their perceptions of the worth of an assessment mechanism, and it relates closely to our notions of validity.

(p. 362)

Orr (2010) reinforces this point, arguing that the students in her research on group work demonstrated complicated notions of fairness, 'indicating that fairness, such as contribution, is not a uni-dimensional construct' (p. 310). Hence, she argues, fairness is not from the student viewpoint a purely technical matter, but a sociocultural one. The sociocultural nature of assessment is a major theme of this book, which I will develop in further chapters. What Orr's work suggests to us is that students' notions of fairness could be contradictory, encompassing both a belief that all members of a group should get the same mark *and* that individual contributions should be rewarded.

The synonymous relationship between fairness and justice is evident in Orr's research:

Fairness was alluded to frequently in all the student interviews, or to be more accurate perceptions of injustice were frequently commented on.

(p. 308)

This is an interesting point, suggesting that students may be more likely to identify examples of injustices in assessment, rather than justice. Orr further observes that, for students, the relationship between effort and mark can underpin perceptions of fairness: 'When students do not feel that their efforts are rewarded through marks given, then they may view the assessment tools as unfair' (p. 308). This accords well with Flint and Johnson's (2011) assertion that

> students believe that assessment is unfair if they have not been given the oppor-
> tunity to demonstrate their capabilities, or if those capabilities have not been
> recognized.
>
> (p. 2)

Flint and Johnson suggest that there 'is a level of acceptance, or tolerance, by students that certain aspects of assessment are unfair' (p. 21). Because students tend to regard their teachers as in positions of power, 'the decisions they make about grades are discussed by students but not challenged' (p. 21).

Crossman (2007) considers the role that emotions play in student perceptions of assessment:

> Student references to emotions and relationships were particularly rich when
> they linked past experiences of assessment with current perceptions, when they
> drew upon descriptions of their relationships with teachers to explain more fully
> their perceptions of assessment and, finally, when affirming the importance of
> being provided with opportunities to express their beliefs, feelings and emotions
> in assessment.
>
> (p. 318)

Recognition of the strong emotional experience that assessment brings is another theme throughout this book. However much academics may try to make assessment an impartial and value-neutral process, for students it is often a viscerally emotional experience.

Clarkeburn and Kettula (2012) highlight this relationship between emotional issues and the perceived fairness of certain assessment methods. They focus on the use of reflective journals as an assessment method and note that this is a method which may unfairly disadvantage nonnative language speakers. They argue that the intrinsically personal nature of the undertaking, of writing one's reflections down, is unfair to nonnative speakers as it is more difficult to reflect in the required way in a second language.

So powerful are some experiences of assessment and perceived fairness and unfairness that people can recall them many years later. This is demonstrated by the personal recollections of some academics writing about assessment. It is clear that they can remember their strong emotional responses to certain assessment experiences and perceived instances of unfair treatment. Thus David Boud writes,

> I have strong memories from school and university of feeling frustrated and dismayed by the capricious nature of assessment.
>
> (Boud & Falchikov, 2007a, p. 6)

Similarly Nancy Falchikov recalls,

> In common with many people, I have a strong memory of dissatisfaction regarding the assessment of some coursework while at university … Being a mature student, I worked diligently and turned in work with which I was satisfied, and which generally received good marks. However, in the lab class, there appeared to be no relationship between the marks I, or any of my fellow-students, received and the quality of work submitted … I guess I had developed a strong capacity for self-assessment and felt resentment at the injustice I perceived to be taking place.
>
> (Boud & Falchikov, 2007a, p. 7)

Here Falchikov also highlights that one's background may influence perceptions of fairness; in her case being a mature student shaped her approach to the given tasks. It is worth reminding ourselves of Carless's (2009) championing of the student perspective when considering assessment. Clearly students cannot be regarded as a homogeneous group – and this has implications for fairness of both process and product. In Sambell et al.'s (1997) study, a mature student made the further argument that assessment through exams is more unfair on mature-aged students who have not come straight out of the school system:

> If you come from a working background, exams are not a lot of use to you … They suit people who come straight from school, who've been taught to do exams and nothing else. I'm out of that routine.
>
> (p. 363)

Indeed, the choice of assessment used raises clear issues of fairness for many students. Exams, for example, are often cited by students as unfair because they rely on the regurgitation of information and do not enable students to demonstrate all they have really learned (Sambell et al., 1997, Sambell et al., 2013). Further unfairness arises due to the advantage held by students in an area not supposedly central to the assessment task itself, let alone the stated learning outcomes. Sambell et al. (1997) quote a student:

> In exams if you have a decent memory you have a 100% advantage over the guy who doesn't have such a good memory.
>
> (p. 360)

Students may even have cause to believe the purpose of assessment is nothing to do with their own learning, and is instead an evaluation of teaching or the quality of lecturers' notes (Sambell et al., 1997). Indeed, Sambell et al. also observe,

> Many other students similarly saw normal assessment as something they did because they had to, not because it was interesting or meaningful in any other sense than it allowed them to accrue marks. To many it was an encumbrance, a necessary evil, and an unfair means of assessment which had everything to do with certification and which was, in their minds, divorced from the learning they felt they had achieved whilst studying the subject being tested.
>
> (p. 359)

The introduction of an element of oral examination into an undergraduate maths course was examined by Iannone and Simpson (2015) who found that issues of fairness 'in one guise or another' were discussed by nearly all students who participated (p. 978). Some students felt that oral examinations were more open to bias than traditional assessment forms; however, this was mitigated by the practice of video recording the presentations as the students seemingly felt that the video recording acted as a safety net. Students also felt that different markers were likely to give different results in the oral examination context, which is interesting as the practice of different markers of written work is widespread. It may be that these students were reacting to the unfamiliarity of the assessment task as much as to particular concerns. Thus perceptions of fairness – or the level of consciousness about fairness – may differ between more familiar and less familiar modes of assessment.

The theme of perceived fairness also arises in literature on peer assessment and the assessment of group work. When faced with group work, Nordberg (2008) observes that 'students regularly question the fairness of the whole process even before they begin to suffer the frequent descent of group work into disagreement and disillusionment' (p. 481). In her study of group work, Orr (2010) found that students raised issues of 'trust and dependability frequently' (p. 307). Typical comments from students included

> You're putting all the work in and it's not really fair.
>
> (p. 308)

In the Portuguese context, Carvalho (2013) found a significant minority of students – 30 per cent – experienced a sense of unfairness in peer assessment, with 'friendship marking' and team conflict being particular problems. These experiences affected perceptions of fairness. Carvalho echoes Entwistle (1991) in arguing that such perceptions of fairness or unfairness can negatively affect the quality of students' learning.

In another study in Portugal, Flores et al. (2015) considered the perceptions of fairness of nearly four hundred undergraduates and found that students undertaking alternative 'learner-centred' forms of assessment were more likely to perceive these as fair than students undertaking traditional (e.g. exam) forms of assessment. They suggest that this

> maybe explained, at least in part, by the nature of assessment methods them-selves, e.g. portfolios and team projects. These are methods that are more sys-tematic, are developed over time and require negotiation, collaboration and the integration of different perspectives amongst students and between students and faculty.
>
> (p. 1532)

What is at play when we consider fairness and peer assessment are multiple, and possibly divergent, understandings of fairness. For educationalists it may appear fair because it enables students to develop requisite and highly valued professional skills (Wilson, Diao & Huang, 2015) and yet students' reactions are based on the fairness of how marking is executed, particularly in a competitive student environment.

A further raft of fairness issues arise if we consider the various forms of assessment that go into degree classification, such as in the UK system. Elton (2004b) is particularly critical of the current UK honours classification sys-tem. The single degree classification is flawed, he argues, as it conflates things that are themselves incompatible 'such as knowledge and practical abilities in a science degree or knowledge and writing ability in an arts degree' (p. 417). The same problem would exist, he argues, with some muted alternatives, such as a grade point average. Only multifaceted forms of assessment, such as port-folios can, Elton argues, offer the required approach to assessing 'high-level life skills and also of academic abilities, such as those contributing to problem solving, criticality and creativity, since students present their learning devel-opment over time' (p. 420). Yorke et al. (2008) also emphasize a concern for fairness when considering the apparent variation in honours degree classifica-tion regulations – including consistency within institutions as well as between institutions.

Similarly, Simonite (2003) considers whether it is fair that different assess-ment methods can lead to different degree outcomes, particularly in highly modularized systems:

The relationship between assessment method and the outcomes of assessment is important when students in a modular scheme are able to exercise a degree of choice in constructing their programme of studies. If students can achieve the same award by following different programmes of study, no student should be disadvantaged by choosing one set of modules rather than another. Systematic differences in the outcomes of assessment by different methods raise questions of fairness to students who aim for the same award, but follow programmes that differ in terms of the assessment methods used to measure performance.

(p. 460)

Elton's and Simonite's arguments resonate with that of Sadler (2010b) concerning the fidelity of assessment tasks; that is, the extent to which a task actually assesses what it purports to assess. Elton (2004b) has also championed portfolio assessments on the basis of greater fairness. However, his argument rests on a rethinking of what counts as "fairness":

Such development is very individual and makes it impossible to treat all students in the same way, which in turn leads to a very different interpretation of what is 'fair'. Instead of fairness being based on everyone being treated identically, in portfolio assessment fairness is based on the concept of all students being given an equal opportunity to show their best work.

(p. 420)

Another key area in the assessment literature which focuses on fairness concerns assessment criteria, particularly the clarity and dissemination of such criteria. Literature on assessment for learning emphasizes the role that the assessment task has in conveying information to students about the expected nature of their engagement with knowledge (Maclellan, 2001). It is for this reason that Taras (2002) considers fair assessment in terms of unambiguity: 'Students perhaps have the right to demand coherent and logical educational processes that are not detrimental to their learning' (p. 501). Worth (2014) argues for assessment criteria that are more student-focused and cites the importance of student perceptions of fairness. She links perceptions of fairness with 'student and staff understanding/ use of assessment criteria *through practice*' (p. 363, italics added). The issue of students' genuine engagement with assessment criteria is returned to in Chapter 7.

Carless (2015) extends the concept of openness beyond simply the criteria, onto the very nature of our relationships and interactions with students:

Openness in assessment is a major means of enhancing perceptions of fairness in assessment. It involves dialogue with students in supporting them to understand various issues, including the rationale for assessment tasks; unpacking the criteria on which they will be assessed and how academic judgements are made; and clarifying the multiple purposes of feedback and how these can support their development of appropriate learning outcomes.

(p. 19)

In summary, fairness and assessment appear inextricably linked, but their explicit discussion is not as widespread in the literature as one may assume. There is more likely to be discussion about whether a particular assessment task is 'fair' than discussion as to what fairness might actually entail. But this lack of clarity, paradoxically, does not diminish the powerful connection between assessment and fairness.

How assessment affects students' lives

The second major way in which the higher education assessment literature connects with issues of social justice rests on exploration of the link between assessment and students' current and future lives: their well-being, self-esteem, identity and social and economic opportunities. Boud and Falchikov make the claim stark and simple: 'Assessment affects people's lives. The future directions and careers of students depend on it.' (Boud & Falchikov, 2007a, p. 3). The authors powerfully drive this point home:

> What is at stake here is the nature of higher education itself. Assessment, rather than teaching, has a major influence on students' learning. It directs attention to what is important. It acts as an incentive for study. And it has a powerful effect on what students do and how they do it. Assessment also communicates to them what they can and cannot succeed in doing. For some, it [assessment] builds their confidence for their future work; for others, it shows how inadequate they are as learners and undermines their confidence about what they can do in the future.
>
> (Boud & Falchikov, 2007a, p. 3)

Similar statements now pepper the higher education assessment literature. Boud, Cohen and Sampson (1999) describe assessment as 'the single most powerful influence on learning in formal courses' (p. 413). Deneen and Boud (2014) state that 'more than any other part of students' learning experience, assessment has the potential to both enhance and reveal the quality of learning' (p. 577). Boud

(2014) also argues that 'assessment is probably the most powerful shaper of what students do and how they see themselves' (p. 24). Sambell et al. (2013) state that

> ideas about assessment relate very closely to ideas about learning. What we decide to assess indicates *what* we value in learning – the subject content, skills, qualities and so on.
>
> (p. 8, emphasis original)

Biggs and Tang (2011) argue that 'assessment is the senior partner in learning and teaching. Get it wrong and the rest collapses' (p. 221). Maclellan (2001) refers to assessment playing 'a subtle, complex, and enormously important role in the students' experiences of learning' (p. 308). Similarly, Taras (2008) argues that assessment 'has been shown to be the single most important component that influences student learning and education in general' (289). Leathwood (2005) states that 'future careers and earnings potential as well as health, status and self-esteem can all be affected by degree results' (p. 318). Zaher (2012) describes assessment as 'a destiny-determining' aspect of education (p. 527), while Knight (1995) insists that 'assessment is a moral activity. What we choose to assess and how shows quite starkly what we value' (p. 13). Sharp and Earle (2000) refer to the 'moral responsibility' institutions have 'to ensure that their assessments are valid and reliable tests of specialised skills and knowledge' (p. 193) partly because the rewards of society tend to be distributed according to the formal qualifications people hold. As Brown and Knight (1994) explain,

> Assessment is at the heart of the undergraduate experience. Assessment defines what students regard as important, how they spent their time, and how they come to see themselves as students and then as graduates.
>
> (p. 12)

In the context of increasing performativity, Broadfood and Pollard (2000) argue that assessment 'moulds' students' views of themselves not simply as learners but more broadly as members of society, 'defining notions of success and failure and the reasons for it' (p. 25). James (2000) refers to 'the immense significance of assignment grades and feedback comments on assessed work for the self-perceptions of these students' (p. 155).

Leathwood (2005) is one of the few authors to explicitly link assessment to social justice concerns. She regards assessment systems as 'rooted in academic cultures and institutional habitus' (p. 315) which are in turn dominated by the 'values of the white, masculinist establishment and a capitalist economy'

(p. 317). It is not just that assessment may shape students' future lives, but that the current system does so in ways that are not as just as they may seem. The experiences of assessment are not value neutral but reinforce particular social structures and divisions:

> Assessment is used to provide a rationale and legitimacy for the social structures and power relations of modern day societies, and for one's place within these. It is concerned directly with what is taught and what is valued within our education systems. It can influence not only how we see ourselves, but also our social relations with others and how we see them.
>
> (p. 308)

Not to underestimate the importance of assessment, Leathwood states that 'it is implicated in "the governance of the soul"' (quoting from Rose, 1991). As with other social institutions, she highlights how assessment systems are fraught with issues of power and privilege. In particular, it is the taken-for-granted status of assessment, our preparedness to just put up with it as the way things are, that enables its pervasive and negative impacts on the social world to continue – largely unnoticed.

At the level of the individual, student assessment can also have devastating effects on a person's self-identity, self-worth and self-esteem. Falchikov and Boud (2007) write,

> In some cases the interaction between the learner and the assessment event is so negative that it has an emotional impact that lasts many years and affects career choices.
>
> (p. 144)

Boud (1995a) describes assessment as working as 'a mechanism to control students that is far more pervasive and insidious than most staff would be prepared to acknowledge' (p. 35). Further, Boud (1995b) explains that 'assessment messages are coded, not easily understood and are often read differently and with different emphases by staff and by students' (p. 39). Indeed, in the previous section we noted how student and staff perceptions can differ markedly. Sambell and McDowell (1998) observe that assessment is 'the element of educational practice which most powerfully determines the hidden curriculum' (p. 392), again emphasizing the ways in which students can be excluded from full participation in assessment and learning tasks. In addition, argues Boud (1995b), each individual student carries with them prior experiences which will influence how they respond to the subject, and how they interpret assessment messages.

It is the failure of assessment to take account, and to assist, students' ongoing and future learning that particularly concerns Boud and Falchikov (2007a):

> Assessment would be less of a problem if we could be assured that what occurs under the guise of assessment appropriately influenced student learning.... Commonly, assessment focuses little on the processes of learning and on how students will learn after the point of assessment.
>
> (p. 3)

While the notion of self-directed learning has gained increasing prominence and credence, we again find dissonance between this and students' assessment experiences. Sambell et al. (1997) report that students often find that traditional assessment approaches leave them with little sense of control over their own learning. Assessment thus becomes 'something that was done to them, rather than something in which they could play an active role' (p. 363).

We can find among the assessment literature heart wrenching stories where students have been harmed or damaged by the prevailing assessment practices. This may occur in terms of their learning, or take more personal forms. Sambell et al. (1997) refer to the 'contamination' of learning by assessment (p. 357). Hughes (2014) argues that the dominance of competitive forms of assessment provide a barrier to genuine learning. Further, Falchikov and Boud (2007) outline how students who do not do well in assessment may describe themselves as being 'the problem' (p. 149). Richardson (2004) relates the story of Pauline, an economics student who learns – through her assessment tasks – *not* to engage critically or deeply with the subject, but simply to provide the expected answers. James (2000) tells the story of Theresa – whose self-image and confidence progressively declined through experiences of assessment. Here Theresa explains her feelings:

> [My self-confidence is] probably lower than it's ever been. That last essay did it, because the first two I had back I thought OK this is good, you know you're doing well kid, hang on in there ... So I felt good about myself for a while, for a week. And then I got the other one back, and I thought I just don't know the game, this is a game ... you know, I'm not playing it right. I'm so dependent on other people's assessment of my work for my own feelings, which is crazy, and I hate that I should be dependent on other people, because they're only assessing a piece of paper, not me. But it always feels so bloody personal ... sorry I didn't mean to swear.
>
> (p. 153)

Theresa goes on to talk about crying for days and needing to see a doctor – she felt so awful. Crossman (2007) reveals the visceral emotions students can feel when talking about assessments and their relationships with teachers:

> The predominant emotions described were anxiety, worry, hate, embarrassment, stress, terror, panic, humiliation, a sense of being under threat, horror, feeling overwhelmed, a sense of pointlessness, being upset, dread, hurt, frustration, boredom, resentment, being under pressure, loathing, fear, nervousness, emotional scarring and anger.

(p. 321)

Conclusion

Assessment is a social justice issue because it can have a profound effect over students' current and future lives. As Boud (1995a) makes clear: 'Students can, with difficulty, escape from the effects of poor teaching, they cannot (by definition if they want to graduate) escape the effects of poor assessment' (p. 35). The profound importance of assessment, and its implications for students' well-being is sometimes given as a reason for excessive caution when it comes to changing assessments. But equally, I suggest, this is the reason why we cannot leave assessment aside when considering social justice within and through higher education: 'Assessment is a moral activity' (Knight, 1995, p. 13). The current literature makes some connections between assessment and social justice, but we can and must do more to shift assessment to the centre of any emancipatory pedagogical project.

2

Theories of Social Justice

Introduction

In this chapter I begin my exploration of the theoretical ground upon which the idea of assessment for social justice rests. I spend some considerable time in this first section of the book on these theoretical underpinnings because I think they are important for establishing the foundations for real social change, and I believe this is an under-explored area of assessment in higher education. My analysis rests on a belief that the notion of social justice is complex and contested. Simple definitions also often hide a more malign intent. They can be used to subvert the very concept itself, making it fluffy, feel-good and devoid of critical meaning. Social justice can be a nebulous term, and one used so broadly and without clear definition as to lose all meaning. Notwithstanding evidence of the increased marketization of higher education (Bok, 2005; Maringe & Gibbs, 2009) pledges to social justice, well-being and civic responsibility feature in the mission statements of most universities and in many government policy statements. However, robust and purposeful links to social justice require more than the right words and must necessarily rest on firm, albeit multifaceted, theoretical foundations. Hence, I spend the first part of this book in this theoretical terrain.

What particularly interests me in an assessment context is that different understandings of social justice can lead to very different positions on what is fair, necessary and appropriate. In this chapter I will demonstrate this point by providing an overview of three different traditions of social justice theory and then considering how the perspectives on assessment that emerge through these lenses differ, and the social justice implications of this. I begin with the social contract tradition, and particular attention to the work of John Rawls and his theory of justice. Known variously as procedural, social contract or distributive theories of social justice, work in this tradition is important to my consideration of assessment for social justice because these are the theories which have been largely dominant within western societies for some time. As such, I argue, they have influenced conceptions of justice within mainstream assessment practices, along with education more broadly. That their influence may have arguably been more implicit than explicit does not diminish their importance. As already discussed, there are few explicit discussions of assessment and social justice in the literature, though there is some exploration of 'fairness' and assessment. I also argue that there is currently a considerable focus on procedures and methods – sometimes summarized under the dubious notion of 'good practice'. These approaches place a high emphasis on getting conditions and processes into ideal states that will then ensure just outcomes. Such literature, I argue, reflects the dominance of procedural notions of social justice in modern societies.

There are alternative ways of conceptualizing social justice within which the emphasis shifts from procedures to outcomes, or lived realities. Both the capabilities approach to social justice, particularly associated with the work of Sen (e.g. 2010) and Nussbaum (e.g. 2006, 2011) and critical theory place a much stronger emphasis on lived realities as a way to understand social justice. After my summary of Rawls and the social contract tradition, I will provide a brief introduction to each of these alternatives. In both examples, easy assumptions of well-behaved processes leading seamlessly to handsome outcomes are questioned. A recurring theme throughout this book is that we need to think about assessment more deeply and in terms of the people and practices that actually take place, and devote less time and faith to procedures alone. What justice means, and what may constrain it, becomes far more complex, messy and unpredictable outside the social contract tradition.

How we interpret assessment through the lens of social justice depends on the conceptualization of social justice we use. I demonstrate this in the final section of this chapter by considering four themes that highlight the shortcomings within an assessment context of prevailing, though often implicit, procedural understandings of social justice. These themes are: procedural or outcome-based approaches to social justice; how our understanding of social justice deals with difference; the extent to which social justice is conceptualized in 'perfect' terms and how the social and economic spheres are understood to interrelate in the theory. This will lay the foundation for the following chapters in which I drill down in greater depth into Axel Honneth's particular approach to critical theory based around mutual recognition, which will underpin the second part of this book.

John Rawls and the social contract tradition of justice

John Rawls's (1971) seminal work, *A Theory of Justice*, is often credited with rein-vigorating debate about the nature of social justice in the late twentieth century. This work has its roots firmly within the social contract tradition that has been a feature in Western thought since the European Enlightenment. Earlier social contract theorists who influenced Rawls include Hobbes, Locke and Rousseau and even a small familiarity with the different character of each of these think-ers' works suggests the diverse forms that social contract theory can take. Social contract theories bring together two traditions of thought with an even longer lineage: first, the notion of a 'state of nature' as a hypothetical time before the establishment of social institutions or political authority; and second, the idea that governments rest on some form of an original agreement between the rul-ers and those ruled (Lovett, 2011). The social contract represents the decisions made by people in this state of nature and upon which the legitimacy of political institutions is founded. On the basis that members of society share the traits that rendered the social contract, it can be assumed that they would then agree to such a contract through this process of identification with those who make the social contract. Having agreed to the contract, citizens are then motivated to abide by that agreement and any subsequent civil laws (Voice, 2011).

Rawls uses the term 'original position' instead of state of nature for this hypo-thetical state, and his version is also more abstracted than that of his prede-cessors in the social contract tradition (Rawls, 1971). This greater abstraction enables greater generalization by Rawls: 'He has no need for the lurid details of Hobbes's state of nature or the arguably more appealing details of Rousseau's alternative version' (Voice, 2011, p. 12). Stripped of these details by his greater level of abstraction, Rawls has more scope in which to consider the principles of justice (Voice, 2011) and thus his emphasis using the social contract shifts from a focus on the legitimate exercising of political authority and turns towards shared understandings of political and distributive justice (Voice, 2011). The heart of Rawls's theory of justice is, however, deceptively simple: justice as fairness. This primacy that Rawls accords to *justice as fairness* is another distinctive feature of his work (E. Kelly, 2001).

Scarcity is another central concept within social contract theory. The need for agreement only makes sense in conditions of relative scarcity. Thus, the social contract is seen as the basis for reasonable agreement about the distribution of benefits arising from social cooperation (P. Kelly, 1998). There would be no need for such agreement if resources were so abundant that everyone could have whatever they wanted, nor if they were so scarce that there was no choice of anyone having any (Voice, 2011). Thus we need to imagine people in the 'original position' faced with scarcity and therefore the need to make choices. Rawls makes the further assumption that these people are rational, reasonable, free and equal (Voice, 2011).

Rawls's primary interest was political in that it was concerned with the basis and operation of institutional frameworks. For example, in stating that people are equal, Rawls's meaning was political in that 'people are equal in the fundamental sense that they have equal political standing with respect to fellow citizens and equal claims on society's institutions' (Voice, 2011, p. 18). This is not about equality of outcomes or moral virtues.

There is one further essential concept that forms part of Rawls's framework, and this is the 'veil of ignorance'. How is it possible to make decisions about how social institutions will deal with scarcity in such a way that everyone will find it rational and reasonable to agree to them? This is where Rawls introduces the 'veil of ignorance'. This veil prohibits those in the original position from knowing how their own well-being will benefit from the agreed social arrangements. As a result, the only rational thing to do is to agree on a position that they would find acceptable even if they were in the group least advantaged by it. Any differences between citizens, notably the pursuit of their own differing interests, are thus brought into a situation of mutuality. Citizens are assumed to share a mutual disinterest about how their own position is directly affected by decisions on justice and to share a mutual interest in a rule of law that prevents any one person's interests dominating another. For example, it would not be rational to choose to live in a society with slavery, as you could not be sure that you were not a slave (Lovett, 2011). However, Rawls does not base his analysis in precise examples such as this, but at a more abstracted level, considering the general principles that can then be used to shape specific institutions (Lovett, 2011).

In describing such people as free, Rawls is explicitly locating his theory of justice within the context of liberal, democratic society. People agree to the social contract because they identify themselves as free, rational, equal and reasonable along with the people in the imagined 'original position' who made the initial decisions. They are assumed to understand the contract and thus be able to make informed decisions. Despite being based upon hypothetical situations and assumptions, Rawls does not see his theory of justice as purely metaphysical. Such assumptions are only useful if they are in some way 'anchored in the realities of human nature' (Voice, 2011, p. 7). Rawls states that his work envisages 'a society in which everyone accepts, and knows that everyone else accepts, the very same political conception of justice' (Rawls, 2001, p. 8).

The twin notions of fair procedure and mutual disinterest, which are central to Rawls's conception of social justice, are replicated in key tenets of what currently 'counts' as good assessment. Mutuality is mirrored in assessment by notions of academic credibility and quality standards. Thus, while all students are assumed to pursue their self-interest of obtaining good marks, it is also in their self-interest for there to be a disinterested assessment procedure which ensures that the interests of other students do not dominate their own. In addition, the credibility deemed to arise from such a system has an added benefit of improving the status of one's achievements. The notions of validity and reliability are at the fore of many discussions of fairness and assessment. I therefore argue that the procedural notion of social justice is pervasive and deeply socially engrained. As such, it is also not sufficiently interrogated.

Alternatives to proceduralism

In the coming chapters it will become more evident that my analysis of assessment for social justice rests firmly within the tradition of critical theory. However, in making the case for alternatives to procedural approaches to justice, I believe it is also important to mention the work of Sen and Nussbaum and the capabilities approach to social justice: not least because both authors have considerably influenced my thinking. Critical theory has much in common with the capabilities approach, particularly through the recognition of how undercurrents of power shape the different life opportunities of people. Both approaches also focus on lived realities rather than procedures and neither subscribes to ideal-type assumptions or the purely transcendental. But critical theory and the capabilities approach are both diverse groups of work, with their own internal debates; they should never be thought of as homogenous or simple conceptualizations.

The capabilities approach

The capabilities approach, as developed by Amartya Sen (2007, 2010) and Martha Nussbaum (2006, 2011) represents the first of my two alternatives to the social contract tradition (though Sen would argue that his version of the capabilities approach is not a theory of social justice). Both Sen and Nussbaum acknowledge the undeniable contribution made by Rawls, particularly in bringing questions of justice back to the fore of social thought. However, they both believe that Rawls's work is insufficient in addressing the breadth of issues required for a modern conceptualization of social justice. There are two main strands to the critiques made by Sen and Nussbaum. First, that Rawls's work is overly abstracted from the lives of real people, and second, that there is too much emphasis on procedure at the expense of focusing on actual outcomes.

The capabilities approach is important for the way in which it shifts the focus of social justice from procedures to outcomes. Rather than working through 'thought experiments' or idealized assumptions, the focus of the capabilities approach is very much on the lived realities of people's lives. This has resonance in my notion of assessment for social justice as I seek to understand the balance and causation between what students do within university and their later actions and dispositions in the broader social field. Both Sen and Nussbaum reject any ideal-type approaches to social justice and instead emphasize the complexity and multifaceted nature of people's lived realities. Key here is justice in terms of any individual's ability to fulfil their potential within whatever social context they live.

Nussbaum (2006) positions her capabilities approach as offering a solution to some of the more intractable problems within Rawls's theory of social justice, and particularly the issue of those people excluded by the initial assumption of sameness in the concept of *free, equal and independent*. Nussbaum argues that contractarian approaches, such as Rawls's, conflate aspects of 'by whom' and 'for whom'. As such, there is an assumption that the parties who design the principles of social justice do so on behalf of human beings possessing the same features as themselves. But what then of those who are different, featuring mental or physical disabilities that mean they are unable to participate in the processes of establishing the principles of justice? Thus, Nussbaum argues, the contractarian approach cannot accommodate the interests of such people under the umbrella of justice, and instead relies on notions of charity or compassion to protect their interests.

Nussbaum explains that while social justice theories should be 'abstract', they 'must also be responsive to the world and its most urgent problems and open to changes' (Nussbaum, 2006, p. 1). Overly idealized and abstracted theories have been guilty, she argues, of failing to confront some of the most serious problems facing the world. Thus Nussbaum offers a list of capabilities that represent common aspects of a fulfilled life, and yet allow room for contextualization in different settings. These capabilities are listed by Nussbaum but still regarded as subject to change over time. They are also subject to local contextualization.

Sen (2010) argues that a fixation on the nature of perfect justice removes attention from present and real experiences of suffering and injustice. He states: 'Justice cannot be indifferent to the lives that people can actually live' (p. 18). Sen is particularly interested in notions of choice involved in moving towards greater social justice, based on the realities of an imperfect world of limited resources. Thus, from Sen's perspective, the Rawlsian tradition has reached something of an impasse and attention must now focus elsewhere. Rather than continue to tweak idealized situations, decisions need to be made *and evaluated* by real people dealing with real problems of the distribution of goods (O'Neill & Williamson, 2012). This is addressed directly by Sen (2010) who states: 'If a theory of justice is to guide reasoned choice of policies, strategies or institutions, then the identification of fully just social arrangements is neither necessary nor sufficient' (p. 15).

Critical theory

Critical theory brings a particular dimension to understanding social justice not only through its complex understandings of power, but also from the emphasis given to the hidden and the distorted forces that shape human experience. To the idea of assessment for social justice, critical theory brings an appreciation of the implicit and unsaid, multiple notions of power and a commitment to change.

Critical theory is a term embracing a broad range of works and is particularly associated with members of the Frankfurt School (the Institute for Social Research) beginning in the early twentieth century. Founded as an independent research institute, the critical theory of the Frankfurt School embraced a commitment to both critical understanding of the social world and working to change that world. Critical theory involves a commitment to both empirical and critical research. It seeks to offer ways to explain the complexities, and apparent contradictions, in industrial, Western society. Critical theory thus seeks 'a foothold in the social world that simultaneously points beyond it' (Fraser, 2003, p. 202). Critical theory's 'primary task is the diagnosis of processes of social development that must be understood as preventing the members of society from living a "good life"' (Honneth quoted in Zurn, 2015, p. 93). Looking ahead to this 'good life' should be as important as looking back to the causes of injustice and suffering, although some commentators on critical theory suggest that a focus on critique and a growing pessimism more accurately reflect the work of the early critical theorists such as Horkheimer and Adorno.

Fundamental to critical theory is its foundation in Marxism; however, critical theorists offer neither blind advocacy of Marx's works nor simple critique. Critical theory grapples to understand a world in which there are no longer any of the 'essentialist guarantees' of the old Marxism (Fraser, 2003, p. 200). Instead, critical theory emerged from efforts to interpret and adapt Marx's writings within a twentieth-century context that Marx could not possibly have foreseen (Brookfield, 2005). In pursuit of new understandings, in new contexts, early critical theorists were notable for the ways in which they sought to bring Marx's work together with other emerging areas of thought. Early critical theorists brought in other bodies of work, such as Freudian psychoanalysis, and wove this with reinterpreted Marxism as they worked to understand the workings – and failings – of early twentieth century society. As Jay (1996) observes, it is difficult, looking back, to realize just how audacious it was to first bring Marx and Freud together. Freud's work was particularly important for emphasizing the role of the unconscious in shaping acts and beliefs. Critical theory pays particular attention to the hidden assumptions which underlie dominant social practices. What Freud's work offered the early critical theorists was an insight into that which is not easily seen – the subconscious – but which nevertheless exudes enormous influence. Freud's work, generally focused upon the individual, but was translated by these critical theorists to the social level, while at the same time understanding the social and the individual as inseparably interrelated.

The Frankfurt School was committed 'to bring about emancipation from ideological blinders by bringing to awareness the material conditions of our own knowledge of the world' (Anderson, 2011, pp. 32–3). Importantly, the implication that arises from this position is the possibility of change – of the social world being constructed differently (Anderson, 2011). This is clearly articulated in Horkheimer's early essay from 1937 on the difference between traditional and critical theory. In Horkheimer's words, 'critical theory maintains: it need not be so … and the necessary conditions for such change already exist' (Horkheimer, 1995, p. 227). In the simple phrase *it need not be so*, I believe Horkheimer delivers both a radical challenge and hope to those of us committed to social justice.

Critical theory has been described as an 'interdisciplinary social theory with emancipatory intent' (Zurn, 2015, p. 4). The contribution of critical theory, according to Fraser, is 'its distinctive dialectic of immanence and transcendence' (Fraser, 2003, p. 202). It is immanent in that its critique is grounded in the empirical world, not some godly perspective. It is transcendent in that it refuses to be constrained by that which already exists.

To achieve the dual purposes of explanation and critique, critical theory draws on a range of different disciplinary fields. In the case of such critical theorists as Theodor Adorno, the range of different areas of scholarly and everyday life which he draws upon is truly staggering, ranging through philosophy, sociology, music theory and down to reflections on everyday practices such as lonely hearts columns. As Goehr (2005) observes, it appeared that 'no place seemed to be protected from Adorno's pen' (p. xix). Similarly, Jay (1996) describes the 'sometimes dazzling, sometimes bewildering juxtaposition of highly abstract statements with seemingly trivial observations' (p. 82).

It is now possible to clearly identify three generations of critical theory, each of which are historical manifestations of their particular times and thinkers. Some caution, however, is needed to avoid presenting critical theory in too neat a way. Much of what I have discussed so far draws upon the first generation, which included Horkheimer and Adorno, and which I continue to find offers clear and critical insights into our social world and the place of justice within it. The second generation of critical theory is associated with Jürgen Habermas. Formerly a student of Adorno and Horkheimer, Habermas critiqued the critical theory of his forebears as being overly pessimistic and somewhat intolerant of modern culture. Habermas's critical theory is grounded in notions of communicative reason as a vehicle towards human emancipation. An example of the application of Habermas's critical theory to higher education can be found in McLean's (2006) book on critical pedagogy and the university. Habermas's influence extends well beyond the confines of critical theory alone, and deserves credit for a broader communicative turn in social criticism. But in recent years it has been argued that a recognition paradigm has replaced the previously dominant communication theory paradigm in social criticism landscape (Rossler, 2010). Recognition is at the heart of third-generation critical theorist Axel Honneth's work and in the next chapter I explore Honneth in greater depth. I do so because I believe it demonstrates a path beyond critique alone, and offers a theoretical lens well suited to the challenges of assessment for social justice. Honneth clearly differentiates his approach to social justice, referring to

> a transition from the idea of 'redistribution' to the notion of 'recognition'. Whereas the first term is linked with a vision of justice that aims to establish social equality through the redistribution of goods guaranteeing liberty, the

second term defines the conditions of a just society through the aim of recognizing the individual dignity of all individuals.

(Honneth, 2004b, pp. 351–2)

Before this, however, I want to explore in a little more detail the implications of assessment being informed, albeit implicitly, by dominant Rawlsian/procedural understandings of social justice, and begin to consider how things might seem through alternative social justice lenses.

The implications for assessment of social contract assumptions about social justice

Procedure rather than outcome

I begin with the clearest distinction between Rawlsian approaches to social justice and alternatives such as the capabilities approach and critical theory. Both the capabilities approach and critical theory reject a focus on procedures rather than outcomes. This distinction must be understood as somewhat nuanced. It is not the case that Rawlsian approaches ignore outcomes altogether, nor do these alternatives eschew any consideration of processes. Sen (2010), for example, is clear that he does not advocate ignoring good process, but rather moving our main focus beyond procedure alone. But the emphasis in these different traditions between procedure and outcome can be contrasted. Nussbaum (2006) exemplifies the difference between these with this example:

> Although the following analogy may strike some fans of procedural justice as a bit unfair, it seems to the outcome-oriented theorist as if a cook has a fancy, sophisticated pasta-maker, and assures her guests that the pasta made in this machine will be by definition good, since it is the best machine on the market. But surely, the outcome theorist says, the guests want to taste the pasta and see for themselves.
>
> (p. 83)

In the previous chapter I discussed the different ways in which fairness is discussed in relation to assessment. I also argued that fairness is for many people the byword of just assessment. The problem, I suggest, is that much of the work, including policies and guidelines, that seeks to ensure fair assessment focuses on procedures alone. While there has been considerable attention paid to setting up systems to ensure 'fair' assessment, these are, arguably, based on false assumptions that any such procedural certainty is possible. Stowell (2004) warns against assuming outcomes will be just simply because assessment procedures are in place. The problem with a reliance on procedure is that it denies the dynamic, unpredictable, socially constructed nature of what it means to engage in an assessment task and in the marking of students' work. But such is the reigning faith in proceduralism and 'fair' assessment that we continue to move more and more resources into shoring up such procedures rather than addressing underlying issues. As a consequence, all the limitations associated with procedural approaches to justice have become ingrained in assessment practices encouraged by unreflective acceptance of the virtues of proceduralism. And yet, as Sadler (2007) observes, assessment policies can sometimes lead to the opposite outcomes as those intended. The resources that go into maintaining a system of extensive procedural checking must necessarily be diverted from other activities which may be more effective in promoting student learning (Bloxham, 2009).

Assessment cannot be ruled by procedure alone because it is not a discrete task such as filling a bucket of water: marking students' work at university is a complex process that requires judgement and experience. Eisner (1985) emphasized this in his notion of 'connoisseurship' and assessment. This reinforces assessment as a social practice which one learns and develops through engagement with the task and interaction with others. The task of assessment must be learned through experience rather than a rule book. This is not to say there are no rules, but rules are insufficient in themselves. Moreover, rules are also social constructions. Critical theory is useful here for highlighting the hidden assumptions which underlie dominant social practices. The decision as to what does or does not get included in an assessment rule or procedure is itself a social construction reflecting many values and assumptions.

From a student perspective, an emphasis on proceduralism can distort the nature of the tasks they should be engaging with. Higher education should be based around complex knowledge, with which we engage critically. There is a tension, I suggest, between tasks that can be easily assessed (such as right/wrong answers or multiple choice questions) and critical engagement with dynamic and contested knowledge. Of course, sometimes there are formative or evaluative reasons for setting simpler tasks to scaffold learning of more complex material. But in the main, students can misunderstand the very nature of higher education if we send out wrong messages through the assessment task. Students can also become too fixated with procedures, and thus misunderstand the true nature of the assessment tasks. Research by Norton (2004) suggests that where students become overly obsessed by the procedural aspects of feedback or advice, it can give rise to a prescriptive approach which inhibits learning. Rather than being empowered by advice given, students may become more dependent, obsessing over details such as how many references they 'should' include and so on. This occurs because such details are easy to proceduralize, whereas the real focus of student work – engagement with complex knowledge – is not. A focus on procedure in assessment thus leads students away from the most important aspect of what they should be doing – critical engagement with complex knowledge.

Assumptions of sameness and difference

Procedural approaches to social justice necessarily work on the basis of assumed commonalities that everyone is free and independent and that people exist in a state of mutual disinterest. Treating everyone the same works, no matter how self-interested individuals might be, because this is the only way to ensure their treatment is not worse than that of others. Such assumptions of sameness and mutuality are closely tied with the emphasis on procedures rather than outcomes. Thus, if we shift our social justice gaze to outcomes, we also problematize the extent to which justice can simply be treating everyone the same.

I suggest that a preoccupation with fairness as sameness is one of the major factors constraining assessment playing a greater social justice role. In a procedural approach, anyone who deviates from the norm can only be accommodated through special allowances or charitable exceptions. But these are only given on the basis of certain circumstances, and the choice of which circumstances count may appear impartial but is actually based on particular values and perceptions. Students may qualify for 'special circumstances' if able to establish they have a medical condition, family bereavement or other factors deemed beyond their control. However, this rests on an ideal-type assumption about the 'normal' conditions under which students live, study and complete assessments. So illness is a socially acceptable reason for deserving different treatment. Contrast this with differences in economic class which lead some students to have to work long hours of paid employment in order to go to university, or to go without useful aids such as laptops, books and even basic necessities such as heating. But these are not deemed reasonable grounds for different treatment. I am not suggesting that we introduce more grounds for special circumstances nor that we abandon the practice altogether. However I am highlighting that these supposedly 'fair' systems are themselves highly selective and based on socially constructed notions of what should and should not count, and these may deserve rethinking. There is no ideal-type point of reference as implied by procedural notions of justice.

Lying on a foundation of assumptions about 'sameness', procedural approaches to social justice risk essentializing identity. We come to see all undergraduates or all chemistry students or history students as the same. Students are an amorphous mass, a mob, and attempts to account for student difference are made to seem unhelpful or even disruptive. From this perspective, accounting for difference must be unfair, because fairness is unquestionably nested with sameness.

A further example of this can be seen in the ways many institutions have responded to perceived student dissatisfaction with feedback. Many have introduced blanket turnaround times in response to complaints that feedback is not timely, and thereby failed to consider the real issues of timeliness in terms of usefulness and applicability to future work. Moreover, there have been drives for standardization of feedback in other ways, such as in what form it is given or how much (even word limits on how much feedback is given are mandatory in some institutions) in a procedural drive to an illusive form of fairness as sameness: driven by the apparent logic that if all academics are doing exactly the same for all students, then surely there can be no unfairness.

Nussbaum (2006) warns about utilitarian approaches to social justice that focus on aggregating notions of satisfaction. In so doing, she argues, these approaches inherently marginalize those who do not gain prominence in the aggregate. Moreover, aggregation ignores tendencies for 'adaptive preferences' (making do in the circumstances). Thus she argues: 'Contentment is not the only thing that matters in a human life; active striving matters, too' (p. 73). As discussed, Nussbaum argues that procedural approaches, such as Rawls's, conflate aspects of 'by whom' and 'for whom'. As such, there is an assumption that the parties who design the principles of social justice do so on behalf of human beings possessing the same features as themselves – the long shadow, once again, of assumed sameness.

The repercussions of how identity, sameness and difference are dealt with in an assessment context are huge, and are influenced by the conceptualization of social justice that one brings into play. Serious tensions in current approaches are easy to observe. On the one hand there is an acknowledgement of student diversity through increasing emphasis on student voice and on the personalization of learning and teaching interactions (McLean, Abbas & Ashwin, 2013) and yet the prevailing system of 'fairness' structured around predetermined learning outcomes and constructive alignment cannot truly deal with individual differences. Indeed, the logic of fairness and justice inherent in this system is to negate differences: it is the level–playing field approach to justice. As such it is an uncontextualized notion of justice that denies all context and temporality. Students line up at the same starting place and have a clearly defined and common finishing line – but all other factors are ignored in the name of fairness. Exceptions are dealt with in terms of charity: exceptional circumstances and benevolent exemptions.

Forced to conform by an assessment process to an essentialized group identity, students are frustrated in bringing individuality and personalization to their learning. This impacts on the social justice outcomes in two ways. First, it is a form of injustice to the student – it is again a mirage of fairness where conformity masquerades as process. Second, it embeds a notion of conformity as civic responsibility which carries through to social practices; hence doctors can go on to expect patients behave a certain way, lawyers expect their clients to accept procedures – rather than have a right to challenge, resist and subvert within a society that is perpetuating injustices.

How perfect can social justice be?

The extent to which we can aspire to a perfect or ideal notion of social justice relates to the two previous two themes. If one's focus is on procedure, and if one works on assumptions of sameness, then an ideal state of social justice makes sense. What distinguishes Rawls's approach from capabilities or critical theory is the role of idealized, perfect notions of social justice in working towards any reality. Nussbaum's (2006) work suggests that a pre-occupation with putting in place the 'right' conditions for social justice may actually obscure our understanding of the multiple circumstances that can prevent or impair different people's experiences of (in)justice in a society. This can be understood from a critical theory perspective in terms of the importance of the immanent basis of any social analysis, and the very real dangers of the submersion, and hence pathologization, of social problems and disparities.

One of the appeals of procedure in an assessment context is building in checks and balances to ensure students get the 'correct' mark. For this to work, assumptions of sameness and a 'level playing field' are required. This notion of checks and balances is not unreasonable in itself, and is entirely consistent with thinking of assessment as a social practice. However, what is not reasonable is to perpetuate myths that assessment can in any way be 'perfected' by procedure or any other means. Many academics still talk about ensuring their students have the 'right' marks and some even try to back up such claims in exam boards by proudly producing bell curve diagrams of their marking distribution as evidence of its *perfection*. Thus their approach to assessment falls victim to the pervasiveness of normative approaches to marking, masquerading as criterion-based. This is process as illusion.

Social and economic spheres

A further problem with procedural approaches to social justice lies in the insufficient attention given to the complex social domain, and the ways in which this intersects with the economic. In contrast, both the capabilities approach and critical theory highlight the many interrelations between economic and social factors that shape our lives and the nature of social justice. Hence social justice cannot be attained by a procedural distribution, or redistribution of wealth or resources, but involves a dialectic between the social and economic on many levels. This impacts on understandings of assessment at a fundamental level because it connects with beliefs about the very purposes of higher education. If social justice involves an interaction of social and economic factors, then connecting assessment solely to the economic realm (as in employability and/or preparation for work) is unreasonable. While work is important for well-being, there is more to well-being than the economic exchange value of our labour.

As I have discussed elsewhere (McArthur, 2011) 'the problem for higher education is not the trend towards it having an economic role, but rather the narrowness of the way in which that role is conceptualised' (p. 738), and particularly its disarticulation from the social realm. Therefore, 'what "the economy" looks like, and what it means to people's lives, interactions, thoughts, beliefs and relationships, may look very different depending upon where one is placed within that economy' (p. 738). A major problem for the way in which assessment in higher education has become so intricately linked to the employability agenda, and even to graduate attributes, is this conflation of the economic perspectives of those who thrive within the current economic arrangements and those who do not.

Conclusion

In this chapter I have reviewed the differences between alternative approaches to social justice. In so doing, I have given a brief introduction to critical theory, which I will build on in the following chapter. Most importantly, I have sought to demonstrate that, in an assessment context, our notions of justice and fairness can differ considerably depending on our conceptualization of these terms. Social justice can be understood in many different ways. What is essential, I suggest, is that we move from implicit understandings to explicitly articulating what we mean by social justice, and then use this to explore assessment in higher education.

3

Social Justice as Mutual Recognition

Introduction

In the previous chapter I demonstrated that different theories of social justice can have very different implications for assessment. I further argued that much of our current assessment policy and practice rests on implicit, and also often unreflective, assumptions influenced by dominant social contract, or procedural, notions of social justice. In contrast, this book is positioned within the tradition of critical theory and critical pedagogy, with an emphasis on hidden and distorted forms of power and the emancipatory potential of change. In this chapter I build on the previous discussion and provide a more in-depth overview of Axel Honneth's approach to social justice – where justice is understood intersubjectively in terms of mutual recognition.

In the first part of this chapter, I provide an introduction to Honneth's conceptualization of social justice as mutual recognition: as the giving and receiving of acknowledgement of one's inherent worth, place in society and contribution to society. Here the importance of the intersubjective nature of this theory is explained. In the second half of the chapter, I consider the nature of misrecognition in Honneth's work. Both recognition and misrecognition are equally important concepts to take forward in our understanding of assessment for social justice. This grounding in Honneth's critical theory, and particularly his understanding of social justice as mutual recognition, is essential for offering an alternative way of thinking about assessment, as developed in Part 2 of this book.

Axel Honneth: Justice as mutual recognition

Axel Honneth represents the third generation of critical theorists, following on the work of the original Frankfurt School. The antecedence of his work in these traditions, notably the works of Adorno, Horkheimer and Habermas is clear, though often manifested through critique. Indeed, he is equally keen to assert the distinctiveness of the direction to which he has taken critical theory, and peeling back the levels of analysis to the realm of recognition is an essential part of his approach. Honneth argues that the organization of society is based on 'certain patterns of recognition': 'Human beings depend on social forms of recognition in order to develop an identity and to gain a certain understanding and a sufficient form of self-relation' (Honneth in Marcelo, 2013, p. 210). Social justice requires social structures that enable undistorted recognition of, and between, individuals. This can start from the very basic level of simply recognizing another person to exist, to recognition of the traits and abilities of that person. Thus our gaze is directed to a different place than, for example, famous second-generation critical theorist, Jurgen Habermas. Rather than positioning his focus on the conflict between the social system and the lifeworld, it rests on the nature and reasons for the systematic denial of conditions for recognition (Sandberg & Kubiak, 2013) of and between individual members of that society.

Honneth (2014a) explains his theory of justice as 'an analysis of society' (p. vii); thus, in keeping with other critical theory, it begins with society as it actually exists, not some idealized or theorized idea. Here the influence of Hegel is clear:

> We would do well to take up once again Hegel's endeavour to develop a theory
> of justice on the basis of the structural preconditions actually existing in society.
>   (Honneth, 2014a, p. 3)

Honneth argues that for anyone in the Hegelian tradition, 'the idea of justice is not an independent and free-standing notion that can be explained on its own terms' (Honneth, 2014a, p. 4). We must examine the shared ideals, values and actions upon which social reproduction is based, he argues, and then subject these to critical scrutiny. Honneth's approach challenges 'the division of labour assumed by traditional conceptions of justice between the social sciences and normative theory, between empirical disciplines and philosophical analysis' (Honneth, 2014a, p. 5). Honneth is clearly reinforcing the essential and inherently interdisciplinary nature of critical theory. Following Hegel, there is no 'external determination of how social reality must be constituted' but instead it is determined 'through the analysis of that reality itself' (Honneth, 2014a, p. 6). This contrasts with the stand-alone or ideal-type approaches to social justice within the social contract tradition.

Honneth (2014a) further argues that the social contract tradition of justice rests on a *negative* notion of freedom; that is, freedom from interference in the pursuit of particular actions. He contrasts negative freedom with two other conceptualizations – reflexive and positive freedom. Reflexive freedom, Honneth explains, is consistent with what Isiah Berlin termed positive freedom (in Berlin's distinction between positive and negative freedoms): that is, freedom to act according to one's own intentions. The problem with reflexive freedom, according to Honneth, is that it naturally limits freedom by failing to allow account to be taken of the institutional rather than purely personal factors 'that are crucial for the successful completion of the process of reflection' (Honneth, 2014a, p. 40). Narrowing our focus to simply that of the personal level fails to take account of the social nature of self and identity. Thus Honneth argues for a third concept of freedom – social freedom – that does take account of the institutional forms essential for its realization. It is in this context of social freedom that the conceptualization of social justice based on mutual recognition lies.

Honneth (2003a) argues that the normative principles of a critical theory should be based on moral claims that are already valid in some way within that social order. At the same time, however, we must avoid being positioned simply within the status quo: critique of what exists and striving for change go hand in hand. A high level of criticality is achieved by the focus on existing everyday practices, small relationships, the easily overlooked and unobserved. Normative reconstruction works to ensure the existing order is not simply reaffirmed, but by revealing existing practices in the social order, the aim is to critique and to explore alternative paths. For example, in our prevailing society we might argue that there is already a valid moral claim that adults should care for children and this is evidenced in many held beliefs and actions. It is not, however, fully realized within the current status quo. Abuse and neglect of children does occur on many levels and in different ways. Thus a gap exists between claims we can make based on existing moral outlooks and the realities of the status quo.

Furthermore, Honneth argues that the gap between 'philosophical theories of justice and political praxis' is widening (Honneth, 2014b, p. 36). In contrast, at the time in which Rawls's work was so dominant, along with other philosophers such as Michael Walzer and Charles Taylor, Honneth argues that there was more widespread discussion about the nature of justice, and also more efforts than today to link these discussions to actual political programmes and actions. The situation today, argues Honneth (2014b), is one of 'malaise' in which there is 'a disconnect between political philosophy and political action, between theory and praxis' (p. 35).

To the extent that there are any agreed normative foundations within liberal-democratic societies, Honneth argues that these rest too much on legal guarantees alone. He argues that the location of social justice solely within the realm of legal rights is too narrow and fails to include many of the key bases on which a fuller account of social justice needs to rest. Moreover, he is placing an emphasis on actions rather than simply what is defined in policy statements. Here again we have the emphasis on social justice in terms of lived realities. In offering his theory of social justice as mutual recognition, Honneth is insistent that 'recognition may not consist in mere words or symbolic expressions, but must be accompanied by actions that confirm these promises' (Honneth, 2014b, p. 92).

Mutual recognition

Pivotal to Honneth's conception of social justice is the relational aspect of such justice, realizing that social justice is furthered, and denied, by the ways in which people interact with each other:

> After all, we can only grasp ourselves as being 'free' to the extent that we are addressed and treated as such by others.
>
> (Interview in Willig, 2012, p. 148)

Mutuality is key to Honneth's conception of social justice:

> The justice or wellbeing of a society is measured according to the degree of its ability to secure conditions of mutual recognition in which personal identity formation, and hence individual self-realization, can proceed sufficiently well.
>
> (Honneth, 2004b, p. 354)

It is important to fully appreciate the significance of *mutual* recognition in Honneth's analysis. Recognition is intrinsically embodied in the ways in which we interact with others and also the ways in which we express our own individuality through that process. People only gain subjectivity intersubjectively (Zurn, 2015). Thus Honneth is offering an intersubjective theory of social justice, which I believe distinguishes him from many other social justice scholars.

Thus the social and the individual are always interrelated and our analysis and understandings must include both. Indeed, the notion of mutuality plays out in two key ways. First, through the mutual nature of recognition itself: moral progress (movement towards greater social justice) only occurs through the giving and receiving of these forms of recognition. For, the act of recognition to occur in a one-sided way would actually mean a distortion occurs, representing mis-recognition and injustice. Second, such mutual recognition is always about both self-realization and social inclusion. We can only think about equal treatment in society, according to Honneth, to the extent that people have chances for the formation of personal identity – which rests on the quality of social recognition relations. We cannot separate individual achievement, for example, from the social sphere in which it occurs, in the same way that social practice theories (which I consider in the next chapter) argue that we cannot separate individual agency from its social context. Social justice, or morality, thus becomes 'tailored to the quality of societally guaranteed recognition relations' (Honneth, 2004b, p. 354). Individuals come to grasp their sense of self in the two senses of being a full member of a social community but also a particular member of that community – through the process of recognition across different spheres and domains. Within the different domains, different examples of the struggle for recognition take place. Here is where I believe Honneth's work adds something to social practice theories, which I discuss in the next chapter. In understanding these different domains we can better appreciate instances of injustice and how to effect change. These are different spheres of human action and the everyday practices therefore play out in various ways. Understanding this moves us forward towards enacting greater social justice.

Contrast this mutuality and intersubjectivity with the dominant liberal, proceduralist theories of social justice where the focus is on being free from restrictions imposed by others. Honneth is challenging the 'individualistic notion of personal autonomy' that has become a foundation of other theories of justice, whereby dependency on others is seen as a threat to individual freedom (Honneth, 2014b, p. 37). In contrast, dependency – interrelations and intersubjectivity – are essential to both individual and social freedoms.

What distinguishes Honneth's approach to social justice is his insistence on recognition as the first order area of concern. In this way his works stands in contrast to other progressive theorists who place primary emphasis on redistribution within society. Honneth regards the distinction between economic disadvantage and cultural deprivation as 'phenomenologically secondary in character', referring to 'differences in the respects to which subjects can experience social disrespect or humiliation (Honneth, 2004b, p. 352). Thus Honneth focuses our gaze on a very different point than either other critical theorists or other social justice theorists. Honneth's position is that we must take our analysis of social justice back to the primary realm of individual self-realisation, because to do anything else risks privileging the groups or issues that are most easily seen. Honneth's concern is that approaches to social justice that are based upon redistribution remain

> blind to forms of disadvantage and harm that are not directly linked to the socio-economic class position or to the reality of working class life. For these types of deprivation only come into view, once the criterion for social justice is not defined as equal opportunity in the narrow sense, but as the integrity of the social life form as a whole.
>
> (Honneth, 2010b, p. 14)

Thus, argues Honneth, classical conceptualizations of social justice are also blind to the myriad forms of discrimination that emerge from membership of an ethnic or cultural minority, because of sexuality or due to religious affiliation. Indeed, he argues that such classical views are based on assumptions of the dominant norm being a household with a white, male head (Honneth, 2010b). The intersectionality between different forms of discrimination and injustice is therefore at the heart of Honneth's work, recognizing that such injustice lies in more than economic or legal relations alone.

In order to reflect the complexity of human interactions, and the potential spheres for justice, Honneth proposes a plural notion of social justice with three aspects of mutual recognition, each of equal importance. These are: *love recognition, respect recognition and esteem recognition*. Each form of recognition relates to different realms of human experience, and each in turn has its own characteristics. But it is the three together that make up this understanding of social justice.

Love recognition is all about affective care. The mode of recognition here is emotional support and the principle that should take priority is that of need: what support and love someone needs to realize a just life. There is a level of intimacy and particularity to this mode of recognition. Thus, for example, it is about the relationship between a particular father and his child, or a particular woman and her partner, or two particular friends. In Honneth's terms this form of recognition engenders self-confidence. Love recognition is essential to become a knowingly confident individual. But this is not self-confidence in the everyday meaning of the term, nor in a strictly psychological sense. It is self-confidence as related to the twin achievements of self-realization and social inclusion. Thus, it is self-confidence to be ourselves and for that self-realization to be socially situated. Self-confidence, argues Honneth, is a necessary prerequisite for us to experience the other two forms of recognition: 'Self-confidence refers to a very basic sense of the stability and continuity of one's self as a differentiated individual with particular needs and emotions' (Zurn, 2015, p. 31). In later chapters I will use the idea of love recognition to explore the emotional landscape on which assessment takes place, with a particular emphasis on relations of trust and honesty.

Respect recognition refers to equal treatment in law. Here, the principle that takes priority is that of equality. The mode of recognition here is cognitive respect and it refers to the development of moral responsibility. What is important to stress is that this is not simply about having certain legal rights. It is about having, understanding and exercising those rights *and* acknowledging the same in others. Having this capacity to understand and exercise one's rights therefore also provides one with a sense of responsibility for one's own actions. Unlike the particularity of the relationship in love recognition, here we must understand respect (or legal) recognition as a universal. Rights are 'depersonalized symbols of social respect' (Honneth, 1996, p. 118). This explains why as a society we might ensure the welfare and well-being of a convicted criminal even though we judge their acts to be abhorrent (Zurn, 2015). Without such rights we are simply at the mercy of the goodwill of others (Zurn, 2015). The practical relation to self that is nurtured by this form of recognition is described as self-respect:

> One is able to respect oneself as a moral agent because one deserves – and is publicly recognized as deserving – the legal respect of others as a moral agent.
> (Zurn, 2015, p. 37)

In Chapter 7 I will discuss the extent to which assessment policy and practice enables students to recognize themselves in this way by being able to participate in assessment practices with genuine responsibility.

Finally, *esteem recognition* refers to traits, abilities and achievements and the ways in which these contribute to society. Thus it is also associated with solidarity – with shared social membership. Esteem cannot have the same unconditional character as love recognition, for it would then arguably not be worth much (Zurn, 2015): it simply is not the case that everything everyone does is socially useful. While it does not have the particularity of love recognition, it does relate to individuals – to individuals' acts and contributions to society – unlike the universality of respect recognition. In all three cases, the recognition nurtures a healthy sense of self – always understood, however, in terms of the dual roles of mutuality. Self-esteem is fostered when our abilities and actions are regarded as socially useful and are recognized as such. Honneth explains,

> When I think of solidarity, what I have in mind as a paradigm is the political group, let's say, the solidaristic group of those who are fighting for the same goal.

They are in solidary relationships with each other. Then the question is to understand exactly that kind of solidarity, and I think the best way to understand it is to say it is based on the esteem of action which contributes to reaching, to accomplishing the common shared goal. So, my solidaristic attitude towards my companion or towards the other members in my political group is based on the fact that I esteem him or her for acting in a way which leads to an accomplishment of the goal we all share with each other. So, solidarity is somewhat based on accomplishment, on each estimation of accomplishment.

(Honneth in Iorio, Campello & Honneth, 2013, p. 250)

It is worth making absolutely clear that Honneth's use of terms such as self-confidence, self-respect and self-esteem should not be confused with popular psychology notions of 'self-help' and self-realization. The emphasis on self is always utterly embedded in the notion of mutuality and social inclusion. Honneth uses a 'specifically philosophical vocabulary' (Alexander & Lara, 1996, p. 1) and we must take account of this, not least when we are reinterpreting his work in different contexts. The problem with these popular self-help 'specialists' is twofold – self is often regarded in starkly individualized rather than social terms, in addition to which they exude an instrumental rationality nested in a belief that people can be 'fixed' by outside experts. Honneth displays a scepticism towards 'the pretensions of rationality, self-transparency, and self-determination' (Zurn, 2015, p. 14). Within Honneth's work, 'social groups represent both driving forces of historical development and essential conditions for human flourishing' (Anderson, 2011, p. 48).

Social injustice occurs when recognition believed to be legitimate is withheld (Honneth, 2004b). By insisting on recognition as the primary foundation for any conception of social justice, Honneth is always foregrounding the relational nature of social justice. Social justice arises from the mutual recognition of others, who they are, what they do and their inherent worth. Justice is inseparable from the social nature of our being, but so too is injustice or misrecognition:

The goal of social justice must be understood as the creation of social relations in which subjects are included as full members in the sense that they can publicly uphold and practice their lifestyles without shame or humiliation.

(Honneth, 2003a, p. 259)

A struggle for recognition is successful when it manages to change the prevailing recognition order in society. This results in new forms of intersubjective practices (hence social practices) that ensure people receive the recognition and hence conditions of freedom that they deserve (Zurn, 2015). Individuals only achieve their true identity through relations of mutual recognition. This entails a range of intersubjective relations. In the context of higher education, we can understand these as between: student and teacher; student peers; members of a particular course or programme teaching team; academics and their managers; students and parents. The possible list of combinations, of realms of intersubjective relationships is quite vast, so here I have just listed some of the more obvious ones. Within each of these, individuals may see themselves, or see others, in terms of other group memberships (e.g. LGBT students, international academics, nontraditional students) adding to the relational intersections. These are all potential spheres of social freedom or of injustice.

Misrecognition and social pathologies

The term social pathologies is used in critical theory to describe prevailing conditions that work against people being able to live good and just lives. A social pathology gives rise to the conditions for misrecognition and hence injustice. The idea of a social pathology encourages us to think in terms of hidden influences and unofficial or unacknowledged forms of power, or, indeed, the clandestine impacts of official power. The emphasis here, as discussed in Chapter 2, is to look beyond official statements or policies and to consider lived realities. Recognition, Honneth is clear, is about what happens in practice, not just about platitudes or promises. This supports the emphasis in this book of not simply idealizing assessment, but looking at real social practices, a point which I take up more fully in the next chapter, and in Part 2 of this book.

In thinking about what helps shape these social practices, it is useful to consider Honneth's notion of *pathologies of reason* (Honneth, 2009). Thus while our focus should be on actions, we must also consider the forms of reason that shape these actions. Here Honneth alerts us to the damaging effects of more instrumental forms of reason dominating all others. Honneth explains this in the following way:

> Its insight is that by means of the structural organization of societies, some of our rational capacities are restricted and others are invited to grow. This is the whole idea behind the notion of instrumental reason. It is a pathology of reason because a certain structure of our society privileges only one dimension of our rationality.
>
> (Honneth in Marcelo, 2013, p. 219)

As academics, the dominance of instrumental reason can help us to understand feelings of powerlessness in not being able to rise up against prevailing practices. Here I refer to the point made near the start of this book that we must have a language that allows thinking and actions outside those of the prevailing – largely instrumentalized – mainstream. Thus we may hold feelings of profound unease about the policies that dominate assessment and learning within our institutions, but not feel able to express quite why they worry us so, particularly within formal committees and even informal collegial networks in which the assumptions of the status quo are made to appear simply as common sense, as though it could not be any other way. Here I believe is another way in which Honneth's work can help by providing a language through which to understand misrecognition that may be occurring around us, even embedded into the institutional weft and weave of our universities. In particular, I believe that Honneth's idea of *ideological recognition* provides a powerful foundation to critique current assumptions about the degree to which our teaching, learning and assessment practices are genuinely student-centred. Ideological recognition refers to forms of recognition that seemingly offer positive affirmations but which actually serve to reinforce the dominant system. By giving people a positive self-image, they will more readily submit to socially prescribed roles and behaviour. Honneth (2014b) offers several examples: the 'Uncle Tom' character given praise for his submissive behaviour, thus reinforcing the dominant slave-owning society; the notion of a 'good' mother and housewife, praised for the efforts which actually keep her trapped in certain roles which reinforce the broader gender-specific division of labour in society; and the soldiers heaped with praise about their valour and bravery, as a necessary way of ensuring so many people are prepared to go to war to support established interests. There is a conceptual problem, however, argues Honneth, with being able to easily identify ideological forms of recognition. It is much easier to identify ideological recognition through hindsight when one is no longer thinking within the confines of that dominant ideology. Thus, he argues,

> we live in an epoch that regards itself as being morally superior to past ages, we are certain that the esteem enjoyed by the virtuous slave, the good housewife and the heroic soldier was purely ideological. Yet if we put ourselves in the past, it becomes much more difficult to distinguish between a false, 'ideological' form of recognition and one that is correct and morally imperative, because the criteria of which we were so convinced suddenly become uncertain.
>
> (Honneth, 2014b, p. 77)

Honneth therefore adds a further criterion to establishing whether a given act is one of ideological recognition. He directs us to consider the gap between the recognition being offered and the material conditions for its actual realization. Thus we can take an example from current society, where we are without the benefit of hindsight, and detect ideological recognition where such a gap exists. Here Honneth turns to the labour market for a useful example. He identifies ideological recognition in prevailing labour relations and the dominant management discourse whereby workers are given more and more inflated terms to describe themselves, reflecting prevailing discourses of individual self-fulfilment. Thus independence, creativity and entrepreneurialism are emphasized as wage labour is relabelled *'entrepreneurs' of their own labour or 'entreployees'* (Honneth, 2014b, p. 91). The material conditions of waged work, however, have often moved further away, rather than closer, to the possibility of achieving such independence and self-determination:

> The new manner of addressing employees and qualified workers as entrepreneurs of their own labour-power might contain an evaluative promise of recognizing a higher degree of individuality and initiative, but it in no way ensures the institutional measures that would allow a consistent realization of these new values. Instead, employees are compelled to feign initiative, flexibility and talents where there is no material basis for doing so.
>
> (p. 93)

Thus there is a gap between the promised recognition and the possibility of its realization. Further, such ideological recognition can have a regulatory character, fostering in workers 'a new relation-to-self, which encourages willing acceptance of a considerably modified workload' (p. 91).

The notion of ideological recognition will be important in Part 2 of this book when we consider movements towards students acting as active agents in their own learning and, by extension, assessment practices. To what extent do the many positive terms we use to describe our students, and their assessment activities, reflect the genuine material conditions for their realization? We use terms such as autonomous learner, self-directed learner, self-regulated learner and student engagement: Are the structures and practices in place such that these are realistic ambitions? These must go beyond feel-good policy sound bites and refer to the lived realities of how our students learn within our institutions. When we make lists of graduate attributes or employability skills and link these to our assessment practices, do the conditions for their realization genuinely exist?

Another form of misrecognition that I would like to emphasis with particular reference to an assessment context is that of *invisibilization*: a process involving the giving and withholding of acknowledgement of a person at the same time (Zurn, 2015). Invisibilization is quite different from oversight, or even ignoring a person, because it signals a very basic and profound denial of a person's existence; someone who is, however, quite clearly in existence. Honneth (2001) recounts Ralph Ellison's famous novel *The Invisible Man*, in which the first-person narrator describes being invisible to others although he is a real man, made of flesh and blood. A few pages into the story, the reader learns that this narrator is in fact black. What is going on in the novel is

> an especially subtle form of racist humiliation against which the black protagonist struggles through the entire novel: a form of being made invisible, of being made to disappear, that evidently involves not a *physical* non-presence, but rather non-existence in a social sense.
>
> (Honneth, 2001, p. 111, emphasis original)

As Zurn (2015) outlines, the invisibilization suffered by the invisible man is not the product simply of a particular interpersonal relationship, it is indicative of a broad set of socially situated attitudes and beliefs. Honneth (2001) argues that 'cultural history offers numerous examples of situations in which the dominant express their social superiority by not perceiving those they dominate' (p. 112). An example of this is the traditional way the nobility behave in front of servants. They can, for example, 'undress in front of their servants because the latter were simply not there in a certain sense' (p. 112). Clearly the nobility know their servants are present, because they deliver things to them and get tasks done – so we have here an acknowledgement of presence at the same time as its denial. There is also an intentionality here which is critical to the act of reinforcing one's superiority: 'It demands gestures or ways of behaving that make clear that the other is not seen not merely accidentally, but rather intentionally' (p. 112). Moreover, this is not purely a metaphorical invisibility. Honneth argues that for those concerned, 'their "invisibililty" has in each case a real core: they feel themselves not to be perceived' (p. 113).

Honneth's concern for invisible and unseen injustice features in his debate with Nancy Fraser about whether social justice should focus on recognition primarily, or on redistribution and recognition, as argued by Fraser (see Fraser & Honneth, 2003). Fraser's analysis places significant focus on various social movements, as a source of the empirical reference point required by the immanent aspect of critical theory. Fraser's (2003) argument is that the public nature of such groups makes their claims open to scrutiny and critique and thus 'normatively reliable' (p. 205), while Honneth (2003b) claims that their public nature may give them privilege over less visible but equally important instances of denial, depravation or suffering. Unlike Fraser, Honneth does not start at the point of social participation, but rather believes we must first consider identity formation – though this is itself a social process. His reason for this is that we otherwise risk missing those less visible – for example, those not belonging to identifiable social groups (Honneth, 2003b). Honneth argues that his analysis goes beneath the levels of Fraser and thus avoids the trap he alleges she falls into, of over-privileging the already acknowledged forms of injustice and missing hidden and unexpressed injustices. In Part 2 I will consider tendencies towards invisibilization of students and academics in certain assessment processes and practices. For example, do promotion policies and workload allocation models render invisible much of the real work academics undertake when assessing students?

We can also use Honneth's notion of *instrumental rationalization* to appreciate another social pathology that can shape assessment practices. Such rationalization reflects a gap between the potential for reason and existing social structures and practices (Zurn, 2015). This is a recurrent theme within critical theory, and particularly demonstrates the resonance between aspects of Honneth's work and that of Horkheimer and Adorno, with their critique of the dialectic of enlightenment (Horkheimer & Adorno, 1997). Thus, while the Enlightenment offered emancipatory promise, 'the depressing dialectic of enlightenment for Horkheimer and Adorno is that, due to social causes, the potential of reason is deformed by the dominance of instrumental rationality' (Zurn, 2015, p. 103). As Zurn observes, there is nothing new in the idea of instrumental rationality, but what is striking is the dominance it has come to have over all other forms of reason, effectively crowding out all alternatives. In the context of assessment practices, this is another useful concept for understanding the claims of student engagement and independence, and the actual conditions in which students learn and undertake assessment. To what extent do we actually ensure the conditions for students to exercise their own unique and independent rationality? Or do students become invisibly inducted into a culture in which a means-ends rationality is the only 'common sense' alternative? Anything else is considered naïve or unrealistic. The dominance of instrumental rationality may run counter to the social conditions required for a genuinely good and just life. And yet, ironically, it positions itself as the only sensible form of thinking: to be driven by a narrow, economic imperative becomes the only show in town.

In such circumstances, students (and academics) can fall victim to another pathology of *self-reification*, whereby we standardize or rationalize our own inner selves. For example, the standardized forms of profiling used by some online dating agencies, whereby things such as life choices and experiences are reduced to the same level as natural hair colour or a birthmark (Zurn, 2015). Or, at the opposite extreme is when individuals take such an instrumentalizing stance towards their own inner states, they view them as though 'wholly plastic material to be remolded in the light of socially defined norms and goals' (p. 109). In both these cases we reify ourselves by denying fundamental facets of our own humanity. I suggest that assessment regimes tied to reductionist employability agendas tend to promote this form of self-reification. Students are encouraged to value themselves in terms of their abilities to act as compliant workers in a dominant system. Indeed, efforts go into conforming themselves to the demands of that system rather than a genuine form of mutuality. Such self-reification reflects a belief

> that we can instrumentally remake ourselves in the interest of selling ourselves to others, or that our inner states can be calculatingly reduced to standardized schemas of categories, thereby locating ourselves in an abstract grid of personality types.
>
> (Zurn, 2015, p. 109)

Under self-reification, our thoughts and experiences become treated 'as fixed, thing-like and as property that can be owned and produced' (Morgan, 2014, p. 227). As Morgan (2014) explains, this involves a focus on happiness that

> produces a form of self-relation that turns opaque, fluid processes of experience into instrumental objects for the production of an empty notion of happiness.
>
> (p. 220)

The final example of a form of social pathology that we can relate to the assessment context is that of *organized self-realization*. Modern societies engender more and more demands for us to take responsibility for authentic self-realization, argues Honneth, but at the same time there are fewer and fewer genuine opportunities. Thus the notion of self-realization has moved from 'once a relevant idea to be strived for … into an ideology and a productive force in a deregulated economic system' (Honneth, 2014b, p. 165). People are expected to be flexible and ready to take on self-improvement (Honneth, 2004a). Indeed, people can become 'psychologically overwhelmed by the diffuse demand that they be themselves (Honneth, 2014b, p. 165). Zurn (2015) describes this as leading to 'symptoms of emptiness and purposelessness arising from institutionalized demands for authentic self-realization' (p. 111). Even the idea of authenticity and self-realization has been instrumentalized by the advertising industry 'by packaging consumer items as aesthetic resources for each person's develop-ment of their "own" lifestyles' (Zurn, 2015, pp. 111–12). Thus in an assess-ment context, the rise of notions of authentic assessment has sometimes gone hand in hand, I suggest, with pressures for an instrumentalized form of self-realization which actually runs counter to the conditions required for a good and just life. Authentic assessment has become a popular concept and can hold considerable radical promise, but we must ensure it means more than simply fitting into the predetermined categories of mainstream employers. Understood at the societal level, Honneth observes that Western capitalism has turned the pursuit of self-realization 'into an ideology and productive force of an economic system that is being deregulated' (Honneth, 2004a, p. 474).

The challenge for assessment for social justice, therefore, is to foster the fundamental interrelationship between what students do at university and the broader social world, without reducing this to some narrow, inflexible set of per-sonality traits – where one size fits all. Where 'individuality' is the latest must-have social fad, and a tick box to fulfil on every job application.

Conclusion

In Honneth's understanding of social justice as mutual recognition, we have a rich conceptualization which ranges back and forth between the individual and the social. It takes us back to fundamental ideas of individual self-worth while simultaneously focused on contributions to a just, social whole. His notion of esteem recognition, that is recognition for one's contribution to society, will be particularly important in the second part of this book, as a recurring theme emerges that assessment is not about an isolated task or a simple mark, but about the ways in which students are nurtured to engage with knowledge through social practices that allow them to recognize their own self-worth within society and to be recognized for this by others. It also means being able to recognize the contributions of our fellow members of society, even when somewhat different from our own.

4

Social Justice and Social Practice Theory

Introduction

In this chapter I weave one further theoretical strand into the conceptual foundations of assessment for social justice. In the previous chapter I explored how
we can understand social justice through Honneth's critical theory. Such a theory critiques the current state of society and also casts our view forwards to
what it means to achieve greater social justice. A recurring problem with critical
theory, it has been argued, is that its commitment to change does not marry with
an understanding of the processes of change. Previously I have also suggested
that critical pedagogy has lacked a sufficiently complex theory of how change
can occur (McArthur, 2010). My aim in interpreting Honneth's theory of social
justice in the context of social practice theory is to overcome this problem. There
is, I argue, a clear operational character to a social practice-related theory of
social justice that gives it added potency and impact. Social justice understood
through social practices meets the demands of critical theory to focus on both
current lived realities and the possibilities of emancipatory change. Honneth's
emphasis at all times on the mutuality of recognition, where social justice is
always about both self-realization and social inclusion, fits well with the focus of
social practice theories. Both traditions focus on joint experience, often played
out through everyday acts. The value of drawing on both bodies of thought is,
I suggest, that it combines the strengths of both elements. A theory of justice
shines light on our aspirations for a better society, while social practice theory
explores the details of how change can actually take place. Through understanding assessment in terms of social practices, we have a clearer perspective on
where to focus our energies to effect movement towards greater social justice.
Thus through the combination of Honneth's understanding of social justice and
social practice theory with its understanding of change, we can move on to the

second part of this book with a social practice version of social justice that is robust and offering practical opportunities to ensure change.

Social practice theory is an umbrella term for a group of theoretical approaches to how we understand human actions and the potential for change. What they have in common is the focus on *practice* as the key realm of analysis for understanding human actions. Whereas other approaches might more commonly focus on a unit of analysis in terms of individual agency, cognition or social structures, here it is social practice that is the focus (Trowler, Saunders & Bamber, 2009). Discursive practices are therefore not privileged over other forms of practice, as has arguably become common in many areas of social science research. Indeed, Reckwitz (2002) claims that within social practice theory discursive practices lose their 'omnipotent status', as enjoyed in other approaches such as textualism and discourse analysis (p. 254).

The antecedence of social practice theory can be found in a range of other traditions, including phenomenology, ethnomethodology, actor-network theory and activity theory. Key thinkers associated with such lineages include Heidegger, Husserl, Wittgenstein, Vygotsky and Leont'ev. Here we can see why the bringing together of social practice theory and critical theory may seem unusual, as their lineages are somewhat different. For example, a strong theme of critical theory is a rejection of the sort of theory offered by Heidegger, while he is key to the work of many practice theorists. But it is helpful to stress the commonality between critical theory and social practice theories whereby proponents in both traditions often see their role partly as rectifying flaws and inadequacies in other existing theories and frameworks. In particular, a common feature of social practice theories is the disruption of the rigid dichotomization of structure and agency.

Having conceptually done away with rigid forms of understanding, social practice theories are able to give emphasis to the 'implicit, tacit or unconscious layer of knowledge which enables a symbolic organization of reality' (Reckwitz, 2002, p. 246). Again, the resonance is clear here with critical theory's focus on the unconscious and unseen. Through the lenses of social practice theory and critical theory, our understanding of life, movement and change within the social world becomes at once more dispersed and more complex.

We can discern two generations of social practice theory (Hui, Schatzki & Shove, 2017). The first generation includes three influential bodies of work: Bourdieu (1977), Giddens (1984) and Lave and Wenger (Lave & Wenger, 1991; Wenger, 1998). Second-generation practice theorists include Schatzki (2002), Reckwitz (2002) and Shove, Pantzar & Watson (2012). Schatzki (2013) argues that practice theorists have three main areas in common. First, practice is conceived as 'an organised constellation of different people's activities' (p. 13) and this combination of activity and organization is fundamental. Second, the appreciation of human life does not rest on examining lots of individual activity, but on 'the organised activities of multiple people' (p. 13), so social groups and interrelations are important. Finally, Schatzki argues that there is something in the account of human activity that cannot simply 'be put into words', and that this 'counters the subject-object split that has defined much philosophical thought in the modern era' (p. 14).

Beyond these points of agreement, however, there are distinct differences between practice theorists, and thus it is not appropriate to adopt a pick-and-mix approach. In this book I draw particularly on the second-generation practice theorist Theodore Schatzki because I think his work marries well with that of Honneth, despite some obvious differences. I am conscious here of perpetrating something of a 'shot gun wedding' between these two theorists. Thus to be clear again, I am bringing these two bodies of work together to the problem of assessment and social justice, but not trying to merge them as such. I do believe that together they advance our aim of thinking through how assessment can reflect and enhance greater social justice. My goal is encapsulated by Honneth's understanding of social justice as mutual recognition. From Schatzki I draw the analytical tools to examine the current organization of assessment and the changes required to pursue the aforementioned goal of changing the prevailing regimes of recognition.

Schatzki and practice theory

An enduring question pertaining to social practice theories is what is actually meant by practice. Some might argue that given the variety of complex and diverse human practices it is little surprise that a range of approaches has arisen. Barnes (2001) is less understanding and criticizes the tendency of such theories to fail 'to make clear just what social practices are' (p. 26). Communities of practice theory has particularly been criticized for the failure to spell out what they mean by practice and this perhaps has contributed to extensive misunderstanding of their work, with people latching onto the idea of community and sometimes largely ignoring the actual notion of practice. Schatzki, however, is clear and explicit about practices: practices are 'embodied, materially mediated arrays of human activity centrally organized around shared practical understanding' (Schatzki, 2001a, p. 2). A practice is 'a "bundle" of activities, that is to say an organised nexus of actions' (Schatzki, 2002, p. 71). Examples of practices can include management practices, policing practices, cooking practices, educational practices and assessment practices. There are therefore 'two overall dimensions' to any practice: 'activity and organisation' (p. 71). These actions are both discursive and non-discursive: 'Practices are a motley of actions of both sorts, and it seems to me an error to grant priority to either type' (p. 77). As such, Schatzki clearly situates himself as a critic of the so-called linguistic turn in social sciences and a tendency 'to overvalue the significance of discourse in social life' (p. 77).

Social life, for Schatzki, is formed by a bundle, or mesh, of practices and material arrangements. For example, material entities such as classroom layout, email networks, data projectors and computers all contribute to the ways in which teachers and students coexist (Schatzki, 2005). Schatzki emphasizes the implications of this point:

> This example illustrates, further, that the site of the coexistence among teachers and students is not practices, on the one hand, and material arrangements on the other, but a *mesh* of practices and arrangements, a mesh in which educational practices are carried out and determinative of, but also dependent on and altered by, particular arrangements. This fact holds of social life generally: all human coexistence inherently transpires as part of practice- arrangement meshes.
>
> (p. 473)

The *site of the social* is therefore 'composed of nexuses of practices and material arrangements' and therefore 'social life inherently transpires as part of such nexuses' (Schatzki, 2005, p. 471). Social existence is understood as occurring where such bundles (or meshes) form 'sites':

> Bundles, moreover, connect, through links between their practices, connections between their arrangements, and relations of the sort that join practices and arrangements into bundles. Through such relations, bundles form constellations and constellations larger constellations. The total plenum formed by this labyrinth of linked practices and arrangements is the overall site where social life transpires.
>
> (Schatzki, 2013, p. 21)

A practice can also be described as a set of doings and sayings, but such doings and sayings can also exist beyond the realms of the practice, and therefore Schatzki uses the terms 'task' and 'project' to clarify further. A task thus 'consists of aggregated doings and sayings' (Schatzki, 2002, p. 73) while a project is an organized collection of tasks: 'A practice thus embraces a set of hierarchically organized doings/sayings, tasks, and projects' (p. 73). At the base of a practice are basic activities that a person can simply 'do', such as picking up a pen or typing on a keyboard. These basic activities then connect with other activities to enact the practice.

For Schatzki there is an important temporal nature to practices. He describes them as 'open, temporally unfolding nexuses of action' (Schatzki, 2002, p. 72). This is key because it encompasses the ways in which practices are extended by new actions. Practices are open-ended in that there is no necessary number of activities involved (Schatzki, 2013). Thus, compared with some other social practice theorists who put a strong emphasis on recurrent or even habitual acts, Schatzki is keen to stress that practices can exhibit regular qualities, but equally, practices can embrace changing, unique or irregular actions. Thus practices can involve unusual doings/sayings, tasks or practices; or infrequent and uncommon ones, and also novel and new ones. In this way, Schatzki's work can be contrasted with that of someone like Reckwitz who places a defining emphasis on routine within his understanding of practices:

> A practice is thus a routinized way in which bodies are moved, objects are handled, subjects are treated, things are described and the world is understood.
>
> (Reckwitz, 2002, p. 250)

To return to the importance of practices as *organized* nexuses of action, Schatzki outlines four aspects that enable the doings and sayings of a practice to 'hang together'. These are: '(1) practical understandings, (2) rules, (3) a teleoaffective structure, and (4) general understandings' (Schatzki, 2002, p. 77). Here there is a substantial shift from Schatzki's earlier work (Schatzki, 1996) which only included the first three, general understandings being an additional category added in his second book. And I will argue that it is this category of general understandings which adds particular power to Schatzki's work in terms of taking forward how we can effect change in the context of assessment for social justice. What makes a practice distinctive is 'the *package* of doings and sayings plus organization' based on the particular combination of these understandings, rules and teleoaffective structures (Schatzki, 2002, p. 87).

Practical understandings enable actions to contribute to practices. These involve knowing what to say and do in the situation (Schatzki, 1996). This is a knowledge of which sayings and doings to bring to the practice at hand. Schatzki (2013) gives the example of knowing how to sort and file papers by moving one's hand back and forth. In an assessment context, it could include the knowledge of how to turn on a computer in order to write an essay, or how to pick up a test tube in the chemistry lab in order to conduct an experiment.

Rules refer to 'explicit formulations, principles, precepts, and instructions that enjoin, direct, or remonstrate people to perform specific actions' (Schatzki, 2002, p. 79). Rules provide a link between doings and sayings because people take heed of them and follow them when acting. An example would be a rule allowing a student to take a calculator into a maths exam: following this rule then links the subsequent actions around the practice of taking the maths exam. Such rules are not tacit understandings, as feature in Giddens's work, but 'they are formulations interjected into social life for the purpose of orienting and determining the course of activity, typically by those with the authority to enforce them' (Schatzki, 2002, p. 80). Further, 'Rules are ubiquitous in human life: humans are always formulating or producing them' (Schatzki, 2013, p. 16). Never has this perhaps been more true than in the context of assessment.

Teleoaffective structures also link sayings and doings. Such structures bring together the elements of teleology, as 'orientations toward ends' and affectivity, as 'how things matter' (Schatzki, 2001b, p. 52). Teleoaffective structures embrace 'ends, projects, tasks, purposes, beliefs, emotions, and moods' (Schatzki, 1996, p. 89). Thus the teleoaffective structures contain 'a range of acceptable or correct ends, acceptable or correct tasks to carry out for these ends, acceptable or correct beliefs (etc.) given which specific tasks are carried out for the sake of these ends, and even acceptable or correct emotions out of which to do so' (Schatzki, 2001b, p. 53). The affective part of a teleoaffective structure reflects 'the emotions and moods that people carrying on a practice should or may acceptably express' (Schatzki, 2013, p. 16). There can be considerable variation between practices in terms of the strength and role of the affective dimension.

Teleoaffective structures are hierarchical in nature, reflecting the different types of actions involved. Schatzki (2013) explains,

> In almost all cases, people perform further actions in performing basic ones. A person, for example, writes an essay or manipulates a PowerPoint presentation by typing on a keyboard, sorts and files papers by moving her hands hither and thither, and takes solace surrounded by noisy kids by thinking that the sunset is beautiful. In turn, these 'higher level' activities typically constitute even higher level ones. For example, in writing an essay a student might be doing the work for a course, and in giving an exam a teacher might be testing student learning and abilities. Action hierarchies such as these are teleological.

> (p. 15)

At the top of such a teleological hierarchy is an activity which does not lead on further to yet another activity: 'Such an activity is a person's end: it is that for the sake of which she acts' (Schatzki, 2013). The same act may be done with different ends in mind. Schatzki uses the example of a student studying. They might study and do their coursework for different reasons: 'For the sake of advancing career prospects, living the good life, or surviving to the end of the semester'. Similarly, a teacher might set an assessment for a number of reasons: 'For the sake of bettering people's life chances, improving society, or just doing her job' (Schatzki, 2013, p. 15).

It is important to understand that in Schatzki's analysis the teleoaffective structures are 'properties of the practice and not the individual' (Schatzki, 2002, p. 80). This means that different people may incorporate the teleoaffective structures of a particular practice to differing extents. There can be discussion and dispute around what is considered acceptable in a given practice, although sometimes there can also be 'decrees of authority' which influence positions (p. 83). While an assignment can serve a hierarchical range of ends for students undertaking it, not all students will be participating with all possible ends in mind. For example, if students are required to do a presentation to the rest of the class, different people will do so with different ends in mind. For some it may just be a case of getting through the ten minutes without making a fool of themselves. For someone else it may be a welcome opportunity to share their interest in the subject. And for another it could be useful practice of presentation skills they believe are important for their future social role. Similarly, when we mark assessments it does not necessarily follow that everyone does so with a social justice intention in mind, though this is clearly one possible end. Ends, however, may also not be conscious goals, and a person at any given time may not be aware 'of the teleological end points that determine what makes sense to him or her to do' (p. 81). Just getting through the pile of scripts may be the only end we are conscious of when faced with a large marking load. In this way, teleoaffective structures are not the same as the general will of the group, or 'collectively willed ends and projects' (p. 81). If we think in terms of higher education, a teleoaffective structure can embrace many ends, such as: 'educating students, learning, receiving good student evaluations, obtaining good grades, gaining academic employment, and enjoying a successful academic career' (Schatzki, 2005, p. 472). When it comes to assessment, I suggest, such are the organizational pressures on many academics that they become conscious of only the most pressing ends and may feel disconnected from the broader ones which would give their role greater meaning and fulfilment.

General understandings are described by Schatzki (2013) as 'abstract senses' such as 'the beauty of an artisanal product or of the nobility of educating students':

> They are not ends for which people strive but senses of the worth, value, nature, or place of things, which infuse and are expressed in people's doings and sayings.
>
> (p. 16)

Here in this notion of *senses of worth* I believe we have one of the clearest links between Schatzki's work and that of Honneth, for with Honneth, and particularly the notion of esteem recognition, we are always brought back to the recognition of worth for one's actions and abilities. Schatzki explains the notion of general understandings in terms of workers in Shaker communities' belief that their labour is connected to realization of a higher, spiritual realm. Using a further example of farm tours, Schatzki (2010) suggests that general understandings may include matters such as courtesy, the treatment of minorities (because of the background of many of the people who work there) or tact in how one asks questions. These qualities, therefore, may come into play to help organize many other sorts of practices.

General understandings can take many different forms but what they share is a role in shaping the nature of the practices that are carried out, so a general understanding of courtesy shapes the nature of the practice of going into a shop and asking for a pint of milk. Here the effect is perhaps small, but equally a general understanding might serve to shape larger practices. For example, a commitment to religious and ethnic diversity would shape the way in which diplomatic relations are carried out. In particular, these general understandings help shape the teleoaffective structures of different practices. A general understanding of the importance of courtesy comes into play and places treating others with courtesy as one of the teleoaffective hierarchy of reasons why we participate in a practice. It may not be an end in itself; that may, for example, be to serve customers in a shop or teach students about chemistry – but a general understanding of courtesy can help determine the teleoaffective structures. It is in this vein that I employ Schatzki's conception of general understandings in the second part of this book, to consider the foundations for assessment for social justice. I will propose five general understandings that, if embraced, would help shape assessment practices towards greater social justice.

There are two final concepts that are central to Schatzki's work which I will outline here. First is the distinction between dispersed and integrative practices, and second is the idea of practical intelligibility. The above categories of rules, teleoaffective structures and general understandings generally relate to integrative practices and indeed these practices are the main focus of Schatzki's analysis. But to understand them, we must also understand dispersed practices. Dispersed practices are generally focused around a single form of action, such as 'describing, ordering, questioning, reporting, and examining' (p. 88). They are dispersed in the sense that they 'circulate through different sectors of social life, retaining more or less the same shape in those different sectors' (p. 88). Dispersed practices thus contrast with integrative practices which are more intricate, involving 'complex entities joining multiple actions, projects, ends, and emotions' (p. 88). For example, walking can be a dispersed practice – something which forms a part of many other practices people commonly undertake. Or it can be an integrative practice on its own, such as the hobby of rambling or hill walking, where walking is not an incidental part of the practice but actually key to what it is all about (Schatzki, 2013, p. 15).

The distinction between integrative and dispersed practices is important to Schatzki's analysis. Dispersed practices are typically rule free and rarely have a teleoaffective structure of their own, which is why they can form part of so many different integrative practices. Rather than rules of their own, they are able to draw on those of the integrative practices into which they are woven (Harries & Rettie, 2016). So the rules that govern walking around a workplace or within a school corridor are not held within that dispersed practice of walking but in the integrative practice of fulfilling one's job in the workplace or attending school. Most social research looking at practices focuses on integrative practices, but we must always remember that these are formed, in part, by a range of dispersed practices.

The last concept that is fundamental to Schatzki's practice theory is that of practical intelligibility. Practical intelligibility is what governs human actions: it 'is what makes sense to a person to do ... by specifying what an actor does next in the continuous flow of activity' (Schatzki, 2002, p. 75). Therefore it can also have a hierarchical character, with one activity giving rise to what makes sense to do next. Further, general understandings can be important in shaping practical intelligibility (Welch & Warde, 2017). If one holds a general understanding that courtesy is valuable then it shapes what it makes sense to do when you walk into a shop or pass a student on campus. Unlike many of the concepts we have considered so far, practical intelligibility is linked to the person, not the practice:

> It is always to an individual that a specific action makes sense. Features of individuals, moreover, are what principally determine what makes sense to them to do. Examples of such features are a person's ends, the projects and tasks he or she is pursuing, and affectivity.

(p. 75)

Indeed, emotion can play a key role in practical intelligibility. Schatzki (2010) explains how a shameful experience might lead a person to do the things that make sense in order to avoid a similar experience again. A student who receives a very poor mark or very critical piece of feedback may then make certain decisions when it comes to future assignments. But I am not referring here to some rational decision-making whereby the student learns through feedback not to make the same mistakes again. Instead I am referring to a more personal sense of failure and shame that might, for example, prevent this student from risk-taking in the future or applying themselves as much to their studies. Here we can see the way in which practical intelligibility is not the same thing as rationality (Schatzki, 2002). Practical intelligibility and rationality often converge but we must understand the ways in which they can often diverge, particularly when emotions and other factors come into play. We can see this easily in an assessment context. It may be rational following a failed assignment to work harder next time, carefully rectifying all the faults outlined in the feedback provided. But this may not be what it makes sense to the student to do, and they might instead decide to be less engaged or to put their faith in better luck next time. This can, therefore, help to explain the phenomenon whereby academics can be mystified and frustrated when students repeat the same mistakes. But it is wrong to assume that all student decisions and actions are made on the basis of a rational form of understanding that we ascribe to them. Sometimes a student who has become disconsolate as a result of a poor assessment may feel it simply does not make sense to keep trying. Or they may misunderstand their feedback and put their energies into the wrong things. It may make sense to listen to friends who appear more confident, and follow their advice. Moreover, explicit awareness of practical intelligibility is itself not necessary – someone may not reflect on why a particular action makes sense for them to do. If we think about issues around how students respond to feedback on their work within higher education then this notion of understanding what it makes sense for them to do is both powerful and useful.

Honneth and Schatzki

How, then, might we come to bring this social practice theory together with a commitment to social justice, and particularly Honneth's concept of justice as mutual recognition? The first point that links them both is the multifaceted and complex nature of our understanding of both what we aspire towards (social justice) and how we might go about achieving that end (through changing social practices). Social practices sustain certain regimes of recognition, and these are what we need to change. Unlike a straightforward procedural notion of social justice, critical theory leads us to consider unseen and hidden features of the social world and to consider power at play across many social levels. Any move towards greater social justice, thus requires this multilevel, multifaceted approach, and I believe this is what social practice theory offers. Schatzki's practice theory is particularly appropriate because it spans a sense of day-to-day actions and broader practices, and the influences that shape both of these. As a theory of change, Schatzki directs our attention to the different levels and different types of doings and sayings, but most importantly to what links these together into the nexus of practices and the site of the social.

Honneth also refers to social practices (though I am in no way assuming his meaning is identical to that of Schatzki) as the necessary sphere of analysis when considering recognition and justice: 'The forms of recognition are institutionalized as forms of social practices in a society' (Honneth in Marcelo, 2013, p. 211). Honneth shares with social practice theory an emphasis on both organized practices (institutionalized) and everyday forms of practice. He states: 'Recognition represents a moral act anchored in the social world as an everyday occurrence' (Honneth, 2014b, p. 80). Honneth further explains that forms of engagement essential to social justice lie in everyday acts and habits:

> The social integration of modern societies requires more than legal rules and procedural mechanisms; it needs the development of everyday habits in which the moral principles of modern constitutions are anchored. If we apply this concept to the present, we face the necessity of making the stability and vitality of our democracy dependent on whether the moral attitudes of equality and respect have also taken hold in our everyday practices. My book represents an attempt to examine how far along Western democracies are in this process of anchoring democratic principles *in the everyday habits and customs of its citizens.*
>
> (Interview in Willig, 2012, p. 146, emphasis added)

Honneth argues that in considerations of social justice, there has been a tendency to reduce all social relations to legal relationships, and that this has been 'fatal to the formulation of a concept of social justice'. He writes,

> This one-sided approach has caused us to lose sight of the fact that the conditions of justice are not only given in the form of positive rights, but also in the shape of appropriate attitudes, modes of comportment and behavioural routines. Most of our individual freedoms, which have become the epitome of a contemporary conception of social justice, we owe not to legal entitlements granted by the

state, but to *the existence of a web – one which cannot be so easily untangled – of routine and often only weakly institutionalized practices and customs* that give us social confirmation or allow us to express ourselves freely. The fact that these conditions of freedom are difficult to determine and largely evade legal and constitutional categories cannot be regarded as a reason to simply exclude them from the framework of a theory of justice.

(Honneth, 2014a, p. 67, emphasis added)

Thus for what Schatzki refers to as nexuses or meshes of practices, Honneth uses the image of a web – moreover, a web not easily untangled. In looking at assessment practices I draw two important points from both Honneth and Schatzki. First, that we must look beyond the formal rules and procedures alone, and second, that we must focus on the networks – the webs, meshes and nexuses – of practices that interact, support each other or sometimes compete.

Honneth warns against assuming or demanding too much rationality from individuals when we consider their motives and actions, a point which accords with Schatzki's understanding of practical intelligibility. To overemphasize or to instrumentalize rationality is ultimately unhelpful for the purposes of understanding real behaviours. This also reflects the importance of psychoanalysis to critical theory, and the need to cast our gaze at the unconscious and the hidden. Thus Honneth emphasizes that any theorization of the social world must be 'as realistic and close to the phenomena as possible' and this can only be achieved by taking account of 'unconscious motives and affects' (Honneth, 2014b, p. 195). Further, 'humans are tied, through unconscious drives or attachments, to their own, unique lives' (Honneth, 2014b, p. 195). We can therefore understand social events, including how students and academics experience assessment, as 'the outcome of actions in which unconscious drives or needs for attachment have left their mark' (Honneth, 2014b, p. 195). This is far more complicated than students simply wanting a good mark or academics hoping their grading has been fair. Assessment plays out over a number of levels of recognition, both tacit and conscious.

The emancipatory potential of Honneth's work lies in the criticality that comes from 'unveiling or unmasking, revealing the deep processes lying beyond the surface' (Toniolatti, 2009, p. 373). Honneth's focus is on the 'hidden aspects and shady areas of social reality' (Toniolatti, 2009, p. 373). This position is important, I suggest, when applying Honneth's work to assessment in higher education. The places that are traditionally associated with justice – such as moderation committees and exam boards – may not be the most relevant to broader justice issues, and may indeed turn out to be not all that just. Honneth's work suggests that we need 'an account of the social that emphasises that society reproduces itself through the often-conflictual interaction of real social groups, which are themselves the products of ongoing activities of interpretation and struggle on the part of participants' (Anderson, 2011, p. 48).

Honneth explains the role of struggle in enabling change:

> You see, I take struggle as being an enormously productive force in our human life-world. And it takes thousands of forms.... It's what's happening in class-rooms in different forms. It slowly changes the way we understand the principles of recognition, the way we understand ourselves, and it slowly helps to make our societies normatively better.... I have a productive, positive understanding of struggle. I'm more interested in the small, everyday forms of struggle and not in the big struggles.
>
> (Honneth in Marcelo, 2013, p. 217)

For Honneth, the reproduction of social practices and social institutions occurs through 'specific regimes of recognition' (Zurn, 2015, p. 7). Misrecognition, such as that evoked by stereotyping people according to gender or sexuality, perpetuates social practices that deny certain groups full and equal participation in social life. While there is an element of legal rights here (for example, the right to marriage regardless of sexuality), it is in the everyday acts that the conditions which lead to misrecognition are so often transmitted and sustained. Legal recognition is not enough; Honneth's other two forms of love and esteem recognition must also reflect the genuine capacity for individual justice and participation in the social realm. This is why social practices are so important. Recognition and engagement are intertwined. Honneth's position is that we cannot understand 'an object or a situation without taking part in it in some manner, without a kind of existential *engagement*, without an active demonstration of concern or interest' (Haber, 2007, p. 161). Thus, there is a strong potential for understanding change by appreciating the different domains of misrecognition – understanding what needs to change at a level of considerable detail – but always looped back in to the wider social.

Honneth further uses the concept of 'validity overhang'(Honneth, 2004b, p. 355) to describe that gap between the moral progress already achieved and the realization of just conditions enabling the living of good and fulfilling lives. He is, therefore, drawing attention to the space to which our energies should be directed, ensuring his theory remains embedded in an active conception of change, not simply critique. But we still need, I would argue, the insights of social practice theory to really tease out on the ground what is involved in such change. Thus a powerful aspect of Schatzki's work is that he does not focus only on habits or recurrent practices, as do some other social theorists, but also on the atypical, the unusual and novel practices – within these we have the potential for change. Social practices must be understood within their contexts. To fully understand a practice is to understand it as situated within particular cultural contexts, which lead to a dynamic character:

> Practices are inherently social and evolving. They are nested in cultures that form a major part of the intellectual, moral and material resources on which the practices themselves depend: cultures and practices constitute one another – they are not separable.
>
> (Trowler et al., 2009, pp. 9–10)

Included in such cultures are the assumptions about justice and fairness. Thus the importance of considering what implicit notions of social justice may currently be helping to shape assessment practices – and the alternatives values and practices that could be nurtured. The belief in the ability of good procedure to ensure 'right' assessment decisions is, I suggest, part of the prevailing academic culture: it is open to challenge, critique and change.

A way forward

> To engage in a practice is to exercise a power.
>
> (Barnes, 2001, p. 28)

In considering assessment practices in higher education, we might argue that a social justice dimension already exists in the teleoaffective structures that link practices. Thus the acceptable end of acting justly and furthering broader social justice could exist on the hierarchy of possible ends. Not everyone has to engage with higher education for these particular ends, but they may be recognized as one possible set of ends. There are two difficulties here. First, for higher education itself we have arguably witnessed a narrowing in its perceived ends. In many countries we can see some disciplines in peril because they do not fit an instrumentalized and narrow conception of the economic purposes of higher education. At the very least, the social justice functions of higher education remain something that need to be actively promoted and fought for; they cannot be assumed or taken for granted. Second, the link between assessment activities and social justice really has not been fully made, except in the narrower sense of fairness, as discussed in Chapter 1. Thus we require a cultural shift such that there is an expansion in the teleoaffective structures that link assessment practices. We need it to become reasonable and widespread to conceive of such practices as working towards both the ends of greater social justice in the broader sense, as well as a more complex understanding in terms of individual engagement with knowledge and individual well-being. Here I plan to build on Welch and Warde's (2017) argument that Schatzki's concept of general understandings has considerable explanatory power. I will take the idea a step further because the aim of this book is not simply to explain, but also to initiate change. In the second part of the book, therefore, I outline five general understandings that could shape and link assessment (as well as learning and teaching) practices towards greater social justice. Of course, social justice itself could again be described as a general understanding. But I consider this rather too broad to work as a mechanism in itself to effect real change, thus I want to focus further down the hierarchy. Seeking to move assessment practices in the direction of greater social justice, therefore, does not involve more procedures in place, but a fundamental repositioning of what academics and our students consider assessment to be for, and the qualities that we bring to those assessment practices. There are two overarching ideas behind these five general understandings:

- a belief that assessment can shape how learning occurs
- a belief that learning is valued for the ways in which it develops the abilities and traits with which contributions to society are made.

Assessment may drive learning, but what we need to drive assessment is the commitment to a shared social good. Rather than prevailing conceptions of assessment as part of some competitive process for advantage in the job market, we must reorientate to consider the ways in which assessment prepares students for a broader social role, particularly where they can achieve mutual esteem recognition through making this contribution. And this general understanding must filter down through the practices, actions and sayings and doings relating to assessment. The power of general understandings is that they relate to the culture of practices, or culture in action (Welch & Warde, 2017), and such culture is fundamental when working towards change (Trowler, 2008). Indeed general understandings become particularly powerful when considered as 'complexes of general understandings, such as cosmologies or teleoaffective regimes [as such they] raise the question of how to understand the relation between culture and action' (Welch & Warde, 2017, p. 188). In particular, Welch and Warde suggest that in general understandings we have the basis for 'a model of culture in practice' (p. 188). Here, then, is how change may occur.

Welch and Warde (2017) suggest that along with the function of integrating and organizing, general understandings can also enable illumination: they shed light on everyday practices and put them in a context that gives greater meaning. To ensure genuine cultural change requires a process back and forth between the everyday, which may be reflected in practical understandings, rules, teleoaffective structures and the general understandings. I hope to achieve this process of back and forth in the second part of the book by putting forward a series of alternative general understandings in the context of assessment. These are then the 'abstract senses' (Schatzki, 2013) that inform and shape how, why and what we assess. I want to propose five such senses, or general understandings, in order to begin to realize assessment for social justice. These are: trust, honesty, responsibility, forgiveness and responsiveness. On their own these may read as a worthy collection of pious traits. This is not how they are intended – though I do believe they are worthy. Each of these in different ways can link the practices of assessment to form certain outcomes and radically change the regimes of recognition towards greater social justice. It is not simply that a person is considered trustworthy, for this may seem naive in an assessment context. The key point is that trust is a feature of the practices we need to engage in in order to move towards greater social justice: we engage with assessment practices as an expression of giving and receiving trust. Similarly, it is not simply that students should *be responsible*, which is a rather abstract and uncontextualized trait to impose, but rather that the assessment practices they engage in should be ones of responsibility. To illuminate the difference, it is a simple but often ineffective matter to entreat students to take responsibility for their own actions. We can even put in place rules and procedures meant to achieve this end – but that does not meet our social justice objectives. It is altogether different to design assessment practices with the characteristics of responsibility – such as doing a project for a 'real' client or attending to the care of a patient in a medical simulation suite. The task itself imbues the sense of responsibility: it is not an abstract trait or personality feature.

Assessment involves a nexus of social practices that are linked together by the four concepts outlined by Schatzki. Practical understandings guide the performance of basic tasks such as knowing how to use your calculator or putting in place the beakers in a chemistry lab experiment. As students become

more experienced, more and more tasks will fall under such practical understandings. Rules are a more obvious part of assessment, although Schatzki's
analysis demonstrates that we need to think broadly about these, perhaps better interpreted as conventions that guide what and how assessment practices
take place. The interesting thing that I have observed in an assessment context, across several different universities, is that rules can be very powerful
even when they do not actually exist; by this I mean that assumed, reported
or rumoured assessment regulations can significantly shape practices. Again,
this reflects a dominant culture in which we give particular credence to rules
and procedures. The hierarchy of teleoaffective structures is evident in the varied ends to which assessment seems reasonably directed, ranging from simply
wanting to pass a subject so that it does not have to be done again, to engaging
with complex and socially useful knowledge, and on further to contributing
to a more just society. Finally, an array of general understandings create the
cultural picture in which assessment takes place, and help shape the nature of
interrelated practices. In an assessment context, we bring together a number
of interrelated practices. For example, teaching, marking, revising, researching, moderating – these are just some of the interrelated practices in which
students and academics are involved. The five general understandings which
I propose can lead to changes in these practices towards greater social justice
by shifting the regimes of recognition. Each of these general understandings
reflects a sense of worth to the practices with which students and academics
engage, and thus link towards teleoaffective structures of social justice. They
are socially constructed, culturally imbued ways of thinking that one brings to
assessment practices. These are not the only general understandings applicable
to assessment, of course, as different individuals bring their own. But I hope to
use these general understandings to demonstrate the sort of shared commitments that could lead to the cultural shift inherent in the idea of assessment
for social justice.

Schatzki proposes a dynamic understanding of practices as more than mere
routine or habit, but open-ended and thus subject to change as their circumstances change. Thus, should any of the four elements that link practices change,
then the practice itself would either cease to exist or split into other new, discrete
practices (Nicolini, 2012). Thus should there be disagreement over the teleoaffective structures applicable to a practice, we might see that practice transformed
into two new practices. What is important for change within assessment practices is to consider the ways in which these aspects are experienced by the people involved in those practices. Thus there is a mutuality here that accords with

Honneth. For practice theory, this involves understanding practices as 'collective possessions and accomplishments sustained through interaction and mutual adjustment among people' (Schatzki, 2001a, p. 6). In this space for *interaction and mutual adjustment*, we have the scope for both serious misunderstandings and for positive change. This is what we will explore in Part 2 of this book.

Part Two

Towards Assessment
for Social Justice

5

Trust

Introduction

Assessment for Social Justice requires practices of *trust*. Trust is important because it manifests assessment as more than a procedural or contractual exchange. Trust places assessment beyond the realm of purely instrumental rationality. It thus requires of assessment practices an appreciation of the position and needs of all the people involved. This is about the sense of purpose and meaning we bring to our assessment practices. The doings and sayings, tasks and projects that form assessment practices should be formed and linked by a general understanding that trust is a quality of significance in what we do. This is about the act of trusting and of being trusted. This is important not just on a basic interpersonal level (it is *nice* to be trusted), but educationally too so as to enable students to be in a position to engage with knowledge in ways congruent with social justice. Understanding assessment as a series of intersubjective practices highlights the importance of trust, for without it the processes of assessment are likely to become distorted and even break down. But the current situation, as will become clear in this chapter, is one of embedded and institutionalized distrust between academics and students, built into the material arrangements of our assessment practices. Thus a major barrier to the realization of assessment for social justice is how we can think differently about each other, and move to relationships of genuine, but not naive, trust.

Honneth's work is important here for the way in which it peels back issues of social justice to the intimate and the personal; such realms are too easily overlooked when we focus only on systems and procedures. The first of Honneth's three forms of recognition, which underpin his conceptualization of social justice, is that of love, or care. In Honneth's work, the emphasis is on intimate relationships of the family: 'Love and friendship are the forms of recognition by which parents create basic trust' (Huttunen, 2007, p. 426). I am stretching Honneth's original intention by aligning love recognition in an assessment context, clearly outside the family context of his work, for two reasons. First, within an assessment (and broader teaching and learning) context I believe it shares the attribute of particularity that Honneth ascribes to relationships of love and care. This means that we cannot objectify or distance our understandings and our practices that involve trust: they need to be understood as particular to real people. The commitment to trust another person as we engage in common practices is intensely personal. I will argue that a sense of depersonalization and instrumentalism has cemented a lack of trust at the centre of our assessment practices, and that this is unhealthy and unproductive. Second, I believe that Honneth's association of relations of love and care with the capacity to develop self-confidence has important resonance in an assessment context. As I will explore further in this chapter, where a lack of trust is fostered by the prevailing arrangement, this can alter the nature of the assessment practices students and staff engage in. This, in turn, has repercussions for other aspects of mutual recognition, such as students and staff realizing the achievements that lead to esteem recognition. My application of Honneth's understanding of love recognition may go beyond his own intentions, but I believe I am representing the spirit of its place within our understanding of social justice. In this way, my use of love recognition arguably reflects that of early Hegel, who Honneth himself acknowledged as trying 'to extend the concept of love beyond the limits of a personal relationship and onto a whole community' (Honneth in Iorio et al., 2013, p. 248).

In Honneth's work, self-confidence or self-understanding is inherently inter-subjective. We gain this confidence partly through our understandings of ourselves: individuals must be able to value themselves in order to value others (Honneth, 2014b). Equally, we gain confidence through the acts of others treating us with care and consideration. The self-confidence engendered in this way is not some instrumental skill or isolated attribute, but a fundamental feature of who a student (or academic) comes to be through their involvement in higher education, and the assessment experiences therein. As Honneth (1996) makes clear, 'if I do not recognize my partner in interaction as a certain type of person, his reactions cannot give me the sense that I am recognized as the same type of person' (p. 38). Such cultural change is difficult, even risky, which is why I argue we need to consider trust at the level of our general understandings of our assessment practices. Assessment activities become crucial to our sense of self-worth, created and sustained through numerous recurrent practices, projects, tasks and doings and sayings. Of course, the issue of trust and self-confidence for both students and academics rests on more than their assessment practices. Both groups bring to assessment a range of other social relations and social sites, including home and family, which may negatively shape their sense of self-worth. I am not suggesting that through assessment we can solve all social ills and all sources of injustice. But we can do more not to exacerbate, and maybe even to ameliorate.

In the assessment context, a belief in the role of trust is acutely important because so much may depend on it, and because emotions and fears often run so high. For students it may, as discussed in Chapter 1, influence their future lives and sense of self. For academics it goes to the heart of pride in one's professional self and the contribution made through their work. When students offer work to academics for comment or grading, it is surely an act of trust. Students render themselves vulnerable for judgement and critique when they submit work for assessment: whatever formal procedures are in place, there is at the heart of this practice an element of trust, not least that the formal procedures will be followed. Harder to define or pin down are a host of sensibilities and dispositions that a student should rightfully be able to believe an academic brings to assessing their work. I suggest that we can neither assess justly without mutual trust, nor encourage just practices without enabling students to give and receive trust. And yet, I argue that much assessment takes place in contexts of distrust and suspicion, circumstances which reveal the distorted relationships between students and teachers and the lack of mutual recognition. Of particular concern, I argue, is any tendency by academics to approach assessment with a one-sided appreciation of the importance of trust, thus a one-sided notion of recognition. I suggest that academics can sometimes use notions of professionalism to assure others that they can be trusted, but demand rather more concrete proof from students about their own behaviour. But, 'there is no such thing as one-sided recognition' (Ikäheimo & Laitinen, 2010, p. 38). Unless recognition is dialogical and mutual, it is incomplete.

In this chapter I will outline two areas of assessment in which, I argue, a lack of trust stands as a barrier to moving towards greater social justice. My analysis uses Schatzki's practice theory to make the connection between the general understandings we bring to assessment practices and the teleoaffective ends we may reasonably aspire to. Where there is a general understanding of trust, the range of reasonable teleoaffective structures made possible through particular practices is expanded, and moves us towards greater social justice. A lack of trust is instead self-limiting. I will explore two instances where trust is largely absent.

- The growth of the plagiarism 'industry' – the distrust of students: here I suggest that technocratic approaches to policing academic writing lead to a self-limiting instrumentalism that offers misrecognition and distorts the ways in which students are able to engage in richer academic writing and assessment practices.

- Movements for anonymized marking – the distrust of academics: here I consider the ways in which fears that marking can be subject to bias have shaped the character of dominant assessment practices and consider what students may lose in these circumstances, particularly in terms of being able to learn through feedback.

Writing in the context of health sciences, Hauer et al. (2014) argue that 'trust acts as a gatekeeper to the learner's increasing level of participation and responsibility in the workplace' (p. 436). Without trust students cannot genuinely take on responsibility and thus prepare themselves for professional practice: 'Trust is essential for informing judgments regarding trainees' readiness for less supervised, autonomous workplace activity' (Hauer et al., 2014, p. 450). I argue that such preparation for independent activity in the world of work, or wider social world, is true of other university disciplines too. Indeed, so important are trust and respect, argues Czerniawski (2012), to 'all teacher/ student interactions' that without them 'any claim that formal education is in some way, a preparation, enactment and rehearsal for democratic citizenship is disingenuous' (p. 136). Thus in our hierarchy of teleoaffective structures, practices of trust can stretch from individual actions to broader social objectives. The overall point I am making is that trust acts as both a cultural conception and a teleological purpose because both tie in to our chances of experiencing mutual recognition. In Schatzki's terms, if our general understandings become characterized by distrust, then the teleoaffective outcomes that seem reasonable become constrained and limited, and the chances for mutual recognition curtailed.

The plagiarism 'industry'

Plagiarism detection has become a big industry attached to higher education. Indeed, I suggest we now have distrust on an industrialized scale. I will argue that the way in which the plagiarism industry has developed and spread within higher education represents an instrumentalization of the practices involved in academic writing, submitting work for assessment and in assessing that work. Where a lack of trust becomes woven into the cultural understandings that inform practices, the reasonable ends of those practices – such as learning about good academic writing or teaching students about responsible referencing become limited and distorted. Thus we need to change this aspect of culture in practice, change the underlying general understandings to ones of trust in order to fulfil more worthwhile educational ends. To be clear, I am not naively arguing that we should simply 'trust' all students and pretend plagiarism does not occur. This would not provide the basis for a genuine relationship with students, nor does it enable true mutual recognition. Indeed in Chapter 6 I consider the sister argument of why honesty is so important. My argument is also not that plagiarism does not matter: students who achieve an unfair advantage through inappropriate means clearly increase the injustice done to other students who have worked hard. My argument, however, is that the way that plagiarism detection and avoidance has been turned into an industry instrumentalizes the relationship between teacher and student and the practices of academic writing– and this does more harm than good because it embeds misrecognition into those assessment practices.

The scale of this plagiarism industry is apparent by looking at one of the leading providers of plagiarism prevention and detection software, a company called Turnitin®. Their software is now bought and used in 140 countries, by 15,000 customers in the form of paying institutions within the secondary or higher education sectors (Turnitin®, 2015b). More than 26 million students have their work passed through the Turnitin® system (Turnitin®, 2015b). Such growth is far from simply good chance. The founder of Turnitin.com, John Barrie, is reported to have said in 2000 that within two years the software would be 'as common as the spell checker' (quoted in Marsh, 2004). Thus the ambition is clear – to have this plagiarism software embedded into everyday writing practices. There is no denying the enormous speed and breadth of this software's growth. Between 2005 and 2014, the number of papers graded online, from secondary and higher education sectors, increased by 1,800 per cent (Turnitin®, 2015a). While Turnitin® is not the only plagiarism detection and prevention software available, it is the clear market leader, a situation partly achieved through the acquisition of key competitors (e.g. see Turnitin®, 2014).

One of the drivers for the growth of Turnitin® and similar plagiarism software has been the growth of the internet. While it may seem obvious to accept that the internet has changed the ways in which knowledge and text can be handled, we have perhaps been less aware of the ways in which online software such as Turnitin® has positioned itself to change the relationships between students and teachers and the recurrent social practices of assessment. It is too modest for such software to claim it is merely another helpful tool, for the company itself makes clear a much grander claim, such as here in one of their press releases:

> Turnitin®, the leader in improving how students write and learn.
>
> (Turnitin®, 2015b)

Thus their explicit aim is to inject this software into the everyday practices of writing assignments. Similarly, Jason Chu, education director at Turnitin® recently stated,

> As education moves to greater use of technology, Turnitin is becoming a *core component* of the writing instruction process around the world.
>
> (Turnitin®, 2015a, emphasis added)

Behind the growth of this industry is a largely unexamined assumption that if the internet makes it easier to plagiarize, more plagiarism must be occurring. The transgressions of the student, real *or imagined*, are thus the starting point for the plagiarism industry: if it is easier now to copy other people's work then, clearly, more students must be doing it. This assumption is unfair and unsubstantiated and is far more easily made by treating students as an amorphous mass, than by appreciating we are in intimate relationships of care with our students. Looking beneath the so-called plagiarism epidemic, some commentators such as McKeever (2006) suggest that what we are partially witnessing is the result of a broader reaction against 'the pernicious impact of the Internet on society' (p. 155). This has therefore led to the 'alarmist tone of reporting' and 'the sensational headlines' (p. 155). Howard (2007) points to the 'sense of impending doom [that] hangs over the academy as the specter of "Internet plagiarism" threatens to undo the entire educational enterprise' (p. 3). The simple causation of increased access to text and increased plagiarism which underpins the 'plagiarism industry' positions plagiarism as a disease-like affliction; easily caught 'in the presence of so much readily available text', whereby writers experience a 'lowering of their moral resistance' and therefore plagiarize (Howard, 2007). Again, Honneth is useful here for reminding us that we should not simply treat students as some mass population likely to be afflicted by this plague of plagiarism. If we value the particularity of our relationships with students, then other ways of supporting academic writing are required.

There is another way of reading the same page in the shared history with students and the growth of the internet. Rather than being quite so quick to assume that it is dishonest students who have capitalized on the ever-expanding supply of texts and references, one could view private enterprise as cleverly capitalizing on the climate of fear, confusion and misrecognition by offering a 'solution' in the form of plagiarism detection software. It is a neat way to position oneself in the market, because by being careful to always phrase it as both detection and deterrent, you really cannot lose. If users of the software find cases of plagiarism then the software has worked: if users do not find cases of plagiarism then the software has also worked, because it cleverly multitasks as a deterrent. If the internet has provided an irresistible motivation for students to cheat, it has no less provided an irresistible commercial motivation to exploit fears and uncertainties.

Students and academics will be aware that companies such as Turnitin® are providing a commercial resource for universities to use; however, many may þe less aware of the contribution students are unwittingly making in order for that to happen. Turnitin® operates by online scanning of submitted work from students and comparing this across three different groups of literature. First, the literature which is freely available through the sort of internet searches anyone can do. Second, databases of journal and other literature which is accessed by paid subscription. In other words Turnitin® pays for access to these resources which it uses to in turn be able to charge for its own software: a fair commercial exchange. Finally, however, Turnitin® compares submitted work against its own database – compiled from all the already submitted work from students around the globe. Unlike the large publishing companies, students receive no payment for the use of their work – a huge power imbalance and an economic injustice. Moreover, what appears on the surface to students as participating in a practice to do with academic writing or assignment submission has another end, often unknown to students (and academics), and this is enlarging the database of this for-profit company. The size of this database can then be used in further marketing activity, and so the cycle continues.

Student advocates in North America have been vocal about this situation, with mixed success. A legal action against Turnitin®'s parent company, iParadigms, failed in the United States because their use of student material was deemed 'fair use' (Bruton & Childers, 2016). But this ruling has not stopped student groups from continuing to try to campaign against such commercial software. At the University of Toronto, the students' union makes the following statement as part of their advice on Turnitin®:

> Essentially, this service uses your intellectual property for profit. Many institutions, such as Harvard, Princeton, Yale and Dalhousie, have decided against using Turnitin.com for this reason.
>
> (University of Toronto Students' Union, n.d.)

Writing for the student newspaper of the University of Georgetown, Tau (2010) argues,

> The thorny legal question remains unanswered. If Turnitin.com pays a fee to license published content from copyright holders like newspapers, magazines, and academic journals, why are student copyright holders any different? Turnitin.com charges schools to use its services, then archives the papers it receives to expand its database. A non-profit foundation or crowd-sourced version of Turnitin.com might have a legitimate case for existing. But paying corporate copyright holders while greedily arguing that students have no legitimate rights is unacceptable.

The issue of these firms' use of students' work casts a question over one of the frequent arguments in favour of this sort of online plagiarism detection software – and this is that it is a largely educational tool, rather than one of crime and punishment. However, if that was where the emphasis really lay then there would be less need to hold this vast – and commercially valuable – repository of student essays. Accidental plagiarism in the form of poor referencing or paraphrasing from published sources could still be highlighted. Using another student's essay is an altogether more deliberate act. It is hard to avoid that it is that vast store of students' work that gives the more successful among these firms – such as Turnitin® – their commercial edge. Handing in an assignment is a stressful time for many students – is this really the best moment or circumstance to make an informed decision of consent? And what alternatives are students given? It is part of the system, therefore you must go along with it? Hardly an argument grounded in social justice. This demonstrates the power of establishing such software among the recurrent practices of assessment submission. It relies on a conformist practical understanding of simply submitting to the system.

What has particularly concerned me looking at the research literature on plagiarism detection software is that the rationale for its use is often instrumental and broader ethical or educational understandings are sidelined. Or when such arguments are raised, they are frequently dismissed in favour of the 'greater good'. Here is an account from Warren, a lecturer in English:

> He was aware of the 'ethical problem' with Turnitin®, which he described as relating to 'a company that is making money off of the intellectual property of others ... who are not being compensated', but described himself as 'pragmatic enough' to realise it was a necessary tool in teaching large online courses.

Similarly, Paul, a lecturer in history

> reasoned that 'the way that Turnitin® is using these documents seems fair
> enough' because it is a 'John Lockean moment where you give up a little bit of
> your freedoms in order to have a little bit more security'.
>
> (Both extracts from Bruton & Childers, 2016, p. 322)

Whether intentional or not, what these lecturers appear to be saying is that students make a sacrifice (give up some freedom) so that academics, as their teachers, get the trade-off reward (convenience and efficiency). In the same study, a more sympathetic response came from Sharon, a lecturer in English who was concerned because 'it does in some ways violate students' rights to their intellectual property'. She also worried about other aspects of its use:

> I do think that it is often used as a sort of scare tactic and a means of not having
> what can be very difficult conversations with students, and with what is a diffi-
> cult skill to teach. I think that because writing is different in every discipline, it
> is a faculty member's responsibility to teach their students how to write in that
> discipline. I think that you can use Turnitin® and still do that, but I do think
> there are some faculty who don't.
>
> I do think there are some faculty that simply use it as a policing mechanism
> and I do think that is problematic.
>
> (Bruton & Childers, 2016, p. 322)

In looking at the literature on Turnitin®, I am struck over and over by how little appreciation of the student perspective is given by academics. There are odd exceptions such as Sharon above, but the majority of this literature is about the amazing efficiency of such plagiarism detection software. Marsh (2004), one of the exceptions among the literature, compares the lure of Turnitin® to that of the textbook industry, with promises of convenience and time saving: 'Like the generic textbook, Turnitin.com offers a prescriptive and normative educational agenda' (p. 433).

Student perspectives from the literature are rather different and express their hurt and anger at a system based on presumptions of guilt. Here I believe it is useful to think in terms of Honneth's understanding of love recognition and the particularity of relationships of trust. What may appear to be a general policy to academics, requiring submission of assignments through Turnitin® is actually a practice of some particularity for students: it is about the way general presumptions of possible guilt make them feel individually. One of the few studies to consider the student perspective on software such as Turnitin® includes the following comments from students:

> When we were told that we had to use Turnitin for this piece of coursework, I think everyone was a bit annoyed because we thought well why should we? We're not cheats and what if it gives an inaccurate result and you know you have not plagiarised anything? Why should you have to reword it just because this piece of software says that you should?
>> It's like being accused of cheating to be honest I thought. It is though isn't it?
>> (Penketh & Beaumont, 2014, p. 100)

Tau from the Georgetown University students' union is also concerned by presumptions of students' guilt:

> The dubious ethics of presuming students' guilt and forcing them to demonstrate their innocence. An ethical education should involve a degree of trust. Georgetown should be confident that the ethical precepts it emphasizes would be reflected in the actions of their student body. A presumption of guilt goes against Western legal and ethical principles and has no place in an academic setting.
>> (Tau, 2010)

Howard (2007) is right when she maintains that it is not simply the relationship of distrust engendered by plagiarism detection software that is the problem, but the mechanized nature of the resulting practices which compounds the dangers. She writes,

> In place of the pedagogy that joins teachers and students in the educational enterprise, plagiarism-detecting software offers a machine that will separate them.
>> (Howard, 2007, p. 12)

As Howard also observes, 'That a mechanized detection system could teach ethics – much less that our culture *needs* such a means of ethical instruction – is, *prima facie*, an outrageous proposition' (p. 12, emphasis original). Ethics is not the sphere of practical understandings where we simply do this or do that; it has a strong teleoaffective quality and an ethical approach involves a certain general understanding, to use Schatzki's phrase. In critical theory and critical pedagogy terms, teaching ethics in this way is the triumph of instrumental rationalism. Howard argues that while there may be some gains in terms of reducing the most 'readily detectable plagiarism' through these mechanized means, 'even more likely, though, is that it will close off possibilities for actually teaching students how to read, synthesize, and write about sources' (p. 13). Marsh (2004) also has concerns about the bureaucratization of pedagogical practices:

> I nonetheless make the specific point that Turnitin.com – as both a writing assessment tool and a kind of authoring environment itself – reifies identity categories via apparent metaphors disguised as informative educational content. Advertised as remedial pedagogy, the Turnitin.com service socializes student writers toward traditional normality and docility notions. Moreover, as a corporate solution to a nagging pedagogical problem, the Turnitin.com phenomenon represents what I see as a continuing bureaucratization of writing and writing instruction consistent with past administrative practices and reflective of emerging corporate management alliances in higher education.
>
> (p. 428)

In Honneth's (2014b) terms, what occurs in such situations is an impairment of subjects' ability to 'learn to experience themselves as deserving respect, thereby attaining autonomy' (p. 46). Furthermore, the problem is that we are dealing here with what he would describe as 'ethically damaged and demoralized social relationships' (p. 48).

The problem of trying to nurture better academic writing practices through such a piece of software becomes further evident if we examine more closely how a system such as Turnitin® actually works. At the heart of the Turnitin® system is an 'originality score' based on the matches the software finds between text in a student's work and other published sources. It totals the amount of matched text and presents this as a proportion of the whole piece of work. It is clear here why such software is often described as a blunt instrument, for the percentage of 'non-original' work includes institutional cover pages, quotes properly referenced, common phrases and the list of references. Hence, the more references one uses (even if properly cited) the less original the work is deemed to be. In fact, it is perfectly possible to have a high unoriginality score when what a student has actually done is a very fine piece of academic writing, richly engaging with the literature and well referenced. Thus it is highly problematic to reduce the learning about academic writing to such a technocratic exercise, and it sends potentially false information about students' achievements. Far from encouraging students to learn more about academic writing, a study by Penketh and Beaumont (2014) suggests that using this plagiarism software can simply create an approach of subservience and/or confusion. Particularly worrying is the associated lack of questioning students seemed to have in this study about Turnitin®'s role in checking so-called originality:

> What is also significant is the ways in which students appeared to respond uncritically to the information that was being presented to them and that the software appeared to be 'telling' them what was or was not acceptable. It is possible that the potential for Turnitin to act as a change artefact could be undermined as it replaces existing habitual practices in writing for assessment with another set of unquestioned practices which appear to have an additional weight by their association with the authoritative and disembodied voice of technology.
>
> (Penketh & Beaumont, 2014, p. 103)

When asked if Turnitin® encouraged redrafting, one student said:

> I think it did but not always for the better I think because I would change something that I was quite happy with because Turnitin said it wasn't happy with it.
>
> (Penketh & Beaumont, 2014, p. 100)

How sad that students would value a disembodied bit of software, more than their own judgement. Some students in the same study chose not to rely on the software because of its association with academic malpractice. Indeed, their insights reveal the ways in which the processes and practices of academic writing and redrafting are simply more complex than can be captured by such a piece of software:

> These students spoke about effective processes for redrafting and editing, drawing on existing relationships with tutors or friends in the final stages of their writing. However, the relevance of using Turnitin during this process appears to connect directly with malpractice. There appears to be a disconnect here with existing low stakes and trust-based strategies for revising texts and the appropriateness of using software associated with plagiarism detection.
>
> (Penketh & Beaumont, 2014, p. 101)

Academic writing is itself a nuanced process that simply cannot be easily mechanized. Indeed, surely the aim we have in encouraging original, independent work is to enable students to transcend mechanized forms of reproducing knowledge. Thus I suggest that if we put more time into allowing students to develop the skills and understanding of academic scholarship, or that particular relationship between their own thoughts and those of the existing research and literature, then the likelihood of poor academic writing may be diminished. As Pabian (2015) argues, we use the emotive term of cheating to describe poor academic writing, and yet expect students to perform within structures in which the uncritical reproduction of knowledge is sometimes the norm. Transmission forms of learning lead to uncritically reproductive forms of assessment. This is a point I pick up again in the coming chapters.

The plagiarism industry creates a situation in which distrust shapes assessment practices. Trust is undermined in two ways. First, it appears clear that academics do not trust students and second, it breaches the foundations of an honest relationship because it creates false appreciation of the practices of good academic writing. I suggest that it is not a pandemic of plagiarism that we should fear, but rather the distortion of assessment practices caused by the growth in what I term *the plagiarism industry*. Many higher education institutions are speeding towards the institutionalization of a technocratic assumption of students' misbehaviour, which then takes a blunt instrument to an ill-defined problem.

If students are to develop their self-confidence through their assessed work, we must ensure our practices contribute to this. Choosing an easy, technocratic fix to the problem of poor academic writing or cheating ignores the nature and importance of the relationships we build with students in our teaching-learning interactions. Nothing short of a serious reconsideration of the place of academic writing, as a foundational practice for what students do and achieve, and within the whole curriculum is required. My fear is that because of such software, some academics are spending less rather than more time teaching academic writing. A culture of distrust distorts the practices of academic writing away from the multidimensional qualities of judgement and reason to an instrumentalized one-dimensional quick fix tool. The heart of this issue can be understood by referring to Schatzki's hierarchy of teleoaffective structures. Do students understand assessment simply in terms of passing or getting a good mark or as the engagement with knowledge in socially useful ways? Do academics see the role of teaching and assessing in university as interlinked with developing good writing practices, and not simply transferring subject content knowledge? Positioning trust or distrust as a general understanding takes it beyond just some easy, superficial virtue. To position trust as shaping academics' practices stresses the importance of academics being there to help students. Assessment is not a trick or a trial, but should be a rich practice aimed at enabling genuine achievement.

Anonymous marking

The issue of trust between students and their assessors is reversed when we consider the arguments in favour of anonymous marking, for here we have evidence of students' lack of trust in academics. Students view anonymous marking as a safeguard against academics' bias, and there is some evidence to support this. But looking through the lens of Honneth's approach to social justice it becomes apparent that there are also distortions in our relationships that give rise to these fears. Where trust is absent from the general understandings that shape assessment practices, anonymous marking seems essential, but may bring with it a distortion in these same practices.

Anonymous marking is now the norm in many cases of assessment in countries such as the United Kingdom and Australia (Owen, Stefaniak & Corrigan, 2010). One of the striking features of this development in assessment practice is that it was student-led. It is clear to me from existing research and literature, and from my own work with students, that many students see anonymous marking as an important safeguard against partiality or error in academics' marking practices. At the heart of anonymous marking, however, are tacit practices which, I suggest, run counter to the just relationships envisaged by Honneth's conceptions of social justice, and particularly the first aspect of love or care recognition. It disables the relationship of particularity which, as I argued in the introductory section, should be a part of our relationships with students. While students feel protected by the veil of anonymity, it is also a barrier to personalization and to ongoing learning through assessment and feedback practices.

What particularly interests me from the perspective of assessment for social justice is the apparent trade-off between the protection of anonymity and the benefits of personalization. Arguments against anonymous marking tend to refer to the importance of closing the 'feedback loop' and the value of being able to appreciate how a student is developing and changing over time. Personalization is also mentioned: students learn better when they do not feel that they are just a faceless member of the crowd. Academics teach better when they are able to tailor the subject to students' abilities and/or interests. Formative feedback requires a social practice in which both students and academics engage; among other things this is how formative feedback can be so effective in conveying the tacit knowledge students need for successful academic work. It is very hard to see how some of the basic principles of assessment for learning, including the provision of good feedback, can be achieved alongside practices of anonymous marking. And yet, even understanding all of this, the evidence appears clear that students believe they need the protection of anonymous marking.

I have argued in the previous section that the marking relationship requires some foundation in mutual trust for two reasons: it shapes the outcomes of assessment practices and contributes to mutual recognition between students and academics. Anonymous marking raises interesting challenges to this position. If, as I suggest, assessment for social justice requires academics to have relationships of particularity and trust with students, then surely the reverse is true? Much depends on whether we consider anonymous marking through the lens of Honneth's love recognition or rights recognition. The former would suggest that anonymous marking places a barrier to relationships of particularity and trust. The latter might view anonymous marking as simply a universal right – part of the architecture of the examination and assessment process.

Students have been central to the drive for anonymous marking, and in many countries the national union of students (or equivalent) remain committed to this principle. In 1999 a campaign for anonymous marking across the higher education sector was led by the National Union of Students (NUS) in the United Kingdom. A spokesperson stated,

> We're not saying that lecturers are racist or sexist, but that bias exists throughout society and sub-consciously it could affect marking. If universities adopted anonymous marking they could put themselves beyond reproach and remove any question of discrimination.
>
> (BBC News, 1999)

Another spokesperson for the NUS explained the need for anonymous marking in terms of facing realities, rather than idealized situations:

> If we lived in a perfect world, students would be able to put their name on their coursework. Students would not have to fear that their work would be marked any differently based on their gender, sexuality or race. Unfortunately we don't live in that world.
>
> (quoted in Baty, 2007, pp. 1–2)

The NUS gained support for this position from influential quarters. For example, Julie Mellor, the chair of the Equal Opportunities Commission, said that a move to anonymous marking would 'remove possible bias' (BBC News, 1999). While the chairman of the Commission for Racial Equality, Sir Herman Ouseley, said that anonymous marking 'is a very simple step which could be easily taken and which would help universities better deliver an educational service which does not discriminate' (BBC News, 1999).

In a report on the continuing campaign in 2007, a piece in the Times Higher Education is illuminating for the attitudes presented by academics and students. We can see in quotes from academics the very same sense of being unhappy at being prejudged to be untrustworthy as we found with students concerning plagiarism software. For example, one academic commented,

> The student union believes that lecturers can't be trusted to mark their students fairly if they know who they are. It seems that lack of trust bedevils both sides.
>
> (Baty, 2007)

Indeed, staff perceptions that anonymous marking creates 'a climate of distrust' and is a 'slur on [the] professionalism' of academics (Brennan, 2008, p. 50) sound very like the feelings students expressed about plagiarism software. The NUS, however, maintained its campaign for anonymous marking, and a striking feature is the way in which they grounded this in academic research. For example,

> Research tells us that black students receive lower marks than their white counterparts. Lesbian, gay and trans students report that their coursework has been marked unfairly simply because of their sexuality or gender expression.
>
> (NUS, 2008)

According to the research carried out for the NUS, the marks awarded to black students at one London university were 4.2 per cent lower than those given to their white peers. And at a Welsh university, 42 per cent of men got first class or upper second degrees compared with 34 per cent of women. In Scotland, Asian students comprised 20 per cent of those on a particular course, but represented 80 per cent of those who had failed. At a university in south-west England, 62 per cent of students said they believed their marks would improve under an anonymous system (all figures from Smithers, 1999).

The victory of the students' movements to bring in widespread anonymous marking surely reveals the strength of feeling held. Those involved in this campaign were tenacious and displayed considerable endurance. We can see, from comments at the time this move was still being debated, the sort of opposition from academics that the student activists faced:

> Students should be assessed by lecturers who know their students as intimately as possible.

I can live with anonymous marking of exams. However, when it comes to coursework it is a different matter.

Coursework takes place in the context of a relationship that informs expectations and the assessment of outcome. In a sense the marking of an essay represents the continuation of that relationship. [Anonymous marking] undermines both the relationship and the effectiveness of a teacher to provide guidance and feedback.

(All quotes from Baty, 2007)

The research literature on anonymous marking is limited, complex and often conflicted. Indeed, Birch, Batten and Batey (2015) argue that given the ambiguous nature of current research in this area, it is perhaps premature to come down too strongly for or against anonymous marking. In addition, 'there is also disparity in the practice of anonymous marking across the entire higher education sector' (Batten, Batey, Shafe, Gubby & Birch, 2013, p. 17). But I believe that we can still go some way to better understanding what the debate over anonymous marking, and especially the strength of students' views on this, tell us about trust in the context of assessment practices.

A significant strand of the research which supports anonymous marking has emerged from psychology and the cognitive sciences. The notion of cognitive efficiency is used to explain how and why a marker might inadvertently allow their knowledge of a student to influence their marking. Amid time pressures and a great pile of marking, the marker may unconsciously, according to the cognitive efficiency thesis, rely on cues as to the quality of the work based on their previous experience:

Specifically, in a university setting where a lecturer is marking a student's assignment, schema-driven theorists would argue that a lecturer assigns a student to a specific category based on the cues in the early stages of an interaction (e.g. seeing their name on the cover sheet and assuming knowledge of gender) and then makes a judgement which forms expectancies for the remainder of the interaction (i.e. the marking process).

(Birch et al., 2015, p. 2)

Bradley's (1984) work is often cited as one of the earliest pieces to demonstrate gender bias in marking, although her results were more nuanced than the way they are sometimes presented in other literature. In a study of student final year projects, Bradley hypothesized, and found to be the case, that second markers would be more prone to gender bias than the first marker who was also the student's supervisor. The first marker's knowledge of the student and the project area enabled a certain moderation of any bias compared with the independent second marker. Bradley (1993) argues that her conclusion was not that bias did not exist with first markers, but rather that those factors helped to lesson it. Thus in 1993 Bradley clearly reiterated her support, based on her research, for anonymous marking:

> I recommend they ... introduce blind marking to help to protect themselves and their students from the risks of sex bias.
>
> (Bradley, 1993, p. 8)

In this way, the case for anonymous marking is made in terms of the welfare of both students and academic markers. But the complexity of the issue is evident in this early work by Bradley. For, while she found support for anonymous marking due to the behaviour of the second markers, she also implies that the personalization first markers brought to the process lessened gender bias.

Another case for anonymous marking is made in terms of avoiding the so-called halo effect, whereby markers familiar with the quality of previous work see similar attributes in further pieces of assessment. Malouff et al. (2014) undertook a study of 159 markers across a range of disciplines comparing grades given to written work after students also did an oral presentation:

> As hypothesized, the graders assigned significantly higher scores to written work following the better oral presentation than following the poor oral presentation, with intermediate scores for the written work of the student whose oral presentation was not seen by the graders. The results provide evidence of a halo effect in that prior experience with a student biased the grading of written work completed by the student. The findings suggest that keeping students anonymous, as in the condition with no knowledge of the student's performance in the oral presentation, helps prevent bias in grading.
>
> (p. 2)

Another study by Batten et al. (2013) comes to the opposite conclusion:

> The specific aim of this study was to examine the influence of reputation information, in the form of knowledge of a student's previous performance and the general quality of their writing style, on the assessment of undergraduate student work. It was hypothesised that those students with a more positive reputation would receive significantly more favourable marks, and would receive more feedback than those students with a negative reputation. The results of the

present study, however, are not only in contrast to the proposed hypotheses, but would also appear somewhat contradictory to the results of previous research.

(p. 427)

These two studies are further evidence of the conflicted research-base upon which arguments about anonymous marking are based. Brennan (2008) asserts: 'Student anonymity in the summative assessment of written work is a matter that goes to the capacity of university teachers to apply objective judgement (p. 43). While he acknowledges some potential limitations with anonymous marking, Brennan further argues that these can be overcome with some thought and planning. For example, concerns that it breaks the feedback loop (which I will return to below) between student and their marker can be overcome, he argues, by the provision of such individualized feedback post marking and before their next piece of work. Suggestions such as these, however, take insufficient account of the workload pressures on academics and the timing issues arising from modularization. There may be no opportunity to give further, individualized feedback. Certainly more possible is the practice of 'feeding forward'; that is, giving extensive feedback on a completed draft and thus enabling students to use this when making their final submission. But unless this is also done anonymously (and thus it does not rectify the problem of depersonalization), the final marking is anonymous in name only. Indeed, to give feedback after the final, summative grade runs counter to much of the research on effective feedback: that is, that feedback must be timely and of use to students. They must have opportunities to engage with that feedback and to apply it in meaningful ways. The writing practices of students in highly modularized systems do not support the reuse of feedback in future courses or assessments.

What I have found striking when discussing anonymous marking with students is that they are very aware of these counterarguments. And yet they simply do not feel safe without the protection of anonymous marking. Thus in a scenario of competing ends, the need to be able to feel protected from bias was stronger than that to receive, for example, personalized feedback or indeed a richer student-teacher relationship. Certainly students I have interviewed about anonymous marking often believe that bias is an inevitable human inclination:

> I think that's [anonymous marking] great, because I feel like there's going to be
> a level of certain bias towards people, even unintentionally, it doesn't have to

be aggressively like I really don't like that person, I'm going to give them a bad mark, but I think it's a great thing that lecturers and teachers don't know, because they can show unintentional bias towards someone.

I think it's quite important, because I know that no matter how much we try, we like some people more than the others. It's true, we can't help it really, we can try as much as we want, you know, or maybe we dislike someone for any reason and we are not even conscious about this so we will be trying to find fault in the person that we you know, don't like I suppose. So I think it's safer.

Students seem clear that they believe bias should be avoided whether it is positive or negative:

Especially if someone particularly wasn't doing well before and they decided to pull together and do something really well and the marker's even thinking I should give them extra marks because they've pulled themselves together and I don't think that's right either, because fairness needs to be fair regardless if it's fair 'cos you're doing worse or you're doing better, someone shouldn't be positively influenced by someone knowing who they are either.

One student introduced a new dimension when she linked anonymous marking to her own feelings of self-esteem:

Like you don't want like them knowing who you are, I think it's just a self-esteem type thing, like if you do really badly then you don't want them to know your name, so it's all just anonymous and if I did really badly at least they kind of don't really know who I am kind of thing, it's purely just self-esteem but I think that's the basis of it for me, I think I'm really worried I'll do really badly kind of thing.

Much of the literature on marking bias focuses mainly on whether or not such bias exists, but there is much less exploration of the sources of such bias (Batten et al., 2013). From a critical theory perspective, it should be equally important to understand why bias occurs, particularly as some assessment practices simply cannot be anonymized (Owen et al., 2010). This is likely to become more the case rather than less as diverse forms of assessment, beyond the traditional exam or essay, become more widespread. In addition, the scope for decisions biased by assumptions of gender or ethnicity, for example, is broader than the giving of marks alone. There has been much less consideration, including by student groups, of the potential for bias in favouring certain forms of assessment or the ways in which assessment questions are framed.

Earl-Novell (2001) considers the gendered nature of undergraduate writing, and the role it has played in the under-representation of women with first class degrees in England, particularly in 'argument-based' subjects such as English, history and sociology:

> They believe that the male undergraduate written style tends to conform to a bold, ebullient and risk-taking approach whilst female academic work can be characterised by a more cautious, diligent and conscientious approach.
>
> (p. 168)

Markers may look, consciously or unconsciously, for other indicators of gender apart from the name of a student: here the tacit nature of much of the knowledge brought into marking practices is clear. One academic from Earl-Novell's study claimed,

> You still get the girly handwriting which is very obvious ... there's the style of handwriting, but it tends to be squared off writing with little Os for a dot and men's tend to be spikier and scruffier ... that's the other way you can tell sometimes. Men's scripts tend to be scruffier.
>
> (Male sociologist, pp. 164–5)

Academics interviewed from economics also perceived different gender differences:

> In written work the girls tend to be much more conscientious ... they tend to have done more work.
>
> (Female economist, p. 165)

> They (female undergraduates) tend to have a better writing style ... men's tends to be a lot sloppier. It's usually less careful. It's usually much more jagged and doesn't flow.
>
> (Male economist, p. 165)

As Earl-Novell concludes,

> In a climate where many academics (as testified here) claim to be able to identify male and female handwriting ... this raises the question whether they are really rewarding the 'style' of the candidate before them, or their own subjective expectations based on the candidate's imputed gender.
>
> (p. 170)

Of course, the handwriting issue is easily resolved by moving to a practice of typed exams, but there are more fundamental issues and biases at play here. In the argument-based subjects of sociology and English, Earl-Novell found that it was the bolder style of male students that tended to be valued, over the allegedly more circumspect approach of female students. This resonates with Leathwood's (2005) argument that certain assessment approaches may favour particular forms of expression and thus disadvantage some ethnic minorities. What this study demonstrates is that bias in marking can run deep and be implicit in numerous practices. The tacit and largely unacknowledged connection of certain abilities and traits with certain students is a clear case of misrecognition, and cannot be ignored simply because procedures have been put in place to ameliorate or limit them. There are, therefore, two lessons for assessment for social justice to draw from this issue of anonymous marking. First, academics cannot simply assume or legislate for students to have trust in them (nor was the solution to the plagiarism industry simply to trust students and not work towards good academic writing practices). Fears, uncertainty and doubts run deep. That these become most obvious in the context of assessment practices should not lessen our sense of them seeping through other aspects of our relationships with students and the recurrent practices of teaching and learning. Second, we need to consider what it means for students to be so worried about academic bias that they knowingly make a trade-off between the virtues of anonymization and those of personalization in their learning and assessment practices. Beyond this, the problem with anonymous marking from a social justice perspective is that it relies on a formal procedure to fix a problem that is located more deeply, in relationships of recognition and recurrent practices. In this example, a procedure was put in place to ensure greater justice. However, introduction of a better procedure does nothing to address the root problem of bias itself, thus the real injustice remains. Consider other professions where such biases might also exist. We cannot solve the problem of different treatment based on gender in medicine or law by hiding the identity of the patient or defendent: these can only be addressed through bringing the problem into the light and through challenge and education. The injustices of discrimination based on gender, ethnicity, sexuality or age may be partially contained by assessment procedures that inhibit their full realization during marking, but the prejudices, and hence injustices, still remain and can become manifest in many other aspects of higher education, and society.

Anonymous marking cannot differentiate between sameness that is helpful, as discussed in Chapter 2 (e.g. consistent standards of treatment), and sameness which is unhelpful (e.g. essentializing or denying identity). Theories of learning often place great importance on student individuality in terms of different approaches to learning. Similarly, research has shown the degree to which students value personalization within a learning environment (McLean et al., 2013). In the context of feedback, this is highlighted through the notion of feedback as a dialogue with students (McArthur & Huxham, 2013) and feedback as an integrated part of the learning experience such that the cycle is only complete when a student has submitted work which demonstrates they have addressed the issues raised (Taras, 2002). Anonymous marking provides an impermeable barrier to any true ongoing feedback dialogue or loop. Here we see the scale of change required to realize assessment for social justice. It cannot be achieved through some light tinkering. As Honneth's work impels us, we must go to the foundations of whether our daily practices sustain mutual recognition or distort it.

Conclusion

Recently Woelert and Yates (2015) discussed the implications of a lack of trust for the work of academics. They point to a dual system in which there is arguably too little trust in academics to do the right thing, and too much trust in procedures to ensure that the right thing is done. Have academics become so used to systems of control and the attendant lack of trust, respect and recognition that accompanies them in an audit-driven sector that they are utterly unaware that they perpetuate this through the practices they share with their students? This is the real danger of the growth of the plagiarism industry. And students do not feel able to trust academics not to display bias when they mark; there is evidence to support students' position on this. And so strongly held is this belief that students knowingly trade the advantages of being known (personalization, the feedback loop) in order to ensure anonymous marking. This speaks to the heart of the relationship between trust or distrust and the perceived purposes of assessment, or in Schatzki's terms, the reasonable ends of assessment. A general understanding of trust projects these ends beyond simply the 'right' mark or a good mark and focuses on the development of knowledge useful for society, and on students' expression of their worth and achievements.

There is a further interrelationship between these two examples of distrust that is worth mentioning. If one is concerned about academic misconduct, the danger of contract cheating is a further potential problem that plagiarism software cannot address. Contract cheating involves students buying a bespoke essay from a (usually) online source. The essay will pass any plagiarism detection because it is genuinely original – just not written by the student who claims it as his or her work. One of the most powerful ways to counter this and other forms of academic misconduct is through a stronger formative relationship between student and teacher. Looking at an early draft of work, seeing how it then emerges into a final form – this sort of formative process is much harder to get around through cheating. But it all relies on personalization. So the point I am making is that the lack of trust that is at the heart of anonymous marking then compounds the problem of trust when it comes to possible plagiarism or cheating. Here we see the mutuality in action.

What I hope is apparent in both these examples is that trust and assessment cannot be reconciled simply through procedures or technocratic means. Trust necessarily involves a whole sphere of human relations and social practices. It undeniably speaks to the essence of who we are and how we see ourselves – am I a trustworthy person? There is an intimacy here that is visceral and profound. It is also multifaceted. Thus trust within an assessment context denotes

> the confidence one has in the likelihood of others (management, administration, colleagues, students) acting responsibly in respect of sound principles, practices or behaviours in assessment. In other words, there are confidence, integrity and competence issues.
>
> (Carless, 2009, p. 81)

But this is only part of the story for, as Honneth insists, these must be reciprocal issues. Trust must be about being trusting as well as trustworthy. To accusations that it is naive to simply 'trust' students, I would make two points. First, my arguments against the industrialization of the fear of plagiarism in no way mean that we ignore issues of academic integrity and good writing practices. Rather, I would argue that the fear of plagiarism created by the use of such software, and the fairly heavy-handed way it is sometimes handled, create such an environment as to distort the ability of students to learn genuinely the academic craft. Second, I suggest that it is more naive to believe that such institutionalized distrust and misrepresentation does no harm, or is not implicated in shaping the resulting outcomes. As students grow and continue to construct their identities through their university experiences, trust remains a key aspect of the people they will become, and how near they are to realizing mutual recognition. As Rose (1997) argues, experiences cannot be independent from who we are. And finally, as Warin (2010) also observes,

When we construct a self we are simultaneously creating the lenses through which we see the world and forming the bedrock of our mental health and well-being. Our ability to be reflexive, that is to be aware of our selves, to watch and evaluate our own behaviour, seems to be an ability that is profoundly human.

(p. 29)

Trust must play an essential part in our assessment practices or we risk both misrecognition, and more limited academic ends. This does not mean that we act with naivety. Some systems are necessary for when things go wrong. But it is naive to believe that a system or procedure can, *of itself*, address all issues pertaining to trust. By its very definition, trust must at some point be given and received willingly. Finally, the place of trust in our assessment practices does not lie separately from the other concepts I will go on to explore. Indeed, it gains strength and resilience through its interaction with the other general understandings, such as honesty or responsibility, which will be discussed in subsequent chapters.

6

Honesty

Introduction

Assessment for social justice requires practices of *honesty*. I propose honesty as my second general understanding because it again emphasizes the essentially interpersonal and intersubjective nature of assessment practices. Honesty forces a public commitment to the just foundations upon which academics and students interact with one another, and should enable open discussion of the teleoaffective structures associated with our assessment practices. It differs in this sense from clarity, a term more frequently associated with good practice in assessment. Clarity is also an admirable feature of good assessment but it is a less embodied notion. Honesty is also closely related to the previous chapter's discussion of trust. In many ways, trust and honesty go hand in hand and are mutually dependent. Indeed, an argument in this chapter considers the role that greater honesty about marking procedures and practices could have in enabling greater trust, for example, in the context of the debate on anonymous marking: if we stopped claiming to mark to high levels of precision, students may have less to fear about marking bias. Similarly, the valuing of honesty as a trait in both students and academics can offer an alternative approach to problems of plagiarism or academic malpractice, compared with the instrumentalism inherent within the plagiarism industry.

Like trust, I suggest that honesty can be partly understood in terms of Honneth's realm of love recognition as it relates directly to the capacity for self-confidence. There is an element of particularity here which I want to emphasize. I suggest there is a world of difference between an academic or institution claiming in a general way to be honest to all students, or a student claiming to be honest to all teachers, and being prepared to be honest to any particular individual: there is a commitment and intimacy in the latter that highlights the harm of dishonesty. Honesty, as my chosen term, is deliberately confrontational, but only because I believe that it is a feature of our assessment practices fundamental to a healthy relationship of mutual recognition. I also suggest it can be a powerful driver of change.

In this chapter I consider two examples of where greater honesty about marking practices is needed. My first example focuses on the conditions under which many academics perform their marking. To what extent are academics in a position to assess to their best abilities, and to what extent does this aspect of their practice cause stress and harm? Second, I consider the precision with which students' work can be marked. How finely defined should our marking structures be? Both these issues are, I suggest, matters of honesty, and both are areas in which I suggest institutional practices are not sufficiently honest, leading to misunderstandings of how marking is done, and the purposes of assessment. These are not the only ways in which honesty comes into play in assessment practices, but they are both fundamentally important to the wider project of assessment for social justice, and I will refer back to both these issues in subsequent chapters. I also use them illustratively to demonstrate how practices may change if subject to understandings of honesty. Here it is honesty as a general understanding that evokes both an explanatory and a transformative power.

Marking workloads and conditions

> Marking, marking, marking! How do I get time to mark everything that comes in – and give my students feedback?
>
> > (Sambell et al., 2013, p. 1)

A lack of honesty about the working conditions under which academics engage in assessment and marking practices inhibits the movement to greater social justice in two ways. First, there is misrecognition towards academics through the undervaluing of their labour and their diminished capacity to feel appropriate esteem in a job well done. High levels of workplace stress may further compound the misrecognition they suffer. Second, this lack of honesty about how much time is spent on assessment also diminishes the students' achievements, if the products of their labour are not given the attention they deserve. I position these problems as ones of honesty because I think this is a powerful lens through which to see that established practices that have long become accepted can, and should, be rethought. I suggest that claims about academic workload expressed through this language of honesty would be very uncomfortable for senior managers and policymakers to deal with.

The current irony is that many academics feel that assessment takes up more and more of their time, but they are left with a diminished sense of achievement for all this work because the workload and time frames can be so overwhelming. Assessment is frequently cited by academics as one of the hardest parts of their role, and many academics share with students a fear of failure when it comes to their assessment tasks. Assessment can be stressful and academics may feel besieged by the volume of assessment they need to do within very limited timelines. Indeed, it does seem that many marking practices are being corralled into smaller and smaller time frames – ironically, often to ensure time for more and more quality assurance or moderation procedures to check on that marking. Thus procedures to ensure a 'correct' mark can dominate the actual practices of undertaking the marking in the first place. In addition, the judgements academics are required to make within these time frames are often unrealistic – such as reliably attributing a mark out of 100 (a point I return to in the next section). Expectations of what is involved when academics assess work have also grown with increasing appreciation of the importance of feedback to ongoing student learning, and significant dissatisfaction among many students about the quality of feedback they receive. A common knee-jerk reaction to student complaints that feedback is not timely is to put in place rules for quicker and quicker turnaround of marking. This completely misunderstands the complex notion of timeliness being alluded to by students, which is not about three weeks rather than four weeks, but about usefulness and the extent to which feedback can inform future work. Thus, for many academics, it must feel as though they are expected to do more and more in less and less time. Marking practices need to be made more just for academics so that they do not suffer unreasonable stress nor be denied satisfaction in this important aspect of their work. Students similarly deserve to know that sufficient time and attention will be given to work they have submitted for assessment.

Marking is rarely done under perfect conditions – fresh at the start of the workday, just a few essays or exams at a time to ensure our minds are not jaded and our concentration remains fresh. Indeed, it has become acceptable, as part of the overriding cultural assumptions, to consider marking as a task undertaken under severe time constraints. This needs to be challenged and, in so doing, ensure that this vital pedagogical practice is accorded the respect it deserves; for in doing so, respect for both students and academics is demonstrated. At the heart of assessment for learning must be a recognition that marking, and particularly feedback, is a form of teaching. Academics risk being alienated from the products of their own labour when marking becomes such a chore, such a relentless process, that they can feel little satisfaction in what they are doing. This was brought home by an anonymous blog posted on the website of the Guardian newspaper in the United Kingdom. The blog was written as a letter to a student explaining the lived realities of marking. It is titled: 'Dear Student, I just don't have time to mark your essay properly' (*Guardian*, 2016). It makes sad and disturbing reading – but for many academics it will ring true. The author writes,

> Dear Student, I have just read your essay, and I must apologise – I have absolutely no idea what it said … Your essay is one of 20 or so I've tackled in one sitting this afternoon…. I'm reading something you wrote on page two and I'm wondering if I just read an explanation of this concept on page one, or if that was in someone else's essay. I have to go back a page, eyes swimming, and check.
>
> Your essay does not stand alone, but becomes amalgamated with the others I've read so far today, all talking about the same things, with varying degrees of clarity. Your words are diluted by the ones that came before, they are lost on me even before I begin.

And the author knows this isn't right, is not how marking should take place:

> It should not be like this. In an ideal world, I would spend my morning carefully marking three essays at most, giving them the thought they deserve. I would … clear my head so I can approach the next batch with a fresh outlook and enthusiasm.
>
> But I do not have that kind of time.

The author is doing her best, but falls short of her own standards:

> I know that I should go back and reread a few essays to compare the marks I've given, but there isn't time. I would like to look up the references you cite, to tell you if there are other gems in those books you may have missed, or suggest other interpretations, but there's no chance. I also have a life – washing to do, family to spend time with, that sort of thing.

And yet there is the guilt of knowing how much the marks the students receive will mean to them:

> I know that you will look immediately at the mark written at the top of the first page. You will make assumptions about yourself, your work – perhaps even your worth – based on this number. I want to tell you not to worry about it.

Not to worry about it, because,

Don't take it too personally. I've tried my best to be consistent and fair, and other lecturers will moderate my marking, but really, by a certain stage, I'm just pulling numbers out of the air. (55? 58? I don't know).

Just pulling numbers out of the air:

Your essay does not stand alone; it's either going to impress me or sap my energy, and if it does the latter, it affects how I read the ones which come afterwards. Too many awful essays and I can't concentrate anymore.

The process of marking must be understood as a complex nexus of different social practices, thus involving a range of sayings and doings, tasks and projects which the marker must learn about through participation in the practice itself. Too often academics are thrown into the practice of marking with little or inadequate preparation. Of all the parts of an academic role, assessment should be the one in which a robust apprenticeship is ensured. Eisner's (1985) notion of assessment as connoisseurship is relevant here: assessing students' work is a skill that develops with experience. The more different essays one reads over time, the easier it is to have a sense of how standards vary; the more student lab reports one marks, the easier it is to understand how students might go about such a task. Importantly, it is also easier to see how very different pieces of work can satisfy the same criteria in diverse ways. Given the importance of marking to students' outcomes and future lives, it is surely scandalous how little time new academics are given to develop their ability to undertake such marking. And what of postgraduate teaching assistants who do so much of the first year marking for large classes? How much genuine professional development and learning do they receive? Surely we should consider putting our most experienced markers to work in first year, as their feedback will help shape students' understandings of assessment expectations at university.

There is also an issue around remuneration for marking. The blogger outlined above was on a short-term, hours-only contract. Sometimes there is little financial allowance, if any, for marking activity. Postgraduate students might be expected to do the marking for no remuneration at all – just to consider themselves lucky to get the experience in the modern academic jungle. Academics can find themselves in a potentially exploitative situation:

With no defined hours of work, no overtime payments and no time off in lieu, coupled with reduced job security, academics are clearly vulnerable to exploitation in this corporate managerial environment.

(Kenny & Fluck, 2014, p. 586)

And of course, in such a situation these temporary workers are unlikely to feel able to challenge the dominant assessment and feedback practices. Are universities prepared to honestly declare that while taking in higher and higher student fees they pay derisory wages to those who assess students' work, if they pay anything at all? If assessment is central to what universities do, how can it be relegated to an activity in which there is no or little training and no or little remuneration? This is where honesty matters. How seriously are our universities taking the assessment of student work – not just in terms of the regulations they have in place but also in terms of the lived realities of how marking takes place? When postgraduates are brought in to mark on large undergraduate courses, the issue of reasonable and effective time to learn the craft of assessment also becomes more acute, but rarely are they afforded such an apprenticeship and they may simply have to sink or swim after one pre-moderation meeting.

Where once there was apparent flexibility as part of the academic role, an increasingly bureaucratized approach to assessment takes this away, along with any sense of control over one's workload. Kenny and Fluck (2014) go on to share the thoughts of several academics, highlighting the issue of workload:

> It seems that academics are losing all control over our work-life, as it becomes more bureaucratised and rationalised.
>
> (My workload) … is ridiculously high and completely unsustainable. I have been probably averaging 70 hrs/week, with some up to 90 hrs/week this semester, which is my busier semester. This is having negative impact on personal life.
>
> There is an expectation that work has to be done regardless of workload models so there is no protecting of overload.
>
> For much of the teaching term I work double the hours I'm paid for.
>
> (All quotes p. 597)

Other academics have expressed feelings such that they are 'drowning', being utterly 'exhausted' and becoming 'a gibbering wreck' (Hemer, 2014, p. 486). The further worry expressed by academics is that they simply are unable to do their work well given the workload expectations and the available time – even when working considerably more hours each week. This problem is particularly acute when teaching large undergraduate classes. As another academic explains,

> You know what it's like when you are juggling so many balls and after a while you feel they will all come crashing down. That's what I feel like. There's no sense of reward because you don't feel like you are doing anything particularly well.
>
> (Boyd, 2014, p. 319)

The workload pressure of marking can then shape the nature of the assessment practices. Evidence from Hemer (2014) suggests that assignment marking was where most teachers looked for strategies to manage their time. Examples could include using online quizzes that got marked automatically or using stock phrases on written assignments to minimize feedback time and effort. Marking rubrics were also regarded as potentially time saving, after the initial time investment to set them up. Hemer also relates how academics might use Turnitin® as a time-saving device, saving them the effort of checking for plagiarism. One academic stands out in Hemer's study – this is Bill, who Hemer notes 'employed more strategies to minimise teaching workload than any of the other participants':

> For Bill, his aim is to ensure that he meets the required thresholds for student evaluations of the quality of his courses. Beyond that, he argues that the value placed on teaching by the faculty is unclear, and chooses to concentrate his effort where he considers it is most clearly valued: in research. Here, Bill demonstrates his agency in shaping his work to maximise those aspects of university employment that he enjoys and feels is most highly valued.
>
> (p. 488)

If assessment tells students what part of a course or what type of knowledge is valued, then academics also have various cues to look towards, as Bill is doing, to decide what is really valued in their professional practice. Unless assessment gets dedicated *and quality* time, its status remains low: a paradox surely as it is so high stakes in determining students' future lives and shaping the ways they apply their knowledge as graduates. Indeed, this paradox plays out in several ways as universities try to encourage and compel academics to give better feedback on students' work, but place them under more and more stressful conditions in which to do that. There is also an issue here about how much assessment is set and Boud (2014) rightly observes that something may have been lost along the way, as pressure has mounted to ensure students get grades for everything they do.

One response to perceived problems with academics' workloads has been the introduction of workload allocation systems by many universities with the stated aim of ensuring a more equitable distribution of workload and greater transparency. Here again, is the addition of another procedure where what is actually needed is an honest rethinking of the conditions under which the practice takes place. Indeed, the ways in which workload models frequently work can obscure an honest understanding of what academics do, rather than enlighten.

This can particularly occur when such modules assume a notional full academic workload and the tasks undertaken are made to fit within this full allowance. This can then render any work done beyond that notional allowance invisible and unacknowledged. Here we can invoke Honneth's sense of invisibilization as a form of misrecognition (Honneth, 2001). Like the servants in the stately homes of the nobility, academic staff exist on one level (they do their marking) but remain unacknowledged on another level (there is no genuine recognition of this marking in the workload model). Some workload models exacerbate this problem further by quantifying the amount of time for marking, but in derisory ways. For example, at some institutions a 2,000 word essay is given an allowance of twenty minutes. *Would institutions be prepared to honestly and publicly acknowledge such time allocations?* To compare this with how much time and effort the student put into that work raises real questions about the basis of honesty in relations between students and the institutions they study in. It is also a case of fair procedure as farce – for it is simply an impossibly inaccurate representation of how long it takes to mark such a piece of work. To fulfil their marking responsibilities many academics must work far beyond the notional academic workload. Indeed, it has been argued that universities could collapse if academics only worked the notional hours allocated under such workload models. In fact, such models provide 'a veneer of objectivity and justification for the continuation of a highly uneven distribution of work' (Malcolm & Zukas, 2009, p. 496). The official 'story' about workloads is thus in serious 'conflict with the lived experiences' of academics (p. 500).

The issue of marking workloads raises again the paradox of the audit culture which has flourished within higher education. Workloads models that hide or dissemble the true assessment practices of academics fit well with a pervasive audit culture. The veneer of transparency and accountability is satisfied, even though the content is utterly discreditable.

Thus I contend that we need to be more honest about the workloads, particularly around assessment and feedback practices, of many academics. This is for their own sakes, their rights to stress-free working environments and satisfaction in a job well done, and for the rights of students who deserve their work to be given genuine and full consideration. Students should be seriously concerned about the conditions under which their work is assessed. I would like to see an equivalent campaign as that by the NUS on anonymous marking around the practices and workload allocations of assessment and feedback. Such honesty would be a necessary step to reforming practices and moving towards assessment for social justice: that is why it matters so much. We should also not overlook the issue of feedback here, and the impact on feedback practices of unrealistic marking workloads. It may well be that we need to reconsider the patterns of assessment within a course to ensure that there is genuine scope for healthy and useful marking and feedback practices. We certainly need to reconsider current responses to perceived problems with feedback, and to realize that timeliness is about usefulness, and not prescribed turnaround times. We may need to resist the temptation to make all assessment high-stakes, for the sake of both students and academics. I strongly believe that more honesty about the workload demands of marking on academics' time – in genuine ways and not through the sleight of hand of some workload models – would force change for the better in assessment practices. It is necessary to fundamentally rethink the reasons for assessment and to put the notion of dialogue to the fore. An assessed piece of work, and particularly the feedback given about it, should exist as an artefact in a dialogue between a student and her teacher. Similarly, it provides the basis for a dialogue between students and their own achievements. Even where assessment is for certification, dialogue is central – as the student should be encouraged to think in terms of how they will go on to use the knowledge for which they have received such certification.

Marking precision and accuracy

In this section, I will suggest that if one of the general understandings we bring to our marking practices is honesty, then this has implications for the type of teleo-affective structures we associate with such marking, and particularly the idea of a 'right' mark. As I have already stressed, higher education is about engaging with complex knowledge, and this impacts on the ways in which assessment should be carried out. My argument is twofold. First, I do not believe that high levels of precision and differentiation are possible in terms of the forms of knowledge that should form the basis of higher education assessment tasks. Second, I do not consider that such precision and differentiation is desirable, and argue that it deflects attention from what really matters, which is the social application of such knowledge to nurture greater individual and social well-being. Freeing assessment from the shackles of rigid marking schemes may allow greater scope for genuine engagement with complex knowledge, and the pursuit of social justice practices and ends.

I propose that the idea of a single numerical grade to represent the quality of a higher education student's work is an historical legacy that is long overdue for much closer scrutiny. It is, however, such a socially ingrained perception of what marking is that we should not underestimate how difficult it is to question or challenge. We talk in terms of 'top marks' or '10 out of 10' as familiar ways to give praise. This is particularly an issue because evidence suggests that students attribute a disproportional significance to numerical grades (James, 2000). Most problematic is when marking occurs across a vast range of possible marks – such as marks out of 100. When a student sees she has got 67 per cent for an assignment but a friend has got 68 per cent, she may reasonably believe that some qualitative difference has been discerned. Many academics know from experience that such precision is unreasonable and so they adapt marking schemes to cut down the number of potential grade points. For example, they may mark to just the second, fifth and eighth point in each grade band (52 per cent, 55 per cent, 58 per cent). This is still problematic for two reasons. First, unless students are fully aware that those other places on the percentage scale are not in use, they may interpret the mark as more precise than it actually is. Second, there are rarely marking criteria for these three places across the grading band. Such criteria most often apply to bands as a whole, not places within them. Thus we have criteria to distinguish between a B and a C, but not a high, medium or low B. This means that making these distinctions is not done according to criteria but some other form of judgement, or even intuition. Attempts to resolve this by more and more complex marking rubrics can so atomize the marking process that the piece of work as a whole is effectively destroyed. Similarly, some people adapt percentage grading schemes by only marking on multiples of five. But why not then simply mark out of 20 rather than give the impression of a marking span over 100?

The anecdotal evidence that students misunderstand large numerical grading systems is extensive. It is common for students who receive a mark in the *8 or *9 range (e.g. 48, 49) to ask – 'how can I get that extra point' or 'those extra two marks'. Academics often find such requests frustrating, but how can we blame students when the marking system encourages such misunderstandings. Large numerical grading scales encourage students to see grading as an accumulation of points, rather than a criterion-based activity, engaging with complex knowledge. They encourage students to see knowledge as disembodied and easily accumulated rather than complex and requiring commitment and engagement. Only in certain disciplines, and in specific forms of criteria, do we genuinely mark by the accumulation of points for individual tasks. Indeed, where we may have simple assessment tasks with right and wrong answers, hence consistent with an accumulation of points, we perhaps should ask ourselves whether this is the appropriate form of knowledge engagement in higher education. Numerical grades make sense in assessments where the type of question or task is closed – that is either right or wrong. But many forms of coursework or exam questions that students are given are open tasks – ones for which there is no one, right answer. Anywhere that a judgement must be made – rather than simply a 'right' answer – we mislead students if we present finely grained marking systems. It is a total misapplication to transfer this to the complex knowledge engaged with in higher education. Even in STEM subjects where the building blocks of the discipline may involve a series of simpler, closed tasks, the ultimate aim is for students to engage with the complex forms of disciplinary knowledge represented in STEM practices and research literature. Across the humanities and the sciences, the problems that face us, from a social justice perspective, require judgement and demand multiple perspectives and insights. There is no one right way. If we take climate change, for example, while we now have broad agreement across scientists about the causes of climate change, such agreement has not come about because there was always one right answer. This broad agreement in the scientific community has come about through multiple insights, questioning and exploring how we understand the natural world, and our human impact on it. Such knowledge cannot escape its relationship to judgement, perspective and context. The ways of assessing such knowledge thus need to think outside the confines of simply accruing marks for right 'bits' and adding them all together.

But the powerful 'gold standard' notion of assessment standards is very persistent (Bloxham & Boyd, 2012). It fits well with an audit culture that believes in measurement and standardization. And yet, much is lost by this instrumentalist view. It takes no account of the socially constructed nature of marking, and that values and issues of power are inevitably involved (Bloxham & Boyd, 2012). The issue then is whether these problems can be ironed out through moderation or second marking – but we end up in a circular argument because the same arguments about social construction apply to moderation as they do to marking.

In his broad ranging calls for assessment reform, Lewis Elton (2004a, 2004b) makes a number of points pertinent to the issue of marking precision. Elton argues that only where engagement with knowledge is at the simpler level can we mark with reliability *and* validity. So purely factual knowledge or the recounting of set knowledge, such as the name of a chemical compound or the title of a film, can be marked in this way. For more complex forms of knowledge engagement, Elton suggests a pass/fail marking scheme, which reflects the notion that the details of judgements about the work can be done with validity, but not reliability on any scale other than pass/fail. Further, argues Elton, there may be some things that simply cannot be reduced to a single grade, even on the pass/fail axis, and must therefore be reported on, rather than graded.

Further evidence to support this more holistic approach can be found in Royce Sadler's work on the nature of the marking process (Sadler, 2009, 2010b, 2014, 2014b). Sadler (2014) argues that breaking assessment tasks down into bits that can then be aggregated might seem helpful to the student (and marker), but is actually misleading. He thereby questions the idea that more and more 'compact, reproducible and portable' specifications will ensure 'appropriate levels of consistency and comparability' (pp. 273–4):

> The elements in progressively more detailed descriptions are intended to make meanings clearer but their specifiers are in turn of the same essence and type as those of the main elements. There is no escape. All of them are fuzzy and do not lock things down definitively. Only concrete cases and contextualisation can allow appropriate interpretations to be found.
>
> (p. 279)

Shay (2004) makes a similar point in arguing that marking rubrics are misleading in the supposed clarity they offer as marking systems. She draws on Broad (2000) to argue that rubrics do not, as their proponents often suggest, eliminate marking disagreements. In Broad's study, a group of faculty explicitly set out to eliminate differences in the marking of a first year English programme. The aim was 'to make their judgements quick, easy, and homogenous' (p. 213). In so doing, they reflected the association of legitimacy with 'scientism and objectivity' that has featured in so much educational practice (Broad, p. 215, referring to Aronowitz, 1988). What ensued was a battle between validity and reliability:

> More often than not, my participants' high hopes for standardization ended in frustration and disappointment, for they felt loyalty to the competing values of both consistency and diversity in their evaluations.
>
> (p. 216)

Indeed, the end result of this drive for standardization was 'a widespread and steadily increasing sense of evaluative crisis' (p. 230). Another study which highlights the difficulty of achieving marking consistency is that of Bloxham, den-Outer, Hudson and Price (2016) in which twenty-four academics in four different disciplines were asked to rank five pieces of work against each other. The authors found that in only one case out of a possible twenty did the participants rank a piece of work the same way. And the differences could be significant, with nine of the twenty assessments being ranked both best and worst by different assessors. The authors therefore claim the study replicates the results 'of other studies in demonstrating considerable variation in assessors' grading where complex higher education tasks are involved' (p. 477). To be clear, however, the authors also make this point:

> It is important to stress that we perceive this inconsistency to be a reflection of the complex and intuitive nature of judgement at the higher education level, and should not be interpreted as criticism of the assessors.
>
> (p. 477)

This study added weight to the already 'well documented' issues of 'inconsistency and unreliability' in higher education marking (p. 466). Bloxham et al. (2016) assert that such inconsistency is found in the marking practices of novice and experienced assessors, and even where there is agreement this can turn out to be based on very different reasons. Academics may have a strong sense of standards and the marking criteria, but these are neither neat nor unchanging (Bloxham & Boyd, 2012).

Indeed, what is revealed by Bloxham et al. (2016) is that marking criteria may be of limited use in achieving consistent marking because they may be interpreted differently, and other sources of guidance, formal or informal, come into play. Trying to tie down the marking practices with more and more artefacts such as rubrics is self-defeating and can 'make marking an overly onerous process' while at the same time limiting 'independent thought and originality in students' (pp. 478–9). The authors propose that a more community-orientated approach to marking may be effective. Here the essentially social nature of such engagement with knowledge comes to the fore. Rather than a procedure of marking and then checking for accuracy through moderation, the processes become blurred and the whole nexus of practices are brought together as part of a communal way of developing the shared understandings required for marking. But this only works if we mark across broad categories, such as distinction/pass/fail or possibly grades, but certainly not highly differentiated marking points. To try to distinguish highly precise grading points would again bog down the processes in a mire of illusionary accuracy.

This is ultimately, I argue, an epistemological issue. To achieve high levels of accuracy, precision and reliability we would have to turn all assessments into standardized tests (Bloxham et al., 2016). This would please those who value measurement and auditing above all else, but be of little other use. For standardized tests only work with simple, closed forms of knowledge. They may have some preparatory, formative place in some subjects – ensuring the disciplinary building blocks are in place – but beyond this they completely contradict the purposes of higher education. Thus, to suggest we move away from highly differentiated marks does not arise only from the practical problems associated with achieving their accuracy, though these problems are real and need to be more honestly faced. What is important here is what the assessment systems convey about the purposes of higher education, the purposes of assessment and the achievements of those subject to assessment.

The answer proposed is also not some parody of 'right on' education in which we shower all students with praise and passes – a general feel-good approach to the otherwise nasty face of assessment. As Honneth makes clear about esteem recognition, it would not make sense if we simply recognized everyone as having the same abilities or achievements. The whole enterprise becomes meaningless. Assessment should relate to a notion of the individual quality of achievement but this is further understood (a) in a social context and (b) as an achievement more complex than that captured easily by a single grade.

Standards in higher education matter, but standards are complex because they reflect multiple, complex, dynamic and contested forms of knowledge. Here Bloxham et al. (2016) offer a way forward:

> We should recognise the impossibility of a 'right' mark in the case of complex assignments, and avoid overextensive, detailed, internal or external moderation. Perhaps, a better approach is to recognise that a profile made up of multiple assessors' judgements is a more accurate, and therefore fairer, way to determine the final degree outcome for an individual. Such a profile can identify the consistent patterns in students' work and provide a fair representation of their performance, without disingenuously claiming that every single mark is 'right'.
>
> (p. 479)

In terms of academics' workloads this would mean a transfer of time from all the procedures that currently go into shoring up this illusionary 'right mark' and more time into genuine engagement with the students' work and, where necessary, formative help for their ongoing improvement. Clearly this also has implications for the issues of trust, personalization and avoiding misconduct outlined in the previous chapter. The common task of students and academics should be the nurturing of socially useful knowledge. Individual achievement matters and individual conceptions of self-worth are legitimate and meaningful, but Honneth reminds us that the individual and the social always go hand in hand.

Why do students believe a number represents all their effort and intellectual creativity better than several sentences of carefully phrased prose demonstrating genuine engagement with their work? It suggests that we are not nurturing students and graduates who understand that their contribution to society, and thus their own self-fulfilment lies with the knowledge practices they are able to engage in, not a mark, number or certificate. This is a deeply institutionalized form of self-misrecognition. It tragically undermines the sense of self and the sense of useful social contributions. It would be more honest to accept that we cannot achieve such precision. But there is a further important point, which is to acknowledge that such precision is simply not relevant to the practices of engagement with complex forms of knowledge. The focus should be on the practices to which students are able to bring their knowledge: problem solving, analysing, researching. Thus it is not the differences between students that matters most, but the contribution they can each make to the social good. As Sambell et al. (2013) argue,

> Discrimination between different levels of attainment should therefore be less important overall than the imperative to ensure that everyone develops and learns to the extent that they can reach their full potential and make their maximum possible contribution.

> (p. 34)

Any artifice that creates the impression that marking judgements can be so finely tuned as to be out of 100 seriously misrepresents the reality of marking to students, and this can give rise to other problems. In the previous chapter, for example, I discussed anonymous marking and the trade-off students seem to accept between personalization and protection from bias. While students believe that there can be such a thing as a 'right' or 'fair' mark of 67 per cent, they understandably worry more about intentional or unintentional bias. And they are encouraged to think in these ways by the dominant marking practices. How different it would be for students to see their achievement through the work itself and the feedback on it, rather than the numerical grade. Even under a criterion-referenced, rather than normative, marking system there is something essentially competitive in the nature of highly differentiated marks. It suggests that there is virtue in separating students. But if we take medicine as an example, then a pass/fail system is frequently used. One either can practice as a doctor or one cannot. We do not say this surgeon is a 67 per cent type of doctor and another an 87 per cent type of doctor. Their competency rests in a complex set of practices developed through their university studies and maintained through ongoing professional development and the socialization of working with other healthcare professionals. And parallels can be drawn here with other disciplines and other professions.

What this opens for us, however, is a real social justice opportunity. For not only do I suggest we cannot mark to great precision, but there are strong social justice reasons for not wanting to. Our students should not associate their achievements and self-worth with a mark, but with what it enables them to do. It is the creation of beautiful music, rather than an A on a music exam that really matters to our social well-being. It is the ability to scrutinize complex scientific data through which important breakthroughs will be made, not the 80 per cent on the exam. What I believe Honneth's understanding of mutual recognition does is to force our gaze to a different place when it comes to assessment: force it onto the qualities and practices that are socially useful. This is the difference between a *culture of affirmation* that sustains the status quo and a genuine commitment to social well-being and justice. Honneth is again helpful here:

> We live in a culture of affirmation in which publicly displayed recognition often bears the marks of mere rhetoric and has the character of being just a substitute for material remuneration. Praising certain characteristics of abilities seems to have become a political instrument whose unspoken function consists in inserting individuals or social groups into existing structures of domination by encouraging a positive self image. Far from making a lasting contribution to the autonomy of the members of our society, social recognition appears merely to serve the creation of attitudes that conform to the dominant system.
>
> (Honneth, 2014b, p. 75)

We would, therefore, be helping students as well as academics by moving away from precise marking categories. We would do so by encouraging their sense of self-worth to move from that of a single grade or mark and to focus instead on their abilities, traits and achievements. A grade might represent an achievement, but it is a poor achievement on its own. What always matters more, from a social justice perspective, is what students can actually do with the knowledge with which they engage. How will students know they are progressing, if not given marks to compare as they go along? Well here again, the emphasis should move to the feedback given, not the singular mark it is represented by. Indeed, for students to learn how to take responsibility for their own learning, as discussed in the next chapter, an informed understanding of how to interpret feedback is much more useful than simple marks. The lone mark promises much in terms of accuracy and precision, but delivers little in terms of genuine learning and achievement.

Thus while I sympathize with Bloxham (2012) when she fears that it is 'inconceivable' to reimagine assessment outside the confines of the technical-rationalist paradigm that today dominates, so strong is the current culture of accountability, I also want to contend that this current situation is both illusionary in its claims to rationality and also unsustainable. Honesty would be a good starting place for how we move to nurture the graduates required in society. Genuine recognition of the complex achievements of students and graduates will move us further towards social justice than easy metrics. Employers often bemoan why universities cannot produce the sort of graduates they want. Perhaps it is time we started asking them why they insist we differentiate students in some pseudo-competitive assessment environment. Real social change comes through working together; there is no reason that we cannot begin to learn how to do this through our assessment practices.

Conclusion

The discussion in this chapter has focused on honesty in terms of what academics and their institutions do. More familiar, perhaps, is a consideration of honesty from the student perspective. We require honesty from our students, as in the case of discouraging plagiarism and promoting good academic writing practices. However, I have sought to propose the consideration of honesty as more than simply not doing wrong, but as essential in itself for mutual esteem recognition; that is, for students to be able to recognize their own achievements and the useful social contribution they can make through these. Students who choose paths of dishonesty close down their own capacity to recognize their achievements: it is a form of self-misrecognition. This has enormous implications for their well-being. It can suggest that the result or certification is viewed as having greater importance than what it actually allows the student to do with that certification. Instead, I argue, the focus must be on the practices of engaging with knowledge and applying that knowledge to real social needs.

What is helpful here is to think beyond the 'familiar but rather shop-worn' distinction between summative and formative assessment (Hounsell, 2007, p. 103). No assessment, I suggest, should serve only summative ends in the form of certification. Indeed, certification itself should not be a purpose or an end in itself. Key here is to engender a sense that genuine recognition of one's worth lies in the contributions that can be made to society. The teleoaffective structures which help shape assessment practices should be ones with a focus on the engagement with and application of knowledge, and doing this in socially just ways. Just getting a pass or a certificate is not an end in itself. So the theme of honesty from the students' perspective runs through the other chapters too, wherever we consider the importance of esteem recognition.

There is, therefore, also an element of respect recognition here. As Honneth states,

> It does not suffice to conceive of autonomy as arising solely from intersubjective respect for subjects' decision-making competence; rather, subjects needs to be appreciated for their particular needs and individual deeds. Only when citizens see all these elements of their personality respected and recognized will they be capable of acting with self-respect and committing themselves to their own respective life paths.
>
> (Honneth, 2014b, p. 48)

7

Responsibility

Introduction

Assessment for social justice requires practices of *responsibility*. In this chapter I consider the importance of genuine, informed responsibility, and how this can then shape the practices of assessment for social justice. It is common to talk in terms of rights and responsibilities as two sides of the same coin. But actually, understood through the lenses of Honneth's critical theory, responsibility is itself a right. It is the right to be an informed and active member of a social group, and in the assessment context this means to be assessed through approaches and practices that enable students to take responsibility for their own learning. In this chapter I focus on the ways in which students should have the full knowledge and active participation in assessment practices to enable them to have genuine responsibility for the roles they play, and thereby to maximize their achievements. Such a sense of responsibility is important for students' self-worth, and their place within society, on two levels. First, it refers to Honneth's respect recognition that arises from authentic understanding of the rules or laws under which you act – in an assessment context, the regulations and procedures that shape practices. Second, it refers to students' understanding of the expectations of the assessment practice: here it is not so much the formal rules but the tacit knowledge and, in Schatzki's terms, the practical intelligibility, which can only be gained through active participation. This is all about students being able to recognize the strengths and weaknesses of their own work and therefore aligns with the notion of esteem recognition: To what extent are students able to understand their accomplishments in a social context? To what extent do they learn to appreciate the contributions of others? In this chapter I consider each of these in turn, and argue that we need to rethink the ways in which we assess in order to give greater power to students, and with that power, the responsibility that enables them to be recognized for their achievements.

The previous two chapters have focused considerably on what the academic or marker does. In this chapter, the focus of my examples moves to students, although it is important to stress that, as with the previous understandings of trust and honesty, I believe that the notion of responsibility should inform the practices of both students and academics. The importance of responsibility also flows on from the earlier chapter's emphasis on trust. For it is in relationships of trust that students are more likely able to develop the confidence 'to take on new challenges and test out new territories' (Broughan & Grantham, 2012, p. 49). Similarly, when there is no sense of responsibility, it can be easier to compromise on values such as trust and honesty. Thus we can understand that the forms of responsibility that align with social justice require more than a superficial engagement with assessment criteria or a symbolic role for students. We must throw open our regulations and procedures to informed student scrutiny. We must ensure the acquisition of the practical intelligibility needed to successfully complete complex assessment tasks through the active participation of students with assessment criteria. We must enable students to be accomplished assessors of their own work, including through the assessment of peers' work, so that the assessment and learning processes are within their control. We must allow students to take part in practices for which they can take responsibility for their actions. It is illusionary to suggest that anyone can take responsibility over anything for which they have neither expertise nor full knowledge. Here again, as with the case of trust, we find that mainstream assessment practices can be very one-sided from the student perspective. Thus, students are meant to take responsibility for their assessment actions, they are encouraged to be self-directed learners, but are often not given the requisite knowledge, skills and opportunities with which to do so.

This chapter is in two parts. I begin by examining the formal side of regulations and consider students' relationships with these. I then look at the more tacit forms of knowledge inherent in assessment practices, and particularly consider how students can become confident and responsible judges of their own academic work. As such, I seek to stress the embodied nature of responsibility and that it is more than another transferable skill but is socially situated and socially meaningful.

Regulations and procedures

The regulations on which assessment practices occur should have the same universal character as Honneth's legal rights. This means that we can, and must, consider assessment rights as given and true for all students. They are not bestowed by apparent acts of charity, goodwill or benevolence but are intrinsic to the realm to which they apply. Honneth uses the example of welfare to distinguish between a legal right to obtain state help and a situation in which poorer people are subject to the kindly whims of the better off (Iorio et al., 2013). Similarly, in an assessment context, different arrangements for students who are differently abled or have particular circumstances is simply an expression of their universal rights, and should not be regarded as charitable exceptions.

The powerful idea I draw from Honneth is that it is not simply a matter of having certain rights by law, policy or regulations, but the importance lies *in understanding one has those rights and in exercising them*. In so doing one earns the respect of being able to act morally within the social sphere. Respect recognition is important because it signifies acceptance 'as an autonomous person who has the right and the competence to take part in the discourses in which people reach consensus about political and theoretical issues' (Huttunen, 2007, p. 426). Further, this is a form of recognition that

> entails regarding this individual as a person who is responsible for his or her own actions. The opposite of this is a paternalizing attitude, which denies the individual's freedom of will, autonomy, and ability to work independently. Self-respect grows out of recognition of responsibility, which the individual gains at the level of the civil society (community of rights).
>
> (p. 426)

So for our students to act with responsibility within the assessment sphere, they need to be genuinely informed of their rights. Moreover, bringing Honneth in here suggests that what we refer to as assessment regulations could be more usefully considered in terms of rights: they thereby move from constraining behaviour to enabling achievement. This highlights the difference between rights, in the sense intended by Honneth, and procedure alone, for the end focus is on what those rights enable individuals, alone and collectively, to do. What is clear from this is that it demands a radical re-conceptualization of the power relations between students and academics. Students move into the arena as active and informed agents, not as passive recipients to whom assessment is 'done'.

Thus the first level of knowledge which students should have, to be active players in their own assessment experiences, concerns the formal regulations and procedures that affect what they do, and how their work is judged. There is, however, relatively little research on assessment regulations as such and so it is difficult to know the extent to which students have a genuine, working knowledge of the regulations that shape their experiences. A notable exception within the research literature is work done under the umbrella of the Student Assessment and Classification Working Group (SACWG) based in the United Kingdom, and I draw on some of their work here (e.g. Stowell, Falahee & Woolf, 2016; Yorke et al., 2008). While these works do not specifically address students' attitudes and experiences, a number of key issues emerge.

Assessment regulations are high stakes – students' lives can be affected by them, as can the reputations of their institutions. Assessment regulations are necessarily complex, having to deal with many potential scenarios and situations. Stowell et al. (2016) outline ten 'often competing principles and interests' that underpin regulatory frameworks:

- safeguarding institutional standards
- ensuring consistency with academic credit principles
- ensuring equitable treatment of students
- promoting transparency and consistency of decision-making
- accommodating disciplinary differences
- retaining students and enabling progression
- supporting student engagement with learning and assessment
- providing for an appropriate degree of flexibility (discretion or 'academic judgement')
- reducing administrative burden and
- alignment with 'customary' sector-wide practice.

(p. 517)

From a student perspective, these multiple purposes may not appear obvious. Indeed, the degree to which students engage with the regulations that shape their assessment practices is doubtful. There appears no natural or easy way for students to obtain this knowledge because only a small part of these are really shared with students, and often only after things go wrong. The regulations may technically appear on a public website, but this in no way guarantees students' knowledge of them. These regulations shape the assessment practices, as Schatzki stresses, and thus students' participation in those practices is necessarily limited if they do not have proper knowledge of the rules. Thus students may know that there is something called moderation, for example, but what this is and how this plays out in practice can remain shrouded in mystery. Indeed, Carless (2006) notes that despite some awareness of marking procedures such as double marking and moderation, there is also an 'inconsistent understanding of how these processes' work (p. 228). For example, when he explained to a student that only a sample of assignments get double marked, this led the student to express 'less confidence in the fairness of marking' (p. 228). Here we can surmise that the student is thinking of moderation in terms of aims of equity and consistency, while it equally serves the rather different aim of administrative efficiency. Thus there is a procedural impulse behind such regulations, even when they are couched in terms of equity and fairness.

Knight (1995) observes that assessment tells us something about the values and commitments outlined in programme specifications and mission statements – are they 'rhetorical, for the benefit of auditors, not students'? (p. 13). Assessment regulations 'reflect institutional cultures and histories' (Stowell et al., 2016, p. 515). They must therefore also be understood as socially constructed (Stowell et al., 2016). As such they reflect assumptions about key issues such as validity, reliability, transparency and also fairness (Stowell et al., 2016). Thus Stowell et al. (2016) characterize assessment regulations 'as being "crafted" and regularly "re-crafted" ' as they respond to different perspectives and competing priorities. Further,

> Assessment regulations are 'sites of compromise' in that they are constantly negotiated through the normal decision-making processes of the academy, where competing perspectives and interests are brought to bear.
>
> (p. 517)

These competing interests are reflected in the many purposes that assessment regulations serve, and they do not necessarily all fit well with one another. Yorke et al. (2008) describe how 'consistency and fairness can pull in different directions' (p. 163). There is a tension between the explicit codification required for transparency and consistency and the judgements that may apply if we foreground fairness. The dilemma outlined by Yorke et al. refers to the situation we find ourselves in when trying to evoke a richer understanding of fairness than simply due process. Thus it may be argued that assessment regulations operate more justly when there is scope for flexibility (Stowell, 2004). But the issue is tricky because that same flexibility can lead to perceptions of unfairness (Yorke et al., 2008).

Thus even here, in the realm of formal regulations there may be tacit knowledge that students are not easily able to access. As Yorke et al. (2008) explain,

> Flexibility adds a further dimension to the complexity of assessment regulations. This complexity, which in part derives from the need to make them watertight, militates against transparency. If the regulations are complex for academic staff

to understand and apply, the challenge of understanding seems even greater for students.

(p. 164)

Thus there is the added challenge for students in understanding the foundations on which assessment takes place, which may be far from obvious. As Boud (2014) explains,

> It is apparent that the present state of assessment in practice is often a messy compromise between incompatible ends. Understanding assessment now involves appreciating the tensions and dilemmas between demands of contradictory purposes.

(p. 21)

We have, thankfully, come some way since the times when assessment procedures were matters of a 'substantial degree of secrecy' (Boud, 2014, p. 15). Boud rightly argues that we should welcome the move towards greater transparency of assessment criteria and standards, particularly compared with past practices when these were held to be confidential – not of concern to students. Recalling his own undergraduate experiences, Boud writes,

> We were not told what the criteria for marking would be and how different subjects would be weighted into final results was confidential. The head of the department in which I studied (Lewis Elton) first took the then daring step of formally disclosing the weightings of the elements that would comprise our degree classification in the year of my graduation. Assessment was secret teachers' business: it was not the position of students to understand the basis on which they would be judged.

(p. 15)

Certainly many institutions have since sought to simplify their assessment regulations, but again there are multiple drivers behind such moves, and not all of them consistent with one another. I know of several universities that have recognized that their assessment regulations have become too complicated to work effectively. In order to better ensure the regulations are followed, they have been streamlined and simplified. But this is often done for the benefit of staff and not students. Perhaps student union representatives have some input, but there is little recognition that students as a whole should be informed about the regulations that shape their assessment experiences. Indeed, regulations are often portrayed by academics and managers as a safeguard against student complaints or disputes rather than enabling the best possible learning experiences.

But I return to the point about the many different purposes regulations can serve, and thus there can be considerable variation between institutions, with emphasis put more or less in different places. There is also variation within institutions, as regulations alter to reflect changes in the institutional values and the social construction of standards. But this is a striking issue from the student perspective, particularly when it means 'that the same academic performance might be "successful" under one regulatory regime, but not another' (Stowell et al., 2016, p. 528). Further,

> It is clear that there are a range of different rules for passing modules, and a variety of possible rationales for each position. It is difficult to avoid the conclusion that the same academic performance may be awarded credit for passing a module in one department/institution, but be classed as a 'fail' in another.
>
> (Stowell et al., 2016, p. 521)

Thus we see the way in which rules, according to Schatzki, help shape different local practices. Yorke et al. (2008) also found considerable variance between institutions in the United Kingdom. For example, the weighting and inclusion criteria for what counts towards the honours classification could differ between institutions. Yorke et al. (2008) describe the 'enigmatic' character of the variations in honours classification regulations between institutions, with little clear rationale for the systems used.

Assessment regulations matter to individual students because they affect their lives and also because they reflect the values of the institution. While simplifying regulations to make them more accessible is a welcome development, there can be other less benign drivers of change. For example, many institutions have sought to attract large numbers of taught postgraduate students from overseas – who bring with them hefty fee contributions – while at the same time changing regulations to arguably disadvantage these groups. In particular, the movement towards denying taught postgraduates the chance to resit a subject they fail – which strikes me as very unfair and educationally questionable (this is a point I pick up again in Chapter 8 when I discuss the relationship between failure and learning). And yet, the rules governing this have been tightened over time, not in response to student needs, but as a means of controlling the flow of resources in the *business* of the university.

A similar impulse has led to the introduction of a 'Fit to Sit' policy at many institutions. This hoists an instrumental form of responsibility onto students in a very superficial and potentially unfair way. 'Fit to Sit' has become a fashionable new regulation whereby if a student sits an exam they are deemed to be fit to do so, similarly if they submit a piece of coursework, they are deemed to have been in the position to do that coursework. It is meant as a neat remedy to apparently rising levels of student requests for extenuating or special circumstances. Rather than this form of procedural quick fix, it would be more useful to consider the underlying reasons for a rise in such requests. The important distinction that needs to be addressed is whether this rise in requests is due to an increase in circumstances requiring special consideration (a rise in student stress, increased financial burdens, the prevalence of mental health issues) or is it because of an anxiety about the results that leads students to pursue any ends seemingly available to help their cause. If it is the former, then Fit to Sit is quite simply cruel, and punishes those who try but fail to cope with assessment tasks under difficult circumstances. If it is the latter, then Fit to Sit does not address the root problem, just papers it over with a new regulation. I return again to two important points. The first is students' unrealistic expectations of a precise mark, and the frequent inappropriateness of this for the type of assessment tasks that are fitting in higher education. This expectation of precision leads to greater assessment anxiety as so much more seems to be at stake in a pseudo-competitive system. Second, and ever more importantly, is the misrecognition of considering a mark as an achievement, rather than the engagement with socially useful knowledge. A concern that students may manipulate assessment opportunities or regulations speaks to a much more worrying phenomenon in which, if students are doing this, they are undermining their own sense of self-worth.

As Bols (2012) argues, students themselves are unlikely to be motivated to learn about assessment policy and procedure if they consider assessment as nothing more than 'a hurdle they have to jump over on the way to getting a qualification' (p. 4). Here we have clear evidence of the fuller meaning of respect recognition – that it positions an individual in being able to take her place within the social world. In an assessment context, students need to recognize that they have a greater role to play than simply being the passive victims of distant assessment regimes. What is at stake here is the difference between students as active participants in their learning experiences and students as merely consumers (Bols, 2012). In a study I undertook with Mark Huxham, we aimed to *share control* with students for the design of a module they were to study, including the assessments. One of the biggest surprises for these students was the extent to which regulations and procedures guided (constrained?) teacher actions (McArthur & Huxham, 2011). We found them largely unaware of constraints we faced, such as going through the appropriate boards or committees for approval, and having to meet regulatory requirements. In their minds there had been a stark power differential between us (having all the power) and them (having almost none). In recognizing the constraints on us, however, these students were then able to negotiate taking more responsibility for themselves. So the shift in power relations necessary for students to be fully informed participants in the practices of assessment regulations involves more than a simple shift from tutor to student. It is about the students' relationships with a large and complex organization, where multiple and sometimes conflicting practices are at play. For example, we entreat students to be independent and critical learners while also imposing regulations to direct and control behaviour.

Assessment regulations reflect forms of explicit knowledge that can be codified, but they still reflect complex social practices, shaped through negotiation and compromise. Thus, tensions can arise, particularly when we consider the many different purposes regulations may simultaneously serve, as outlined previously by Stowell et al. (2016). Thus there may be a tension between consistency and flexibility. Codified knowledge with no scope for interpretation and judgement becomes brittle, and potentially quite cruel. Sitting in exam boards, trying to apply regulations and consider individual student fairness, can lead academics to 'frequently irresolvable tensions between these responsibilities' (Stowell, 2004, p. 502). The solution is not for more regulations, or for instrumental quick fixes such as 'Fit to Sit'. We will never get regulations that can justly promote learning and nurture individual and collective social justice until we enable our students to be fully responsible – in genuine and meaningful ways – for their own learning and assessment practices. This involves a fundamental shift in thinking about what assessment is and a fundamental shift in power and trust within our relationships.

Knowledge of assessment practices and expectations

Sambell et al. (2013) pose and answer a simple question:

> Why do good and conscientious students fall at assessment hurdles? They don't seem to understand what they are supposed to do.

(p. 1)

Similarly, they ask another question familiar to many who assess students' work: 'How often do I read a good paraphrase of what is in the key texts when I really want to know what the student made of the topic?' (p. 1). Sadler (2014b) also observes the common occurrence of students who 'focus on the subject matter itself, rather than on what is to be done with it' (p. 152) and, as a result, are surprised and dismayed when they fail to perform well. The knowledge required here, to understand what they are supposed to do, is rather different from the knowledge of regulations and rules discussed in the previous section. In Schatzki's terms, this is about how students acquire the practical intelligibility to decide what it makes sense to do. One of the reasons why students find it so difficult to know what is expected of them is that much of this knowledge is tacit – bound as it is in the social practices of assessment tasks. Tacit knowledge is a defining aspect of social practices, as knowledge is negotiated and formed through the act of participating in such practices, rather than contained in canonical, set forms. Thus such knowledge can also be very difficult to acquire for a newcomer or outsider. Without an understanding of how marking will take place, or indeed the purposes of the assessment, the possible actions that may seem reasonable for students to do may be misguided. It may, for example, seem reasonable to memorize a list of facts, take detailed notes from a particular book or keep reading over the lecture notes. But what if the assessment was aimed at a different way of engaging with the subject? Students may then experience surprise, even rejection, if all that work seemingly comes to nothing and they perform badly in the assessment – because what they thought made sense to do was not what was actually required. But this is not a form of understanding that can simply be handed over; it is an understanding of a social practice which comes through participation in that practice.

It is also important to remember that a critical pedagogy perspective insists that we do not position students as passive in this regard. It is not about them simply coming to know what the teacher wants and faithfully reproducing it. Rather, it is about students developing their own capacity for judgement, and the ability to recognize work – their own and other students – which is socially useful. This therefore aligns with Honneth's esteem recognition. Esteem recognition relates to the abilities and accomplishments of individuals, thus it has a character of individuality, and the ways in which these contribute to the social good. Thus there are two powerful ideas to draw here about assessment: the first is students' capacity to identify for themselves the worth of their achievements; second is the association of such achievements with social usefulness in its many different forms, and not simply an economic or instrumental imperative.

Thus simply sharing marking criteria with students, as has become established good practice, does not by itself help solve this dilemma of what is really expected. To publish such criteria in a course handbook or on a VLE site is an uncontextualized form of knowledge which denies the fuller understanding that comes with genuine engagement. Even students who do read this material are given no context in which to understand it. How, for example, does a student know how to use both the learning outcomes and the assessment criteria? They say different things: How do they interrelate? Which should they follow? The answers to these questions are not objectively obvious. Similarly, we have witnessed some welcome changes in assessment policy and practice over recent years, most notably the move from norm referenced to criterion referenced marking. But it is unclear how much students understand this important shift and certainly the evidence is patchy about the extent to which students genuinely engage with the criteria that underpin criterion-based marking.

Students are in an ongoing state of processing the information they have about assessment in terms of perceptions of justice. Thus profound senses of injustice can follow if students perceive their and others' results to be different from their expectations. Nesbit and Burton (2006) found that students made 'equity calculations' about the marks received by others, and this too fed into perceptions of assessment justice:

> Perceived discrepancies between expected and actual results can lead to negative perceptions about the fairness or justice of the outcome received and about the fairness of processes used to make outcome decisions.
>
> (p. 656)

The problem with such calculations is that students frequently do these without a clear understanding of the basis on which marks have been awarded, without a real working knowledge of the marking criteria. In a project I did exploring the experiences of students who repeatedly failed exams, I found that such students were often conceiving of passing as a matter of good luck, rather than an outcome within their control, or for which they had responsibility. They did not connect their mark with a failure to meet certain criteria. A fail meant bad luck on the day – perhaps the wrong questions. Passing on a resit would therefore involve better luck on another day, rather than a change in their engagement with the assessment task. We should not criticize students for these views and assumptions if we do not adequately provide the opportunities for a more directed and meaningful approach to assessments. Boud (2014) argues that we must not consider students as passive parts of the assessment process 'but conscious, thinking agents of their own destiny'. He asks, 'How can student agency influence the processes of feedback?' (p. 23). But the issue of student agency is itself problematic. There can be numerous barriers and constraints that students face which academics may never come to see. I am reminded of Broughan and Grantham's (2012) account of a first year student who left after just six weeks 'feeling isolated, unsure and floundering in an unwelcoming environment' (p. 45). Such stories are not uncommon. Thus when we consider the tacit knowledge that students need to take responsibility for their assessment practices, we must think about the nature and health of our relationships with students, and theirs with each other if we are to make genuine progress. As Boud argues,

> Students must leave university equipped to engage in self-assessment throughout their professional lives ... Too often staff-driven assessment encourages students to be dependent on the teacher or the examiners to make decisions about what they know and they do not effectively learn to be able to do this for themselves.
>
> (p. 39)

To gain the sort of tacit knowledge required for this type of socially driven responsibility also suggests that the move over recent years to more and more continuous assessment might not be all beneficial. Indeed, Boud (2014) suggests that much has been lost in the move to believing that everything students do should 'count' towards their final grades: 'Trust that work suggested by teachers will necessarily be worthwhile has disappeared in an economy of grades' (p. 16). Also lost sight of is any reason to undertake the assessment other than for the grades, and grades on their own can lead to only a very superficial form of recognition.

The issue with tacit knowledge is that it is hard to proceduralize, and yet we are experiencing a dominant culture, with its emphasis on audit and quality assurance, in which the desire to proceduralize is strong. As Rust, Price and O'Donovan (2003) observe, in debates over setting clear standards there is often 'the implication that if all were made explicit this would be sufficient to establish standards' (p. 148). But this is not how tacit knowledge is gained. Indeed, it can only be meaningfully acquired through participation in the social practices to which it refers. Thus students need to engage in the practices that will nurture their assessment literacy, to give them access to the components of the practices, such as the practical intelligibility that helps to make sense of things. Such literacy, as with other forms of literacy (such as language, academic or digital) is a process that takes time and requires considerable practice (Margaret

Price in Bols, 2012). It involves more complex knowledge than simply how many references a student is expected to use, or the layout of an assignment. As students become more proficient in such knowledge, they are in a better position to work together with staff to ensure 'the assessment process work well' (Margaret Price in Bols, 2012, p. 17). Price goes on to argue that this can include making informed choices and students being active in the making of decisions based on scarce resources.

Developing practical intelligibility about assessment

There are several ways in which students can be supported to gain the tacit knowledge about assessment, and thus be able to take genuine responsibility for their own achievements. These approaches range from working with the marking criteria to actually undertaking assessment marking or determining what that assessment might be. In each there is a rethinking of the locus of power in the student-staff relationships, and indeed in how students are positioned in terms of their own work.

In recent years there has been an increase use of exemplars as a means of enabling students to grasp this tacit knowledge about the nature of quality in assessed work. Here the work of Sadler (eg. 1987, 1989, 2002, 2005, 2010a) has been particularly important. The really useful point to garner from this work on exemplars is that it again emphasizes the importance of participation. Thus, it is not enough to simply give students examples of other students' work, just as it is not enough to simply give them a copy of the marking criteria. Rather, it is the active engagement with such work, ideally in conversation with the tutor and other students, that is key to students gaining this crucial insight into what counts as 'quality', and it is on this basis that they can take greater responsibility for their own work. It is also about ensuring students have a clear teleological sense of the reasons for doing a particular task or project: What will the desired end result look like? Only when they appreciate what the end result might look like are students in a position to make informed choices about what it makes sense to do next.

In the assessment context, 'exemplars convey messages that nothing else can' (Sadler, 2002, p. 136), but only if understood in terms of students' active engagement with them. Thus it is the process of making judgements which defines the practices around using exemplars. Students are not simply given examples of good work, but are also given a range of work judged to be of different quality. This is much richer and more authentic than a disembodied rubric or marking formula. Over time, the students can become connoisseurs of quality work. But I would add two things to the current literature on exemplars. The first is that we clearly need to consider the temporal implications of this form of learning about assessment. It does not fit easily with highly modularized systems and instead works best when there is some pattern of continuity through which students can continue to develop and apply their assessment literacy. Throwing multiple, diverse forms of assessment at students for the sake of variety can make it very time-consuming to gain all the requisite knowledge about what is expected in each form of assessment. Thus while we are rightly moving away from the dominance of traditional essays and exams, we should not underestimate the learning challenge for students in coming to know what is expected of different forms of assessment. Second, in terms of assessment for social justice and ensuring students are situated to experience esteem recognition, we must ensure that our understandings of academic quality are also socially situated. This means that the knowledge we value is knowledge that has broader social usefulness. This should not be confused with narrow economic interests and applies equally to arts and humanities and STEM subjects. Is the music student learning composition that will bring pleasure? Is the accounting student developing a sense of ethical professional practice? Does the history student think in terms of inclusive forms of research? Does the engineering student understand the social context in which a new bridge or office block is being built?

In engaging with the work of other students through exemplars, students then develop the capacity to also judge their own work. Crucially, engaging with exemplars can enable students to understand the teleoaffective structures of their assessment tasks; thus, in Schatzki's terms, they are enabled to envisage the end purpose and value that as something positive. Such self-evaluation is crucial and 'underpins an individual's capacity for independent, reflective thinking and the aptitude to take responsibility for one's own actions' (Sambell et al., 2013, p. 121). To be clear, we are again not talking about such responsibility simply as a desired 'soft skill' or graduate attribute. It must be more roundly linked to an overall, useful social role in the way envisaged by critical theory and critical pedagogy. We must be cautious about encouraging dispositions of compliance or convenience with regard to students' future economic and social roles. Instead we must demonstrate that we value genuine criticality, such that we nurture graduates able to question the status quo and mainstream ways of living and being in society. Thus it is an altogether more critical role that students need to have with regard to assessment practices in order to nourish the dispositions and capacities to critically negotiate social injustices.

Feedback on their work should offer rich opportunities for students to take greater responsibility for their ongoing learning. Some academics express frustration that students complain about the quality of feedback but then do not pick up their essays or assignments and actually read the feedback provided. But the problem here lies in the type and timing of the feedback given. To genuinely enable students to take responsibility, such feedback must be given in a dialogic way that encourages engagement, conversation and application. Feedback on end-of-course assignments or exams has limited potential use in terms of future learning unless bridges are built between courses and across programmes. Academics have a responsibility themselves, from a social justice perspective, to provide feedback that challenges students and promotes future learning, rather than simply justifying a mark for the sake of the external examiner. Furthermore, students who take responsibility for their own learning do not simply react to feedback but use it in a constructive dialogue with their own learning and the ways they approach engagement with knowledge. Mark Huxham and I have explained the relationship between feedback and responsibility in these terms:

> We must therefore understand feedback as a piece of knowledge, with all the attendant virtues and respect that deserves. If students are to be able to actively engage with feedback, to be part of a dialogue, then that feedback cannot be presented, or regarded, as a static canonical statement. By thinking of it in terms of knowledge to be discussed and interacted with by both parties, we also introduce the notion that it is dynamic and contested: not only do students have a right to challenge the feedback; they have a responsibility to determine for themselves its validity, usefulness and implications.
>
> (McArthur & Huxham, 2013, p. 95)

The response to student dissatisfaction with feedback is therefore not to standardize it or employ gimmicks to highlight so-called examples of feedback. Rather, what is needed is to genuinely build this link between feedback and students' capacities to take responsibility for the future paths of their own learning. I will return to this point further in Chapter 8 when I consider the ways in which students gain confidence to learn from their mistakes or misunderstandings and use these positively to further their engagement with complex knowledge.

Students' active engagement with assessment, in order to nurture responsibility, can also be developed through peer and self-assessment. Here the process is similar to the use of exemplars. Indeed, self- and peer-assessment arguably work better if combined with exemplar engagement. Students need this capacity for self-assessment to ensure they are not passive actors in the assessment practices, but also to ensure they do not develop as passive citizens. Again, if we think back to the idea of esteem recognition outlined in Chapter 3, what is important is *recognising oneself* as a person of worth and positive contributions within the social group, not just being recognized as such by others. This is a capacity that should develop over time and be one of the key qualities that a student leaves university with. As Boud (2014) argues,

> Self-assessment, then, should be seen as a marker of how well students are tracking in developing the capacity to judge their own work.
>
> (p. 25)

A companion idea to this is that of ipsative assessment (G. Hughes, 2011, 2014, 2017). Ipsative assessment is where students' work is not judged against external criteria, but against their own previous work. It therefore resembles the notion of a 'personal best' in sporting activities (G. Hughes, 2017). Such judgements can be made both by students themselves and by their teachers. It is argued that ipsative assessment can therefore provide strong motivation for all students, not just those who are already doing well or have already grasped the subject. If students are to learn how to judge their own work, as argued by Boud, then an ipsative approach helps nurture the skills necessary to do this:

> Ipsative feedback informs the learner how s/he has progressed since the previous assessment, and how effective response to developmental feedback has been.
>
> (G. Hughes, 2011, p. 354)

What is crucial here is the practice of reflection on one's own learning and also a clear-eyed capacity to assess change or development, or the lack of it (a point I develop further in the next chapter). Too often some students, especially those who struggle, confuse effort with achievement. Recalling the previous work I have done on students who repeatedly fail, the heartbreaking story from their experiences is the genuine confusion they have when they return another poor result, despite working *really, really hard*. It is not obvious to them to ask a different question about their own work – do I understand something now that I did not understand before? Again, it is hope over actual engagement.

Taking responsibility for their own learning means that students must develop and nurture the capacity to think reflexively and critically about their own work. Such reflexivity is inherent in critical theory notions of social justice, and particularly being able to distil truth from mere appearance, substance from window dressing. Without self-assessment experience, 'it can mean that students leave our modules, and even the university itself, having learned to rely almost exclusively on *others* to make judgements and evaluations of work on their behalf' (Sambell et al., 2013, p. 122, emphasis original). Students cannot appreciate that responsibility, in its broadest social sense, is inherent in their assessment practices if they are not able to develop the capacity to evaluate their own achievements. If students are to take genuine responsibility, then assessment must

> contribute to students developing the necessary confidence and skills that will enable them to manage their own learning and assessment. Understanding is not sufficient; showing that they can perform certain tasks is not enough. Capable beginning practitioners need to be able to become increasingly sophisticated in judging their work. In particular, they need to be able to do so when working effectively with others, in order to assist each other in their learning and mutually develop informed judgement.
>
> (Boud, 2014, p. 29)

This should not be confused, however, with the way a form of ipsative assessment has taken hold in higher education circles with an instrumental notion of *learning gain*. Here the meaning is very different to that evoked by Hughes's work. Linked to the audit culture and the marketization of higher education, some proponents of the idea of learning gain aspire to a simple metric that can *prove* learning has occurred and the university has done its required job. This is starkly different to the developmental sense of students internalizing this capacity to reflect upon and review their own learning. An instrumental form, aimed at the most efficient metric will necessarily privilege certain forms of learning and experience over others. And as I have already stressed, the sort of engagement with knowledge that supports greater social justice is likely to be complex and not easily measured. Such knowledge will also become apparent, and will change over time.

In the case of peer assessment, we see another shift in power between the players in the assessment activity. Work in this field has found that students can initially have overconfidence in the judgement of their teachers, and little confidence in their own and their peers' assessment abilities. McConlogue's (2012) study of peer assessment found that the tutor grades have a 'gold standard' status in many students' minds. The same tendency was found by Wilson, Diao and Huang (2015), with students expressing very little confidence in the ability of other students to mark fairly. The academic marker is seen as the professional, the student a slightly suspect amateur. But if they believe students are insufficiently able to assess work, how then do they believe they are in a position to produce work *for* assessment? The same practices of judgement apply to both.

At issue is the way in which students conceive of the responsibilities of the marker, and a strong theme within students' attitudes appears to be that such marking is objective and that there is such a thing as the 'right' mark (this is also discussed in Chapter 6 on Honesty). McConlogue (2012) used a system of multiple peer markers plus a tutor mark to highlight to students the possible variability of marks. This came as a shock to many:

> Multiple markers and mean grades are common practice in PA [peer assessment]; what is less common is returning *all* grades and comments ... so students saw inconsistencies in marking. We anticipated that this would be a new and perhaps unsettling experience for students, resulting in complaints about grades.
>
> (p. 116)

McConlogue found that seeing multiple marks caused students to question the process. One student was clear that she would not have done so if only presented with the mean mark derived from all markers:

> If I'd only just seen the overall grade, I probably wouldn't have questioned it. So, maybe that's one thing to think of, working out the mean but not actually putting the different grades on. Because if [the tutor] had given me that grade, I'd have been happy with it, but because I'd seen everything else, I'm thinking, well, hang on a minute.
>
> (p. 118)

In this study it was made apparent to the students that there could be a range of marks given for one piece of work, and further that there could be 'no clear pattern in the marks' (p. 120). McConlogue explains,

> For many students, this was perhaps the first time they had seen a range of marks and were confronted with subjectivity in marking. I think students would have accepted peer assessors' marks more easily if only the mean grade was returned to students, a common practice in PA [peer assessment], but this would skirt the issue of marking vagaries.
>
> (p. 120)

For these students, the variability of marks – and how this impacted on the final mean mark they received – was clearly an issue of fairness. Their response was a procedural one: 'There remained a firm belief that ever more explicit assessment criteria and grade descriptors would lead to "objective" marking' (p. 118). McConlogue acknowledges that 'raising students' awareness of subjectivity in marking may be opening the Pandora's box of HE as it entails a shift of power away from the tutor to students who then become more involved in, and possibly more critical of, assessment decisions' (p. 121). But she also hopes that

> by challenging students' assumptions that marking is objective, we may develop their sense of the value of their work, help them make and defend judgements about their own and others' work.
>
> (p. 121)

Thus peer and self-assessment have come a long way since the early days in which there was a 'fixation with figures' and the perceived legitimacy of these activities rested on being able to prove quantitatively that student-derived marks could be as reliable as those derived from tutors (Stefani, 1998). But as discussed in the previous chapter, the reliability of tutors' marks, in many of the assessment forms appropriate to higher education, and when considered over highly differentiated marking schemes, are highly variable. It has taken some time since the pioneering work of Nancy Falchikov (1986) for the message to have become accepted that the point of peer and self-assessment is not as a replacement for tutor marking, some convenient labour-saving device. The point of peer and self-assessment is that participation in the practices of assessment enables one to know better what is required of those practices when developing one's own work.

Another form of participation in assessment comes with student involvement in the selection and setting of either the assessment and/or the criteria on which it will be judged. Deeley and Bovill (2017) recount how students were involved in setting essay titles and in the co-creation of the marking criteria. Indeed, Stefani (1998) argues,

> If students are not involved in the process of setting criteria for the assessment of major learning tasks how can academic staff be sure that students understand imposed assessment criteria?
>
> (p. 345)

Stefani calls for a 'consensus' between staff and students about the aims of any assessment task and for them to work on shared interpretations of any marking criteria. Here we see a movement to staff and students as equal partners in the assessment process; neither assumes a purely passive role. Rust et al. (2003)

consider how students can be invited into a shared experience regarding assessment processes and standards, and thus improve their performance through increased knowledge of such processes and standards. Based in a large, first year undergraduate business module, Rust et al.'s study placed particular emphasis on tacit knowledge acquisition though engagement in assessment activities that included discussion of exemplars and marking criteria, actual marking exercises and self-assessment. But despite this, the study demonstrated the difficulties of fully grasping tacit knowledge and found that students most easily understood the more visible and straightforward criteria such as presentation, structure or referencing (Rust et al., 2003). Socialization can be a slow and resource-greedy process, but what Rust et al. demonstrate is that in an assessment context we might be talking about a relatively modest intervention that can have a significant impact.

The remaining problem, of course, is that many of the projects mentioned here are isolated examples of where particularly motivated teachers have sought to enable students to take greater responsibility. What is needed is to draw from these examples and turn them into a foundation for all assessment practices. Responsibility cannot be a one-off, given in one course then taken back in the next. It must be built into the practices, expectations and values of assessment as such.

Another way in which students can develop their assessment knowledge is by taking an active role in the setting as well as the marking of assessment. Here we have another shift in the power balance between students and their assessors. In the project with Mark Huxham (see McArthur & Huxham, 2011) in which we sought to share control for curriculum and assessment design with students, it was important that such responsibility, and the negotiation which underlay it, be genuine and not merely superficial. We were particularly influenced by Rowland's (2000) distinction between surface and genuine negotiation. Thus it was not just about getting a few bits and bobs of ideas from students so that we could claim to have 'consulted with students'. We sought to genuinely share control, and thus responsibility. To do this, students needed to be informed. For example, students could not meaningfully agree to a particular assessment method – such as the traditional unseen exam – without knowledge of other alternatives, such as a take-home exam or a short-answer assignment.

We found that the students were strongly motivated to try to develop assessment systems that would be fair to all students with different aptitudes and preferences (see McArthur & Huxham, 2011). Thus, rather than mutuality being achieved through the ideal-type assumptions of disinterest, as underlies social contract approaches to justice, it was fostered through the open acknowledgement and engagement with the potential differences in student preferences and needs. Students were clear that they had *responsibility for others*, not just for themselves. Typical comments included:

> I'm still a bit iffy about the [take home] exam ... I know some people don't like exams but I feel I do fairly well in them as proven by my recent exam results I got today ... However, I'm happy to go with a majority so that everyone has the best and equal chance to do well.

However, our work with students also highlighted the constraints on their genuine participation in assessment decisions. For our project to succeed, we had to build in opportunities to enable the students to learn about different assessment methods before they could make an informed decision. Thus the students volunteered over the summer break to be involved in discussions about the design of the course and assessments, and to learn about possible alternatives. Again, the limitations of isolated projects to share control are apparent here: we need to take these lessons and find ways to make them work more generally.

These students' final decision to go with a 'take-home exam' instead of the traditional unseen exam arose only out of this process, as this was not an option they were previously aware of. Indeed, what became evident in this project was that bright and committed students could go through several years of university and simply not have the opportunities to develop a working knowledge of assessment practices. Thus, to be genuinely empowered they first needed to be genuinely informed.

Conclusion

Responsibility as a general understanding emphasizes that both students and academics need to be enabled and informed when they engage in assessment activities. Indeed, they each rely on the other to understand that a commitment to responsibility will shape the outcomes of these activities. As Stefani (1998) has argued, assessment should never 'be a unilateral activity' (p. 340). In a time when the discourse of student engagement pervades higher education, we must be careful of ideological forms of recognition of students, to use Honneth's term, that promise to share authority with them, that promise a fully engaged course experience, but in reality offer only a veneer. Thus we must resist managerial initiatives that promise levels of student engagement, when other processes and practices simply do not allow to be realized. Assessment should enable students to be responsible for their relationship with knowledge and their practices across a range of spheres, from understanding the rules of the game, both explicit and implicit, to being able to evaluate their own learning and finally to working on tasks that genuinely relate, and contribute positively, to the social world.

Acting responsibly in how one undertakes an assessment task requires students to be given alternatives from which they make socially just decisions. They cannot simply be corralled into a particular outcome and then expected to accept responsibility. And the scope for such choices makes assessment more rich, but also more unpredictable (a theme I return to in Chapter 9). It is also likely to make learning more uncomfortable for students, and highlights that the type of knowledge about assessment expectations, as discussed in the previous section, goes well beyond knowing marking criteria or how many references to include, but is all about the nature of the actions and ultimately the goals for which one is responsible. But students are, by definition, still learning so we have to understand this responsibility in a nuanced way. It also has implications for teaching, and particularly requires a supportive and caring environment if students are able to take these chances, make these decisions (Vy & Dall'Alba, 2014).

As academics we may feel powerless to influence institutional regulations, including the ways in which such regulations are shared and negotiated with students. But there are other actions well within our control. For example, we can initiate programme-level discussions about the ways in which we scaffold and support students to gain a genuine sense of assessment responsibility over time. The development of so-called assessment literacy does not simply happen, nor can it meaningfully occur in one module, isolated from the rest of the programme. We need to work with our colleagues to consider how this assessment literacy is nurtured over time. Within our own modules we can build in the opportunities for students to actively assess for themselves – making judgements, decisions and choices – the work they are undertaking through peer and self-assessment. Instead of berating students for only being interested in work where there is a mark to be gained, we can understand the pressures such students are under and how this myopic interpretation of assessment has come into being. Being able to explain assessment needs to be as central to our teaching role as knowing the fundamentals of chemistry, history, law or whatever our disciplinary area is. There is a challenge to find time for this within an already busy curriculum, but very often it is about transferring time resources from one part of our teaching to another. Consider how much time is spent explaining the same mistakes over and over to students when assessing their work – sometimes to the same students over and over. When we separate assessment from the broader practices of teaching and learning, and when we backload most of the work of assessment to the summative stages, we unnecessarily end up working inefficiently. There are conversations to be had here with colleagues, and with students, about the nature of assessment and how students genuinely learn the craft of assessment.

8

Forgiveness

Introduction

Assessment for social justice requires practices of *forgiveness*. In many ways this follows from what has been discussed in previous chapters, for forgiveness is, I believe, closely associated with trust, while a capacity for forgiveness suggests a sense of responsibility for our own actions and their effects on others. Forgiveness requires a capacity to understand both our own contexts and those of others, thus reflecting the intersubjectivity inherent in Honneth's work. Again, what is important here, in terms of esteem recognition, is the capacity of our students to value their work, and the contribution through that work which they can make to society.

Forgiveness is perhaps, among all my suggested general understandings that shape assessment for social justice, the most surprising. It seems, I imagine, a step too far in terms of its emotive nature and vague qualities. However, I argue it is as fundamental as each of the other foundations upon which I seek to develop the notion of assessment for social justice. Forgiveness is a kindly term; it inspires one to focus on understanding and compassion. Forgiveness, I suggest, also has a vital temporal quality which coincides with a pedagogical role. It is looking back with a focus on moving forward. This reflects what we know, and praise, in formative assessment, sustainable assessment and dialogical forms of feedback.

We need forgiveness because learning, teaching and assessment are all an awful lot about making mistakes. Indeed, we could not do any of these without making mistakes. Hence, it follows that we also need to be forgiving about such errors. Forgiving towards ourselves and towards others. This is a long way away from saying we should pass students so as not to hurt their feelings or students failing to meet assessment criteria should be allowed to go on and on. Clearly, robust assessment criteria exist not just for students, but also for the people they may later encounter as qualified professionals and members of society. But if we have a commitment to learning as an iterative process, we must allow *space* for students to learn through the experience of undertaking assessments. Understood as a social practice, not a discrete act, assessment thus requires the time and space for learning.

It seems odd to me that we build in room for trial and error, making mistakes, iterative learning at the doctoral level, for example, but arrangements for undergraduates or taught postgraduates are sometimes far less forgiving. Driven by instrumental proceduralism, some institutions have closed down the options for those who fail – no opportunities for resit. This situation is particularly bad at the level of taught masters' programmes, a growing field, in which failure is sometimes not an option. It is hard not to interpret this in terms of allegations of such students being 'cash cows' for universities. The structure of many taught masters programmes is hard to reconcile with our understandings of how learning takes place. And it would seem that what drives such regulations is the resource implications (Stowell et al., 2016). Indeed, the different ways in which institutions allow for opportunities for reassessment reflect the fact that 'complex pedagogic and pragmatic assumptions lie behind these positions' (Stowell et al., 2016, p. 522). But there can be tensions between the pragmatic and the pedagogic, and my fear is that increasingly it is the pragmatic, in a cold managerialist sense, that holds sway.

As with the other concepts discussed so far, that of forgiveness stretches across different aspects of the assessment terrain, and involves both students and staff. In the first part of this chapter I discuss the powerful social construction of failure as a notion and an experience in our society. While this discussion is largely on students, many of the points could refer equally well to the experiences of academics who can also often see assessment as a test of their abilities and competences. To what extent do we need to reconsider both our conventions and our expectations about failure? The next section considers the importance of feedback to student learning and argues that students can only really fulfil their potential if they are able to cope with failure on some level – be it underperformance, making mistakes or misunderstanding expectations. There must be some resilient capacity to project forward onto improved performance and greater understanding. Thus I make use of the metaphor of the feedback loop and discuss why forgiveness (towards ourselves and towards others) is essential for its realization.

Challenging the social construction of failure

There is a disjunction, I suggest, between the ideals promoted by an understanding of learning as an experiential and iterative process and a deeply ingrained social aversion to failure. Indeed, when I have tried to discuss with colleagues the need to reassess our relationship with failure, I am often met with the response that we need another term – failure is just too negative. But this sort of misses the point I am making. I suggest that we need to be able to cope with the negative aspects of learning and assessment – and these include failure. This will not always be failure of a particular exam, assignment or course, but also those little failures along the way: the misunderstandings, wrong turns, muddled comprehension or a concept repeatedly eluding our grasp.

Elsewhere (McArthur, 2014) I have discussed the odd relationships we can have with success and failure:

> We may fail to catch the fly that has got into our house, while succeed in getting pregnant. We may fail to save our marriage, while succeed in finding a car space at the supermarket. So wildly various are the potential uses of these terms that it is tempting to think they must now be empty of substantive meaning; however, this is not the case.
>
> (p. 177)

Notions of success and failure have strong influences on how we live our lives and our conceptions of our own worth. I discussed this in Chapter 1, considering the ways in which assessment outcomes shape students' current and future lives. Jackson (2010) describes the overwhelming nature of failure and fear of failure for many students. Issues of failure reveal the complexity of student and teacher roles within the assessment context. The threat of failure can make students feel vulnerable to the assumed power of the academics, while academics can feel their own credibility is at stake both on the grounds of their students' performances and also their own marking practices.

Indeed, a great and unacknowledged problem in higher education rests around student underachievement, which is very hard to accurately grasp. For example, what about the student who regularly gets a 'D' grade and so just slips into the pass category every time? Naturally the student might feel some relief at passing. But they also need to recognize an element of likely underperformance in such a grade. Eraut (1997) observes that students who develop a pattern of 'just pass' can find further progression opportunities closed to them: 'Who benefits when students just achieve a target, but lose interest in learning as a result of their experience?' (p. 284). It is now common to give make-up classes or an extra revision session for students who have formally failed a subject and need to retake it. But what about those who regularly fail to improve on their personal best or languish in the margins of a grade band, unsure or unable to know how to achieve higher results? This is Hughes's (2011, 2014, 2017) point about the importance of ipsative assessment, and of students and their teachers being more aware of the extent to which students move forward and develop on the basis of their personal best.

The situation of these, sometimes overlooked or forgotten students, brings to mind Bengsten and Barnett's (2017) understanding of the *dark side* of higher education, not as a place of evil in comparison with the good of light, but as a place of complexity and nuance. The dark side is a place necessarily brought into existence in comparison of the light and the more easily known. It is the 'other side of the coin' to the light side: it is 'the darker sides of higher education in everyday practice, which are less easy to catch in the spotlight and define in functional and explicit terminology' (p. 115). Remember that Honneth too casts his gaze at the 'hidden aspects and shady areas of social reality' (Toniolatti, 2009, p. 373).

I believe that failure is an idea that exists within this darker realm. Importantly, the dark side is not negative or bad, rather it is formed by that 'which may be dim, obscure or caught in a blind angle' (p. 115). I'm drawn by Bengsten and Barnett's entreat that

> we need more elaborate language and subtle concepts for grasping students' experiences of failure and let down, when struggling with and withdrawing from difficult courses never completed; for half-formed ideas and crippled thoughts, full of passion and heart, but unfit for the academic genre of writing; and for interior imaginative wanderings that seldom see the light of day.
>
> (p. 115)

They include here in this darkness 'all the failed attempts, forced detours and dead ends that make up a great deal of everyday higher education learning processes' (p. 124). This also relates to the uncertainty about what students should actually be learning – which is often not nearly as well-illuminated as academics may suppose. As discussed in the previous chapter, until students are in a position to take genuine responsibility for their assessment practices, they cannot fully grasp what is expected of them. But it is an iterative process – each feeds the other, for better understanding expectations also leads to greater responsibility.

It is a problem if students doubt their self-worth when they perform badly in an assessment task, because this may say more about the task than their actual achievements. Highly standardized, rigid approaches to assessment can only reveal so much about what students have actually learned. Engagement with complex knowledge can be tricky, and frequently elusive. This is why students need to be able to critique their work, and thus also find more constructive ways to deal with negative feedback. As academics we know that writing is sometimes a tortuous process. In the course of writing this book, my emotions have swung between despair and excitement. Some bits of text fell easily into place; others eluded my hopes for them despite numerous attempts. As Brodkey (1996) observes of her own work – 'My prose falls apart far more often than it comes together' (p. ix). But through this, she argues, we can develop patience and understanding, and an appreciation of the real joys of writing. Similarly, we need more stories of how learning occurs – the thoughts only half-formed, and the ideas unfinished (Barnett, 2007; Bengsten & Barnett, 2017). Or as Brodkey (1996) puts it, *the writing that falls apart.*

But the pain of apparent failure can be great. Yet students need to be able to confront any flaws or weaknesses in their assessment tasks, and responsibly work through these towards a better end. Even when there are opportunities for formative assessment and feedback, these do not necessarily instil in students an understanding of the messy and circuitous ways in which knowledge is often developed. We can, perhaps well-meaningly, cleanse and simplify the learning process by giving apparently simple tips for improvements when what students might really need is simply an acknowledgement that what they are doing is really, really difficult and may take some time to develop.

Academics can express surprise and frustration at students who make the same mistakes repeatedly, despite being given clear information about what they have done wrong and what is required instead. But this is to confuse rationality and practical intelligibility. Caught in the shadow of perceived failure, students may have mistaken ideas about what approach to study or revision is wise to adopt. And we underestimate how difficult the learning task is when situated in the context of experiencing failure. As Jackson (2006, 2010) observes, we can become so obsessed by failure that fleeing failure becomes a proxy for academic success. But it is a poor proxy, and a poor pedagogical approach.

Indeed, speaking with students who have failed exams, then in turn failed their resits, I have found that their main study approach is to just really, really hope they do better the next time around. Inevitably, this leads to further failure – and not of the good sort. This is why I have suggested we consider two forms of failure: passive and critical (McArthur, 2014). Passive failure looks neither back at what was done nor forward to what should be done differently. Here failure *just happens*, or so it seems to the student. There is little connection between one's activities and the outcome. Indeed, assessment is regarded rather like a lottery: it is all about the luck of the draw. Failure suggests that luck was against you. In different circumstances, with different questions or on another day, you could just as easily pass. As a result, the approach to redoing the assignment or resitting the exam is to cross your fingers and hope really, really hard. The same approaches to revision are earnestly retaken, the same study skills brought to the task. Next time, you might get lucky. Sadly this seldom works and rarely is a poor performance due to just bad luck (unless there is something seriously wrong with the content and structure of the assessment).

In contrast, critical failure positions failure in terms of the factors that led to it (other than luck) and the different actions possible in the future (other than hoping). Thus the experience of failure, while disappointing, comes to be seen positively and linked to a different future outcome. The forgiving nature is needed here to ensure that this positive outlook can be harnessed to aid learning. Rather than being like frightened creatures rendered mute and immobile in the face of failure, students who can adopt a critical perspective understand that they have a role in shaping a different future outcome. The focus becomes sharpened onto the practices of learning and revision – and how these could be done differently. There is even evidence to suggest that students who do well in a first year resit may go on in second year to outperform those who passed first time around (Proud, 2015): so something has been changed, and something gained.

There can, however, be unhelpful approaches to trying to link the failure with academic success, and these lack the forgiving quality I seek to emphasize. I recall an academic telling a class they would need to take a change of pants with them to the exam – it was going to be that scary. Many of us are familiar with tales from first year lectures when students are told to look right, then look left – because one of those people will not still be there by second year. It does a serious pedagogic injustice to students if such a fear of failure is encouraged, and the idea maintained that assessment failure somehow stigmatizes and sets apart those who experience it. It is particularly unfair coming from academics who themselves know the pain and hurt of failure – the article rejected by a prestigious journal and the sharp and unkind comments of the anonymous reviewers. Academics know the difference between comments that aim to help build a better piece of work, and those which simply aim to maim and hurt. But the way forward lies in neither just saying pleasing things for the sake of it nor being destructive and cruel. Part of the purpose academics should bring to the assessment practices they engage in with students should be to school them in this understanding of coping with failure and taking charge of their own future. Again, some rethinking of the temporal structures of highly modularized systems is likely to be needed. If students are not experienced in how to cope with pedagogic failure or disappointment, they can become isolated and inward-looking. Bengsten and Barnett (2017) refer to feelings of 'self-doubt or shame' (p. 118) when students identify flaws in their own thinking. They may also become less likely to seek out the social interactions on which successful learning depends. They may, for example, withdraw from participation in class, or be less likely to discuss their ideas with their peers. The practices which we know can nurture learning and responsibility – such as peer assessment – become tortuous and frightening.

In considering failure we have to return to the nature of knowledge with which we engage in higher education. As I have written previously, it should be knowledge 'that is not easily known'; that is, complex, dynamic and contested knowledge (McArthur, 2013). This is what defines the purposes of higher education. A further feature of such knowledge is that it is difficult to grasp at one's first attempts. Thus there is a mismatch between social expectations that success involves passing first time, and the reality of knowledge engagement. Moreover, I go so far as to suggest that unless students can grasp the pedagogical usefulness of failure, they can remain limited in the extent to which they participate fully in disciplinary discourses. This is not to say they have to fail a particular assessment as such. But what is vital is an ability to view one's accomplishments clear-eyed and see where they have not yet been successful, where further improvements are possible. This should neither be something to be feared, nor to be ashamed of.

Forgiveness and the feedback loop

I turn now to the ways in which an understanding of forgiveness can enable students to complete the feedback loop. Hounsell et al. (2008) introduced the notion of a feedback loop to capture several important aspects about feedback. It can occur at multiple moments within a course. And one experience of feedback sets the basis for how students then engage with the next moment. The feedback loop is closed only when a student is able to do something useful with that feedback – apply it to their work, in such practices as researching, writing an essay, doing an equation or developing a multimodal portfolio. Feedback has become more and more central to our thinking about student learning in higher education. Increasingly it has become clear that one cannot think in terms of feedback as a simple action – something that is given over entirely to a student. Rather feedback involves a set of social practices with which both students and academics engage.

Just as assessment moved within general understanding from an isolated bit at the end to being central to student learning, so too has feedback come to be understood in more and more complex ways. Thus I suggest there is a triumvirate of learning, assessment and feedback (McArthur, 2014). Such a triumvirate emphasizes the ways in which students can only learn effectively, and thus do well in their assessment tasks, when they are able to review and improve their own work, through both tutor feedback and their own reflexive approach. In such an approach, the student moves to a position of actively looking for areas to improve in her work, not fearing or shying away from possible errors. Thus forgiveness engenders responsibility.

It is useful here to say something on the well-known distinction between summative and formative assessment, which was also raised in Chapter 6. The idea of the triumvirate of learning, feedback and assessment casts further doubt on the wisdom to rigidly separate these two forms of assessment. Taras (2008) highlights the way in which this distinction has been perpetuated:

> Current discourse emanating from assessment for learning portrays formative assessment as the ethical face of assessment, as opposed to summative assessment .... The ethical dimension in assessment for learning in the United Kingdom serves as an argument both to support the use and dissemination of formative assessment and also to attack and demonise its evil counterpart, summative assessment.
>
> (p. 393)

But turning our attention away from final forms of assessment, and assessment for certification, risks losing sight of some of the greatest issues around potential justice and injustice. Boud and Soler (2016) also connect the welcome erosion of this 'unhelpful binary division' with students taking a more active and responsible place in their own assessment practices: they refer to a shift in 'assessment discourse away from the notion that assessment is a unilateral act done to students, to assessment that is mutually constructed between learners and assessors/teachers' (p. 402).

A more useful distinction than summative/formative is that of Knight (2000) between high- and low-stakes assessment. Low-stakes assessment is far more conducive to learning than high-stakes assessment. So if we inflate the sense of 'stakes' using devices and conventions designed to scare students, it is simply misrepresentation to present this as some form of motivation. Low-stakes assessment highlights its forgiving nature – this is why it is central to learning. Of course, there needs to be some form of high-stakes assessment at the end of a programme – when the stakes literally are high: when students are on the verge of graduation and going out to apply the knowledge they have gained at university into professional or social practice. It matters that our doctors, lawyers, teachers and so forth can do the work and perform the social roles that are reflected in their degrees. But the point that Knight makes so well is that if better learning occurs in low-stakes environments, then we should have more of these along the way to that final destination. It unnecessarily disadvantages students' learning opportunities to make everything high stakes along the way. This is a point Boud (2014) has also made again more recently:

> When all work is summative, space for formative assessment is diminished. Poor work and mistakes from which students could have learned in the past and consequently surpassed are now inscribed on their records and weighted in their grade point average. Space for learning is eroded when all work is *de facto* final work.
>
> (p. 16)

Indeed, something of a 'grading arms race' (Harland, McLean, Wass, Miller & Sim, 2015, p. 534) can be encouraged, which does little good for the students or hard-pressed academics. In their study, Harland et al. found that grades had become an essential form of motivation for students to study, but this in turn just kept inflating the stakes, and led to other problems:

> Students were experts in grade calculation and tended not to speak in terms of the subject or the type of work they were doing. They did not, for example, say they were doing 'a science essay' but would substitute this with a number: 'I am doing a 25%' or 'I have a 20 due on Friday and a 10 on Monday'. Such expressions reflect a fixation with marks that must partly be determined by the culture of grading frequency. Overall, students thought that all work should be rewarded with a grade … It was clear that student demand contributed to the proliferation of assessments and so also shaped the arms race. Both lecturers and students seemed trapped in a system that would inevitably escalate grading

frequency, although there must be limits to this in all subjects. The largest number of graded tasks found was 31 for a single module.

(p. 535)

What the authors also found was that the frequency of high-stakes assessment made it more difficult to devote the required time for learning more difficult or advanced subject matter. We can see here how the rules or expectations of graded assessment shaped the nature of those assessment practices, and the associated learning practices. Indeed, Boud (2014) refers to Black and Wiliam's observation 'that the provision of a grade may distract students from engaging with more detailed information about their work' (p. 20). The workload for students of repeated high-stakes assessment also becomes unforgiving, despite it seemingly being something that the students in Harland et al.'s study wanted. One student explained,

> When you're doing three or four papers, there's an assessment at least once or twice a week and also you can't really, you're just trying to stay afloat and trying to keep up with the next assessment and not putting the effort and time into it that you should be to be able to get good marks … and it takes away from studying for the next one or learning the content that you're being taught in the lectures because you're just trying to keep up with the assignment load.

(p. 537)

Thus the pursuit of so-called good marks appears to be a motivation, but it is a motivation for taking an assessment and not for learning as such. The two, in these cases, have quite different teleoaffective structures. And yet, when asked about more time for independent learning, students expressed concern that they might not use this time wisely. Throwing off the bindings of continuous assessment similarly raised lecturer concern about whether students would do the required work. The authors observe that

> it raises questions about who is ultimately responsible for student learning. If the grading habit is seen as problematic in terms of how students are using time in relation to educational achievement, then the academic community needs ways in which to re-think practices and provide alternatives.

(p. 537)

We must think imaginatively about how we deal with this apparent paradox – we clearly need some high-stakes assessment, yet students *learn better* when it is low stakes. In turn, however, we want the best performances from our students in their high-stakes assessments, indicating they can take responsibility for going forward and applying the knowledge they have engaged with. In a digital era, possible solutions to this paradox should not be hard to develop. An excellent example comes from Cook (2001) in an account of a large, first year economics course. Assessment for the course is a mid-semester exam, computer-mediated-learning (CML) quizzes over the semester and a final exam. When all of these were compulsory there was admirable variety in assessment tasks for students of different preferences and abilities, but there was also a lot of high-stakes assessment. Making the quizzes and/or the mid-semester examination purely formative would only then make the final examination even more high stakes. This is the high/low-stakes assessment paradox. Instead, this course team came up with a set of options and students were given responsibility to make decisions about the approach to *learning through assessment* (not the assessment as such) that suited them best. So the final exam remained compulsory, but students had the choice about whether to engage with the other assessment tasks. This meant that the final assessment for each student would be determined by one of four options:

Option 1: End-of-semester exam 100 per cent
Option 2: End-of-semester exam 75 per cent; mid-semester exam 25 per cent
Option 3: End-of-semester exam 85 per cent; CML 15 per cent
Option 4: End-of-semester exam 60 per cent; mid-semester exam 25 per cent;
   CML 15 per cent.

(p. 544)

Students chose whether to take part in the CML quizzes or the mid-semester exam but they did not have to choose which of the four options their work would be graded by. A simple computer programme would determine which option gave the best result – and that would be the student's mark. So a student who did all the assessments but performed much better in the final exam would get a mark under option one. A student who did not do well in the quizzes but did very well in the mid-semester exam and okay in the final exam would get a mark under option two. Thus there is a really interesting safety net here – a forgiving structure – that comes pretty close to solving our high/low-stakes paradox, particularly for students who decide to do all assessment tasks. Thus, the 'freedom in assessment actually creates more student responsibility for their own learning' (Cook, 2001, p. 544).

In addition, such an initiative makes it legitimate for students to take time to grasp complex knowledge. The forgiving nature of the four options means that someone is not penalized for poor performance on the continuous assessment aspects, and even if their performance is poor they may learn from it, particularly if they are not fearful of failure. There are some interesting outcomes in Cook's study if we examine the decisions that students made about the now voluntary assessment activities. Of 900 students, only thirteen sat the final exam and no other assessments, and the majority of these were students who were struggling, sometimes with repeated failures. So being a strong student did not lead to them taking the high-stakes option. Students who performed best were those who fell under options three or four – who had therefore been engaging with the continuous assessment tasks regularly, but not necessarily in a high-stakes form.

We damage students' abilities to engage with complex knowledge if we stigmatize them for not grasping it easily or on their first attempt. There are challenging issues at play here in terms of students' perceptions of their own achievements and how they believe others perceive these: the mutuality of esteem recognition and the ways in which they develop and demonstrate socially useful traits and abilities. Sambell, McDowell and Montgomery (2013) use similar terminology to my own when they refer to 'forgiving' spaces in which to learn by taking risks and through trial and error (p. 52). Similarly, Bengsten and Barnett (2017) make 'a plea for an institutional attitude that acknowledges that education and educational institutions sometimes *hurt* people and break things':

> We need pedagogies and institutional frameworks that are able to deal with the fact the higher education sometimes wounds people, makes them doubt themselves and disrupts their plans for life as it may change people's needs and ambitions in life. We need more elaborate pedagogies that build on the premise that institutions *will* lose sight of certain students, and that students should not merely be managed – they should also have room for getting lost and to lose their way in order for them to be able to come back as different persons.
>
> (p. 121, emphasis original)

When it comes to feedback, there are still some widespread misunderstandings and misinterpretations of its role in student learning. It is revealing to consider the way institutions in the United Kingdom have responded to poor results in the National Survey of Students (NSS). In particular, assessment and feedback have routinely been the areas of greatest student dissatisfaction (Bols, 2012; HEFCE, 2010). A common solution is to blame the students: they are getting good feedback, they just don't recognize it. This has led to strange and bizarre actions to try to shape students' perceptions of feedback practices. I know of one institution where academics are required to hold up a large 'F' sign to tell students that a feedback moment is upon them. Others put an 'F' next to key places in their student handbooks – to ensure they know that these are the times they will be getting feedback. This is trivializing a deeper problem. And such approaches completely underestimate our students. I even know one institution that claims their poor NSS scores are the result of their students being particularly bright, and hence more likely to critique practices (but why they would particularly critique assessment practices more than other parts of their experience is unclear). The point remains, even if students do not recognize feedback, this surely suggests some limitations in it being helpful to them. Students and academics need to understand the social nature of the practice of giving and receiving feedback, and the importance of dialogue to any feedback practice. As such they are better positioned to appreciate where the other partner may be coming from.

At the same time that some institutions are making trivial changes in desperate attempts to resolve the publicity crisis of the perceived NSS feedback problem, they are making other changes which will arguably make substantial negative impacts on the opportunities for constructive feedback, and for students to critique and improve their own work. Here I refer to the increasing pressure on the pace and rhythm within courses. Where are the spaces for engagement with feedback: the forgiving spaces? When is there time to learn from one's previous mistakes and misunderstandings? Feedback must be understood as a curriculum design issue and we must actively build in the places in which students can genuinely reflect on their work. We also need moments when it can be considered okay not to understand everything and to need further help. As Mark Huxham and I have argued (McArthur & Huxham, 2013), feedback moments can occur in many places within a course and take many forms. But a crowded curriculum and inflexible timings can make it very difficult to provide students with the necessary time and space to genuinely reflect upon, and learn from, their own work.

The idea of a feedback loop should not be confined to formal systems and structures within a course. It is just as much about students' disposition towards their own learning practices, and indeed them identifying learning as part of the teleoaffective structure of participating in assessment and engaging with the feedback received. Do they ask themselves questions about their own understanding? Do they seek to join up points where there are gaps in their understanding? Thus feedback is not just something done or given to students – it is equally about what students do. A good example of this is the notion of 'boot grit feedback' developed by Mark Huxham (see McArthur, Huxham, Hounsell & Warsop, 2011). The genesis of this idea is a metaphor drawn from hiking and climbing. Imagine you have a stone or bit of grit in your boot. You can keep walking with this but over time it will cause more and more damage until eventually it impairs your ability to walk well. To stay healthy you need to regularly 'tip out' the boot grit as you go. Similarly, we need to have practices that enable students to check on their own understanding, seek clarification, tip out the boot grit of misunderstandings as they go along. A particular place where this works is at the end of a lecture. Here Mark Huxham turns the end of a lecture, even with large numbers of students, into a rich learning moment by asking students to write on a slip of paper anything they do not think they have understood in the lecture. These are anonymous and Mark then commits to putting answers on the virtual learning environment within a set time after the lecture. Students get to see whether other people also don't understand something (which is reassuring) but have the safety of anonymity (which is comforting and better enables them to engage with the subject matter).

The practice of boot grit is clearly a forgiving one. Students are not berated for failing to understand concepts the first time they are explained. They are not blamed – there are no suggestions that it is due to them not listening or paying attention. Rather, it is acknowledged that anyone may not quite 'get' a concept, theory or example the first time around. Large lectures can be busy places that proceed at a fast pace. Boot grit ensures forgiveness for those who struggle. There is also here a strong sense of mutual recognition of the roles of lecturer and students. The lecturers are recognized as maybe not always able to explain a concept the best way for maximum understanding the first time around. But that's okay – they find out that they need to try again from the boot grit and that's what they do. Students are similarly recognized as legitimately not always able to pick everything up first time around in the lecture. There is here a strong relationship of trust also – in being able to recognize one another as fallible and in recognizing learning as complex and temporally unpredictable.

In part, mutual recognition and a spirit of forgiveness remind us not to assume what we say is self-evident and obvious to students. Such assumptions are, however, not uncommon and carry with them the view that students will obviously know how to rectify any problems identified (Hounsell et al., 2008). What makes this particularly challenging for students is that the nature and helpfulness of feedback can vary between tutors and courses (Hounsell et al., 2008). There is nothing more perplexing for a student than to try to follow the advice of one tutor, only to have the effort criticized by another tutor.

The crucial aspect of feedback for students' sense of self-worth is their ability to recognize for themselves both when their work needs further improvement and when they have succeeded in their task of engaging with complex knowledge. The two inevitably go together. The more one recognizes the trials and pitfalls of a complex task, the more one can rightly feel pride or esteem in one's achievement. Feedback in this way helps to enable students to recognize their own worth and the traits and abilities they have to contribute to society.

I am reminded of Maxine Greene's (1995) idea that learning is about imagining otherwise. This can be more difficult than it may seem. From a student perspective, the placement of feedback on their work requires them to imagine the work could be different, at least in part, to what they have already done. When a student has worked hard to construct a particular essay, perform an experiment or develop an online presentation, it can be hard to picture it any other way than what they have already done. This is where the combination of resilience and forgiveness comes in. There is something quite hard-edged to be able to look at one's own work and recognize flaws and failures: it is a task requiring clear-sightedness and an unswerving gaze. And we can only achieve this if we are forgiving of the problems we see.

Conclusion

As a general understanding that can help shape assessment practices towards social justice, forgiveness offers a supportive path between present and potential achievement. It is particularly important in the context of higher education because the knowledge we are – or should – be dealing with is complicated, contested and dynamic. Many of the current ways in which assessment is organized force the pace of student learning to an unforgiving degree, leaving little scope for the reflexivity needed for proper responsibility, as discussed in the previous chapter, nor for genuine learning through feedback and an iterative sense of improving on one's mistakes. The knowledge that students engage with in higher education, which lays the foundation for the contributions they can make to society, is complex and not always easily known on first attempts.

9

Responsiveness

Introduction

Assessment for social justice requires practices that are *responsive*. This concept very much builds on all those that have come before. Such responsiveness plays out across many different planes and through diverse relationships. In some ways responsiveness may seem a gentle term, but I mean to use it with radical intent. I regard the trait of responsiveness as active and powerful. It involves a dialogue between positions and an openness to have one's thoughts and actions shaped by one's encounters with the world in which one is placed. It is, therefore, arguably different from mere reaction to events around oneself, and brings with it a considered nature, a thoughtfulness of response. Assessment that nurtures responsiveness encourages people to see themselves as interconnected with the world in which they live, interconnected with fellow citizens and interconnected with the knowledge with which they engage. It is thus closely connected to the mutuality at the heart of Honneth's conceptualization of social justice. Here again, it is Honneth's realm of esteem recognition that ties in most clearly to this trait of responsiveness because one of the ways in which students can appreciate the social usefulness of the complex knowledge they engage with is by seeing it clearly in its social context. There are also echoes here of rights recognition and the importance of actively using the rights one has. Similarly, students must be able to genuinely use the knowledge they acquire through study. Thus participation again becomes a central focus of both knowledge engagement and of social justice. Honneth (2010b) explains,

> The opening and extension of opportunities for participation is an imperative of social equality because it is the only path through which the citizens can make use of their political right to actively contribute to the shaping of their social environments.

(p. 16)

Participation in terms of one's rights, knowledge, traits and abilities is fundamental to social justice. Thus responsiveness is an ongoing commitment and suggests the qualities of appreciating one's connectedness with the social world. Responsiveness necessitates looking outwards, a view beyond oneself or one's current context. It requires sensitivity; responding not only to the loud and obvious, but also to the quiet and nuanced. Responsiveness includes a preparedness to change and to challenge the status quo and habitual practices, along with the movement or response to a different position than that held previously. And this has real implications for the extent to which we can predict the outcomes of student learning. For academics seeking to genuinely take a learning-oriented assessment approach, this may often require transgression of prevailing norms and practices.

Assessment shapes students' lives, as discussed in Chapter 1. Assessment nurtures the ways in which students do – or do not – engage creatively with complex knowledge, and then apply this to social needs. As Knight (1995) puts it, assessment can play a role as 'a vital ritual in the maintenance of some hazy features of the social order' (p. 16). Thus the impact of assessment is far from neutral or benign. Indeed, from a critical theory and critical pedagogy perspective, our aim, through our assessment practices, should be to disrupt the existing social order and to champion and enable ways to question the status quo, mainstream and taken-for-granted. Radical change of the social order is at the heart of critical theory and critical pedagogy, and no less is required if we are to move closer to the genuine forms of recognition outlined by Honneth.

In this chapter I will examine the concept of responsiveness in two different but clearly related contexts. The first looks to the ways in which assessment practices are structured into curriculum design – and particularly the amount of scope for responsive practices that is enabled by the organization of learning and assessment. The issue at stake is the degree to which we believe assessment should be characterized by clear goals, determined in advance, or by a more fluid and responsive pathway, shaped during the experience of learning and thus more likely personalized by the student. I contend that we must challenge assumptions that learning is a linear experience, and the dominant forms of assessment that therefore follow. The distinction between self-limiting and more expansive general understandings, as discussed in Chapter 5, is important here. A linear and closed approach to assessment closes down the likely teleoaffective structures that come into play, thereby encouraging the idea of assessment as simply a hurdle to be overcome. Second, I consider the ways in which assessment practices respond and interact with the wider social world. Here I explore the importance of assessments that are shaped by the social world in which students will go on to apply and use their knowledge, and be valued as citizens for that participation.

Responsiveness to knowledge

Assessment should be responsive to students' engagement with knowledge and thus leave room for an iterative experience that is far from fixed, linear or predictable. Something different and new is produced when students genuinely engage with complex knowledge, but mainstream assessment often relies on treating all students the same way and defining in advance all the parameters by which students will be judged. I have used the metaphor of a palimpsest to suggest the ways in which students should be able to leave their marks on the disciplinary knowledge with which they engage (McArthur, 2012, 2013). The term palimpsest comes from old manuscripts upon which revisions are written over the original text. It evokes both a sense of active engagement with knowledge – the rewriting of what we know – and the scratchy and imperfect nature of such engagement. What I am particularly keen to show through this metaphor is that learning is about 'participation and engagement, rather than transfer' (McArthur, 2013, p. 91). And if students are to genuinely participate in this process of engagement with knowledge, we cannot restrict their activities to rigid and predetermined ends. Indeed, Parker (2005) goes so far as to argue that it is improper to seek to predetermine the outcomes of student learning. Eraut (1997) reminds us again that students must be able to apply – to do something with – their knowledge in order for it to be valued:

> If students find themselves unable to apply their academic knowledge or use their cultural knowledge in situations which are important for them, they take no ownership of it and the justification of preparation for life loses its validity.
>
> (p. 287)

Thus students must be able to respond to real problems and situations with the knowledge they acquire. As such this knowledge informs their practical intelligibility and influences the ways in which they engage in a multitude of social practices. What is always crucial is that students learn to use knowledge, not simply acquire it (Eraut, 1997). Freire (1996) makes the same point in his critique of bankable knowledge, an approach where we simply 'fill up' the students with knowledge, and assessment requires no more than students laying out the contents that have been deposited.

There are, thus, two threads here to my argument if we are to genuinely enable students to actively engage with knowledge through their assessment tasks. The first is that we cannot rigidly dictate the outcome of such engagement: students bring their own minds and experiences to the projects and tasks we set for them and we cannot entirely know the outcome of this in advance. Second, such engagement is not neat, perfect and linear, but a messy dialogue and thus still further unpredictable. But there is clearly also a conundrum here because it makes no sense to say that assessment tasks can be just *anything* – endlessly open-ended and adhering to no particular criteria. There is a practical and ethical responsibility to ensure students are learning at certain levels and engaging with the forms of knowledge appropriate for their disciplinary area. We want to know that our doctors, engineers, lawyers and teachers, for example, are equipped to deal with the professional roles they will inhabit. The *holy grail* here, therefore, is to enable students to have genuinely responsive engagement with assessment tasks while also meeting the purposes of the curriculum underlying them.

By far one of the most influential and long-lasting influences on how we organize assessment has been Biggs's (2003) notion of constructive alignment. Indeed, this seminal work was instrumental in assessment being reigned in from the wild reaches of practice and seen as integrated with what we wanted students to learn and how we facilitated that learning. There is enduring good advice in Biggs's analysis:

> In aligned teaching, there is maximum consistency throughout the system. The curriculum is stated in the form of clear objectives, which state the level of understanding required rather than simply a list of topics to be covered. The teaching methods are chosen that are likely to realize those objectives; you get students to do the things that the objectives nominate. Finally, the assessment tasks address the objectives, so that you can test to see if the students have learned what the objectives state they should be learning.
>
> (p. 27)

Constructive alignment provides the foundation for much mainstream assessment literature and the practices of academic development. However, there is a problem with any concept that becomes overly reified. It can lose its critical potency and radical charge. I am not arguing against the inherent logic that motivated Biggs's development of the notion of constructive alignment, later developed further with Tang (Biggs & Tang, 2011). It is a fundamentally good idea and such obvious common sense that one wonders how people could ever have thought to act differently. The problem, however, is that this notion has become embroiled in the rise of an audit culture and an associated dominant proceduralism. Constructive alignment thus becomes the feted objective, rather than a pathway towards some richer and more complex end. As long as academics use the 'right' verbs when describing their learning outcomes, all is well: more complex discussions of the purposes of assessment can be ignored.

The real problem in terms of enabling a responsive engagement with knowledge is the instrumental rationality underpinning the predetermined learning outcomes on which constructive alignment rests. My juxtaposition here will grate with some readers because, in fact, predetermined learning outcomes have been associated with the movement towards more student-centred approaches to learning and assessment. They marked a transition from a focus on what the teacher did to the placement of students at the centre of their own learning processes. The argument is typically made along these lines:

> Describing and making clear and public what the learner is intended to achieve changes the nature of assessment from a tutor-led system with fuzzy objectives and undisclosed criteria, to a student-led system with greater emphasis on formative development and personal responsibility.
>
> (Otter 1995 quoted in Ecclestone, 2001, p. 301)

Indeed such is the powerful rhetoric of student centredness behind predetermined learning outcomes (Ecclestone, 1999) that it may seem impossible to challenge them from a student perspective. I argue, however, that as with the case of ideological recognition, as discussed in Chapter 3, predetermined outcomes promise a far higher degree of student-centredness than they actually deliver. In fact, severe and fixed approaches to predetermined learning outcomes hold echoes of behaviouralism and thus are far from promoting student agency, independence or responsiveness. Here the purpose of education is seen as a change in the behaviour of students – but this is a set and fairly rigid sense of change. The core tenets of early behaviouralists remain central to the dominant educational approach. Hardarson (2017) demonstrates that education, in this behaviourialist view, should be

1. causally brought about by administering educational experiences
2. specified as objectives that can be attained, reached or completed
3. [and involve] changes in students that are described in advance.

(p. 62)

The assessment practices that one should engage with to meet such concrete objectives are shaped by the need for efficiency and realizing the outcome already set in place. To be clear, the alternative is not to approach education in some aimless way. But the key to a more socially aware learning is that the process is more than simply what is prescribed by the outcome. As Hardarson argues,

> It does not follow from this that we should conceive of education as aimless, but it does follow that some of the aims are constituted by the process of education rather than caused by it.
>
> (p. 63)

Ecclestone (1999) notes the ideological and epistemological challenge of prescribed specifications for anyone 'committed both to more transparent, accessible forms of assessment and to responsive, genuinely critical learning experiences for students' (p. 31). While Biggs talks positively of students being caught in the safe trap of alignment outcomes, methods and assessments, Ecclestone writes of being *ensnared* in restrictive forms of learning.

The predetermining of a learning aim has a long history. In fact, we can find a critique of it in Richard S. Peters's paper from 1959, 'Must an Educator Have an Aim' – outlined in Hardarson (2017). In this paper Peters criticized the prevailing view that 'teaching and learning are instrumental means to terminal endpoints that students are supposed to reach' (Hardarson, 2017, p. 59). Hardarson also quotes Peters from 1973,

> The model of adopting means to premeditated ends is one that haunts all our thinking about the promotion of what is valuable. In the educational sphere we therefore tend to look round for the equivalent of bridges to be built or ports to be steered to.
>
> (p. 59)

In other words, clear, discrete tasks are best if one wants to predetermine ends. The endeavour comes better suited to simple tasks rather than complex problems: 'objectives-based planning fails to address the open-ended nature of human endeavour and, in particular, social change' (Swann, 1997, p. 41). This loss of a connection between ideas and the social realm necessarily limits the nature of what one can engage with: 'Objectives-based planning is likely to promote mediocrity because it provides no social mechanism by which bold and potentially valuable ideas can be discussed' (Swann, 1997, p. 43). Moreover, it is in coping with unforeseen or unexpected ideas that the real nature of learning becomes apparent (Swann, 1997). What is key here is the distinction between performance and learning – and the two cannot be understood as synonymous (Swann, 1997).

To predetermine learning is to render students again as passive recipients of assessment processes. In contrast, learning should necessitate

> autonomous activity on the part of the learner, and is always based on the skills, knowledge, values and attitudes which the learner brings to the situation. Quite simply, we cannot determine the nature of another person's learning.
>
> (Swann, 1997, p. 45)

Not only do these predetermined ends tend to be more concrete, but often also necessarily less complex. Predetermined outcomes fit well with an audit agenda. If we set out in advance what we want to achieve, we can then clearly measure if we have achieved it. But only if the resulting output comes in certain forms. The need to specify what is learned gives rise to the privileging of certain forms of learning and certain forms of knowledge. Outcomes-based assessment is posited on a positivist rationality (Ecclestone, 1999). While the question of knowledge in education is surprisingly difficult (Young, 2008) and is inclined to 'take us back to some of our most basic assumptions … in the broadest sense, philosophical and political questions' (p. xvi).

The connection between an audit culture and predetermined learning outcomes is central to the position adopted by Steadman, and quoted by Ecclestone: 'If learning is important, measure it … If you can't measure it, you won't improve it and if you won't measure it, you probably don't care' (Steadman quoted in Ecclestone, 1999, p. 201). Such an approach is also reflected in Bloom's famous work on a taxonomy of learning outcomes. Thus Bloom stated that

> only those educational programs which can be specified in terms of intended student behaviors can be classified.
>
> (Bloom quoted in Hardarson, 2017, p. 61)

Indeed, Bloom's taxonomy has become canon in some circles as part of the proceduralization of predetermined learning outcomes – viewed as a sure-fire way of ensuring the right results, just so long as the approved verbs are used to describe it. But as Bengsten and Barnett (2017) observe, 'Students learn in ways difficult to measure on the scales of Bloom's taxonomy' (p. 118).

In the end, I argue, the stress on predetermining students' learning is not empowering. As Ecclestone (1999) argues,

> This is ultimately disempowering because the processes of action planning, review and self evaluation also require people to regulate their own behaviour through the minutiae of the assessment regime.

(p. 39)

The problem becomes acute if it encourages tacit dispositions that promote assessment practices that privilege narrow, predictable knowledge rather than open, challenging engagement. Consider the economics student named Pauline (Richardson, 2004) who is asked to explain the concept of opportunity cost using *real world* examples. Pauline can think of several real world examples drawn from current social debates. In Melbourne, where she lives, there is controversy over plans for a new casino and debates about the value of holding the Grand Prix. These are the examples she first thinks of when asked to do this assignment. However, Pauline has learned from previous assessments. She has learnt that expressing her own opinions is not wanted. Thus she decides on a safer example – one she cannot make the mistake of being opinionated about – and uses one from her textbook on the price of cotton during a shortage. There is no cotton industry in Melbourne. There is no imminent threat of a shortage. But this is an example Pauline knows her assessors may be anticipating – it has been already discussed as part of the course. Bringing in the casino or the Grand Prix would be risky: these are not the examples the assessors are expecting.

I have used this example of Pauline several times before because I never cease to be surprised and enraged at the ways in which assessment can *teach* a student to turn off her critical abilities: teach her to go for the safe and predictable rather than the risky and unexpected. Indeed, such assessment has succeeded in enforcing a behaviourialist approach to engagement with disciplinary knowledge. It is her conscientious attention to the assessment specifications that causes Pauline to curtail her intellectual curiosity. She does not put forward knowledge with which she has actively participated and engaged to meet the assessment task.

But what alternatives are there between extremes of tightly prescribed outcomes and being entirely aimless and unaccountable? A good place to begin lies with the distinction Hardarson (2017) makes between closed and open aims. Hardarson puts forward this distinction in which open aims, which we could call ideals, are characterized by working towards something that can never be fully completed. In Schatzki's terms these are hierarchically different teleoaffective structures. Hardarson contrasts open and closed aims with the following examples:

> Going for a swim this afternoon, painting the kitchen, and going for a walk with one's life partner next Sunday are aims of the first type. Staying healthy, keeping a beautiful home and having a happy marriage are lifelong tasks of the second type.
>
> (p. 65)

The problem in education, argues Hardarson, is that we too often focus on closed aims and give insufficient attention to the open aims which actually underpin the purposes of what we do. To illustrate this he gives an example on learning about Newtonian physics:

> Learning to use Newton's inverse square law to calculate the gravitational force between two masses may be understood as a closed aim in this sense, but understanding gravity is better seen as an open aim that cannot be conclusively reached. When has a student understood gravity? When she has learned to do simple calculations based on Newton's formula? Is able to explain how massive objects affect space-time? Has mastered the concepts used to describe black holes? Knows what the long search for the Higgs boson was all about? Can participate in debates about the differences between gravity and the other fundamental forces of nature? Understanding gravity is an endeavour which, arguably, cannot be completed.
>
> (p. 65)

In this example, we see the relationship between open and closed aims. The latter, in some cases at least, can become pointless without the former. In this distinction between open and closed aims, a vital space is opened up for students to build their engagement with knowledge through their responsiveness to the challenges, rocky outcrops and steep slopes which they encounter. This example also highlights the ways in which this can apply to all disciplinary areas, stressing that the sciences themselves are also complex, socially situated sites of enquiry.

It is the open aims which matter most to social justice. Any endeavour to understand our social world requires more than pre-specified outcomes reached through mere memorization of fact (Hardarson, 2017). To work towards open aims, the student must actively engage, for there are fewer certainties on which to rely:

> Ideals, or open aims, are needed to choose and criticise objectives, and modify them in an intelligent way in light of changing circumstances and unforeseen opportunities.
>
> (p. 66)

Indeed, more rather than less emphasis is placed on what students can do when the aims are open rather than closed.

A practical example of this comes from another project I have done with Mark Huxham. Mark and I share a commitment to social justice through education and to considering issues of power and sharing control with students through teaching and assessment. It was in response to the challenge of more responsive ways to include students in curriculum design that Mark developed an alternative to constructive alignment based on the mountaineering metaphor of *natural lines*. In work we did together with students, we sought to reconsider how the curriculum, including assessment tasks, could be reconfigured to enable the space for less linear and bounded engagement with knowledge. A key departure point, we felt, was the prominence we gave to issues of power, and particularly the ways in which power could be shared across the course. Table 9.1 below compares the two metaphors of course design.

Table 9.1 Comparison of natural lines and constructive alignment approaches to course design (developed by Mark Huxham)

Natural lines	Constructive alignment
Mountaineering metaphor	Surveying/engineering metaphor
Identifying an elegant route	Creating an efficient route
Team effort	Individual effort
Process informed by outcome	Outcomes determine process
Bounded flexibility and spontaneity	Carefully planned and predictable
Requires risky commitment	Risk is minimized

(from Huxham, Hunter, McIntyre, Shilland & McArthur, 2015)

Natural lines is a mountaineering term which refers to the route taken by the climber. The emphasis is not on the fastest or most efficient route to a particular end, but rather it focuses on a route that evolves through the process of undertaking the climb, unfolding as the climber interacts with the mountain, makes decisions and chooses between options. It is an approach more risky, challenging and ultimately satisfying. The student is in an uncertain situation – no longer protected by the 'trap' of the net woven between objectives, methods and assessment, as outlined by Biggs, with constructive alignment. But the student is also more powerful and much greater independence and responsibility for task accomplishment is required. Our assessment practices, therefore, need to account for student responsiveness to the task ahead – maintaining standards while maximizing effort and responsibility.

So how were students assessed after this immersion in a responsive form of curriculum design? Well in this case the assessments had been decided by a previous cohort of students, who engaged in the sharing control project for that purpose (McArthur & Huxham, 2011), and discussed in Chapter 7. But the ways in which students engaged with the assessment were congruent with their engagement with knowledge over the course. The same key aims of flexibility, commitment and responsiveness were brought to assessment practices. Here one student (and co-author), Robin, explains the impact it had on her:

> In the past we have been taught to take widely accepted theories for granted, so it was interesting to think of it from a different angle. It was surprising how easy it was to think like this, in a way we haven't done before but once we start, it seems fairly obvious e.g. finding evidence that competition is not important, as opposed to evidence supporting theories of competition. It was also interesting to think about how to interpret the same results from different angles … a valuable skill to have next semester when we are writing our honours projects.
>
> (Huxham et al., 2015, p. 539)

The natural lines metaphor leaves knowledge more open and thus more sensitive and responsive to individuals who engage with it. Thus, our mountaineer is working towards ever honing her skills of physical and mental navigation; each climb in itself is a subset of this, a particular closed aim contributing to the larger open aim. To extend the metaphor further, what adds richness to the natural lines experience is that the rock face is not smooth, even and predictable. Extra challenge and greater accomplishment lie in working with the fissures, crevices and geological character of the rock face. Here we can see the resonance of this metaphor with Bengsten and Barnett's (2017) consideration of darkness in the university, introduced in the previous chapter: darkness understood in terms of the contrasts with light, the shadows and angles thrown into relief. Students at work in these dark and shadowy spaces must be responsive to the contexts created by these complex shifts between light and dark. They must learn to move with confidence between certainty and uncertainty.

Such dark places reveal the complexity on offer once we move beyond the artificial brightness of the easy-to-audit world. They entreat us to consider the alternatives to these easy measuring systems if we focus on the shadows of higher education. Most importantly, the emphasis is not on the product of learning alone, but also on the processes. Set apart from the presumed certainties of an audit culture, the darkness of our institutions reveals 'the ambivalent and slippery nature of everyday institutional practice' (Bengsten & Barnett, 2017, p. 120). Here again we can see why students' outcomes cannot be fully predetermined but require a responsiveness to the contexts in which they find themselves and the genuinely original outcome of any engagement with knowledge.

A more responsive approach to assessment also transforms the role of academics involved, making their part also richer and more meaningful. Lum (2012) makes the distinction between prescriptive and expansive modes of assessment:

> In the prescriptive mode the assessor's role is essentially that of passive, non-judgemental facilitator tasked with gathering rigidly prescribed, pre-determined data. The assessor's function is essentially binary: to indicate the presence or otherwise of a given behavioural manifestation.
>
> (p. 597)

Here the practices of judgement are clearly limited. An expansive mode of assessment offers much more for the academic involved, as well as the students:

> In contrast, in the expansive mode the assessor's role is essentially active and judgemental with judgements being potentially a matter of degree.
>
> (p. 598)

Keeping the space open for students' genuine responsiveness to the knowledge with which they engage makes teaching a far more difficult undertaking, but surely also more rewarding. It moves from the artificial light of an audit culture to the shadows and rich nuances of Bengsten and Barnett's (2017) darkness:

> It is tempting to react to the darkness of teaching with doubt and sometimes guilt. It seems like the easiest way out, and fits with the contemporary mainstream understanding of teaching as a liquid form of technology adaptable to all situations if done properly. Another, and much tougher, way would be to react with resilience and recalcitrance and to step up to the next challenge, not with uncertainty and insecurity, but with an eagerness to show that you can endure the darkness of teaching as a condition for your endeavours and an aspect of fate.
>
> (p. 123)

Despite frameworks such as Bloom's taxonomy claiming to show different levels of complexity in terms of what a student does, it remains a framework more rigid than the realities of engaging with complex and troublesome knowledge. If we tie things down too tightly, to meet instrumental ends, then we truncate the possible joy and commitment students can have in their assessment tasks.

If assessment and learning are understood as intertwined, we need to consider what scope we have for students to experience both this joy and commitment through the practices of assessment. As Sambell et al. (2013) argue,

> Assessment is arguably most productive in terms of promoting genuine, valued learning if it fosters individuals' own interests and concerns. There is a world of difference between students feeling they are doing an assessment because they are required to slavishly conduct an activity for the sole reason that their teachers require it, and one in which they feel a sense of ownership and responsibility.
>
> (p. 14)

Thus we can relate this back to Chapter 7 and the importance of student responsibility in assessment. We can now see that to take genuine responsibility students must have some real investment in the assessment task. Similarly, a feature of the natural lines approach outlined above is that it was not necessarily 'a more "pleasant" learning experience; all of us experienced anxiety about the risks involved. The challenges should not be underestimated, but therein also lies the joy' (Huxham et al., 2015, p. 539). Angela (both student and co-author) explains the mix of emotions she felt after handing in her take-home exam:

> I am left feeling restless after handing in the take home exam. After sitting a conventional exam I am always used to feeling negativity – realising afterwards that I have written the wrong answer, remembering facts I had forgotten during the exam and complete dread that I have failed. It is the lack of this negativity that has left me feeling restless, I am simply not used to the positive after effects that the take home exam has filled me with. I feel like I have learned so much, like I have done the best I possibly could and I know there is very little chance that I could fail.
>
> (p. 540)

Contrast this with a student named Karl, discussed by Sambell et al. (2013), who reveals the superficial, and temporary, nature of engagement with knowledge encouraged by traditional exams:

> Exams are not a normal way of working. Actually, when you think about it they're rather pointless – they just say whether you're having a hard time remembering or an easy time remembering. So you revise in a way that means you just thinking 'Let me remember this for a short while'. You try and cram for an exam. When I know I have got an exam on a module I revise by writing down all the information I have to learn on post-it notes, which I stick up around the flat.

The house gets covered with them! It's a shallow learning which doesn't stick. Actually, you try to forget it before you take the next exam, because you don't want to get the two papers muddled up.

(p. 10)

A theme running through this book is that highly rigid and proceduralized forms of assessment run counter to social justice concerns. We need to have approaches to marking that allow us as assessors to be genuinely responsive to what our students have done, even when it falls outside the norm or what we had expected. As Sadler (2014) argues,

> Experienced assessors are open to those criteria that come legitimately into play only rarely and build these into their judgments when they apply. Fixed codifications do not allow for such eventualities. This reflects the reality that it may not be possible to predict with certainty the variety that can arise through students' ingenuity, originality and creativity.

(p. 278)

Responsiveness to the world of work

This section builds on the notion of responsiveness and considers the ways in which assessment practices are responsive to the social world in which they are situated. This connection is a quality highly valued by students and evidence is clear that where students perceive their assessments tasks to be 'inherently meaningful, interesting, relevant, and have long-term value' they learn better (Sambell et al., 2013, p. 12). Students relish opportunities to 'communicate, discuss or defend their ideas' (p. 12). The idea of *authentic assessment* seeks to capture this link to activities with a clear alignment in the social and economic world. We therefore require flexible approaches to assessment that can be responsive to students' needs and interests (Eraut, 1997; Swann, 1997), which should themselves be nurtured through a responsive relationship with the wider social world. Students can feel discouraged by being forced to go through processes that bear little relation to what they will later go on to do in their chosen career. In our sharing control project, Mark Huxham and I (McArthur & Huxham, 2011) found that our students were committed to forms of assessment that mirrored real world applications. Thus they did not want to critique a 'model' scientific paper, but insisted on the somewhat harder task of writing a critique of a real scientific paper from one of the leading journals. Most striking was the student who said she did not want to be examined on perfect, textbook style examples of botany, when her future would be formed by dealing with the muddy, messy realities of real nature. It is, therefore, not just the profound and grand aspects of the wider world that students should respond to, but much meaning and richness lies in the everyday. Indeed, it is beneficial for students to harness everyday experiences as part of their assessment activities (Sambell et al., 2013).

There is resonance here with the notion of responsibility, as discussed in Chapter 7. Students respond well to being given real challenges and, as such, real responsibility. They can be quick to criticize forms of assessment that seem unrelated to the ways they will go on to engage with knowledge after university. Consider this observation from Karl, the second year electronic engineering student mentioned earlier. Exams, he argues are 'not a normal way of working':

> But it's odd, because normally, if you were in a working environment, say, and someone came to you with a problem to solve, you wouldn't necessarily have to know the stuff, and remember it, there and then. You'd say: 'hang on a minute, I see there's an issue, so I'll go away and find out more about it, get to the bottom of what's going on here, and come back to you with a solution once I've talked to people and done some research'. That's the way of working you might use in a project-type assignment, where your lecturers ask you to work on something in a more realistic or relevant way. But not in an exam.
>
> (p. 11)

In order to be genuinely responsive to the social and economic contexts in which students will go on to use their knowledge, our assessments must be relevant to those contexts and to the likely nature of future applications. Looking across assessment practices at many universities, it is hard to escape the realization that they have been resistant to change. Despite the rich scholarship on assessment, the predominance of unseen exams remains in many disciplinary fields. What arguments are made in their defence? Often there is a link to tradition, or the argument that this is the way things are done here. Or arguments are made that they are easily managed and marked, again suggesting the dominance of proceduralism. None of these reasons are sufficient. In a multimodal world filled with diverse forms of technology and in which knowledge itself is understood as more than text alone, the suite of assessment forms on offer in some universities remain terribly narrow.

Thus, interconnectedness to the outside world, which in turn necessitates responsiveness, is prized by students such as Karl. It was also highly prized by the economics student Pauline, until assessment experiences 'taught' her otherwise.

It is further clear that for many students, consideration of the wider social world is closely associated with the world of work. I do not want to dispute this connection, but I do want to problematize the ways in which it is currently manifested in assessment practices. As I have argued previously, the problem lies not with higher education having an economic purpose, but with the narrowness of the ways in which that purpose is understood (McArthur, 2011). Responsiveness to the world of work becomes problematic when it privileges the views and interests of a powerful elite over everyday working people. The world of work is much more than the supposed desires of large or powerful businesses and employers.

Certainly research suggests that students value links between their studies and their future world of work. But to position themselves to be able to genuinely contribute to social good, in terms of esteem recognition, necessitates a rethink of the nature of such work. It must be formed by a web of practices that highlight a complex web of social relationships. Work connects multiple social practices wherein lies the potential for justice or injustice. Consideration of these practices should not be left to some special cases or minority interest (as one reviewer of my work once described critical pedagogy) but must be utterly central to our engagement with knowledge. When students work with knowledge and apply it to the social realm they are always participating in a process of justice or injustice.

I am therefore calling for a new way of conceptualizing and responding to the world of work within and through our assessment practices. A way that recognizes that this world of work cannot be conflated with simply what employers want but is formed by a nexus of social practices and a myriad of interconnections and relationships. Work is important for social justice because it includes many of the practices through which we engage with fellow members of society, both those known and unknown to us. When we think of esteem recognition, of being valued for the social contributions we can make, the world of work is clearly an important aspect of this. Similarly, work has an important impact on our sense of well-being (Winch, 2002). I therefore argue that assessment practices should be responsive to the requirements to participate in the world of work, in fulfilling and socially just ways. I want to cut down to the ways in which assessment can positively shape our understanding of what it means to be part of the workforce, and the place of such work within broader society.

I begin, therefore, with a critique of the current ways in which work and assessment are frequently brought together in higher education. Here I refer to the progression over the past twenty or so years from a stress on transferable skills to the notion of employability and employability skills and through now to the ascendance of graduate/generic attributes. The notion of transferability of skills and knowledge from university into work is clearly more familiar than that of responsiveness. However, I use the latter because it brings with it a sense of change occurring through the process and a sensitivity to context. Bankable knowledge can simply be *transferred*, complex engagement with knowledge involves an interconnection, a change or a rethinking.

With each new iteration from transferable skills to graduate attributes the problem, I suggest, is that they have been driven from the perspective of what employers are thought to want. The broader notion of our participation in work as part of our social development is given scant attention, and connections to broader social issues, including social justice, often act as window dressing and little more. Thus one of the earliest definitions of graduate attributes, and widely cited, comes from Bowden et al.:

> The qualities, skills and understanding a university community agrees its students should develop during their time with the institution. These attributes include but go beyond the disciplinary expertise or technical knowledge that has traditionally formed the core of most university courses. They are qualities that also prepare graduates as agents of social good in an unknown future.
> (Bowden et al., 2000, cited in C. Hughes & Barrie, 2010, p. 325)

But such appeals to a social good are meaningless without a robust sense of the nature of that society. Too often such connections are made on the basis of a benign view of the social world, as though injustice and inequality were not major problems: as though the world of work is a positive and fulfilling place for everyone within it and misrecognition never occurs.

Moreover, with graduate attributes, as with constructive alignment, we see the almost inevitable force towards proceduralization, crushing in its relentless march forwards the qualities that originally seemed to make such sense. What is lost is the space in which genuine, socially relevant learning and teaching can take place. When everything is tied to a metric, nothing can flourish and bloom to full effect. Thus, once again, only that which can be easily measured is valued. What is lost is the space in which genuine, socially relevant learning and teaching can take place. Thus another paradox presents itself (recall the high/low-stakes paradox discussed in Chapter 8). With moves to measure and audit the attributes that graduates leave university with comes a necessary simplification in order to make them suitable for measuring. But, as such, they then become less valuable in terms of ongoing learning and ongoing social practices. The literature supporting graduate attributes places significant emphasis on this demonstrable quality (C. Hughes & Barrie, 2010). And we can observe graduate attributes finding their way into the rubrics used to assess students. But the tension is clear. As Jones (2009) found in her study of academics implementing graduate attributes, the qualities most valued might also be very difficult to assess. Thus what can be assessed, as one of Jones's participants observed, is what is easy, where simple questions can be asked. I return again to the importance of understanding higher education as a site of engagement with complex knowledge. My concern is that once we begin to think in terms of what is easy to assess and measure, we lose sight of the real purposes of assessment in higher education. It is useful to recall Elton's (2004b) argument that some forms of engagement with knowledge may be best reported on, rather than given a mark as such.

The problem at play here, I believe, is the focus on attributes rather than social practices, and particularly the disarticulation of such attributes from engagement with knowledge. A better approach is to consider how our practices of knowledge engagement, which are at the heart of higher education, foster social justice. A focus on attributes rather than practices also leads to a decontextualized understanding of students' abilities and achievements. And the move towards generic attributes that can be compared across disciplines and institutions necessarily loses much of what was at the heart of the original concept (Jones, 2009, 2013).

A more important point, however, is that concepts like graduate attributes do not sufficiently, and fundamentally, challenge our understandings of the world of work as is necessary to move towards greater social justice. It all ends up, like transferable skills and employability before them, with an appeal to *what employers want*. Too often claims to employability or graduate attributes simply perpetuate the world of work as it is, perhaps adding some decorative trimming of social responsibility to it. But the world of work is not a neutral place: the prevailing regimes of recognition are not all just. Current Western societies are beset with issues of workplace stress, erosion of workers' rights, more unforgiving working practices. If we are to nurture social justice through assessment then it must be done by equipping students to become critical and informed members of the workforce, not compliant and willing servants. As Honneth (2014b) argues,

> After all, the theory knows too well that such decisions are only provisional, partial and distorted as long as citizens cannot raise their voices free of all anxiety and shame. For the sake of this element of individual autonomy and elementary freedom of public expression, this theory of justice must demand advocative relations in which subjects attain self-respect not only in the democratic public sphere, but also in their familial relationships and in their working life.
>
> (p. 50)

My concern with the employability/graduate attributes approaches is that they reinforce a mainstream instrumentalization of what is an enormous part of most adults' lives. The soft touch of these approaches, with their words about social good, should not divert us from tackling the assumptions underlying them, and these assumptions speak to a yielding, compliant workforce. Even traits such as critical thinking are tamed and only valued in terms of their instrumental ends, and not genuine, emancipatory projects.

Movements such as employability and graduate attributes risk fostering two forms of misrecognition. First, they run the risk of promoting a form of self-reification, as discussed in Chapter 3. Here students come to identify themselves with set categories and to judge their worth by these set terms. Preparing oneself for work becomes a matter of ticking off qualities defined elsewhere and by others. The relationship is utterly one-sided. It is not focused on students' own sense of self, developed through responsive engagement with the social world. Instead what we should do is nurture students who think in their own terms, closely linked to social solidarity, about the nature of their relationships in work. And we can do this through assessment practices that nurture a sense of responsiveness to the social world – to poverty, climate change, violence and other forms of injustice, as well as taking joy, inspiration, creativity from the world around. This is about a sense of moral interconnectedness that transcends utilitarian sets of skills or attributes.

The second form of misrecognition is that of ideological recognition (also discussed in Chapter 3). Here students are feted for having certain attributes, such as independence and critical thinking, but the realities of their working lives may be quite different. Honneth is helpful here, observing the ways in which 'employees are compelled to feign initiative, flexibility and talents where there is no material basis for doing so' (Honneth, 2014b, p. 93). The problem is that such traits are heralded without there being genuine paths to their realization. Think of some of the zany, carefree working practices we are told are typical of some of the large software firms, and contrast this with the demands for other forms of conformity and compliance within them. Personal identity, as a worker contributing to the social good, becomes a simulacrum. It is simply not enough for students or graduates to have certain attributes if they do not bring these to bear on the practices with which they engage, and if they do not engage with a committed sense of the teleoaffective structures that guide socially just engagement.

The problem, I argue, with these dominant approaches to linking assessment and the world of work is that they instrumentalize what is a moral relationship.

Thus a new approach to the world of work is called for. Indeed, Honneth argues for

> the need for our present societies to radically redefine and open up the concept of work on a social level. It is much too restrictive to really compensate for all those contributions which we, using fair principles, have to describe as forms of work.
>
> (Honneth in Petersen & Willig, 2002, p. 274)

Honneth also observes that intellectuals, feeling disappointed, have 'turned their backs on the world of work in order to focus on other topics far from the realm of production', having lost hope in 'the humanization or emancipation of labour' (Honneth, 2014b, p. 56). He argues that 'never in the last two hundred years have there been so few efforts to defend an emancipatory and humane notion of labour as today' (p. 56). And yet, he argues that 'labour has not lost its relevance in the social lifeworld ... the longing for a job that provides not only a livelihood, but also personal satisfaction, has in no way disappeared' (p. 57). This observation is at the heart of assessment for social justice. All along in the discussion so far I have tried to emphasize that it is not a mark or a certificate that really matters, but the knowledge with which students engage and what they are able to do with that knowledge. This is where genuine satisfaction and a sense of self-worth reside. It is, therefore, as already mentioned, an essentially social understanding of social justice – it can never be about isolated individuals or discrete acts. Here we begin to look upon our fellow members of society in new ways, recognizing them in terms of the contributions they make to the social good. Employers thus cease to be considered as some homogeneous or amorphous mass, but as key players in the moral and social construction of society.

I believe it is a worthwhile and radical position to suggest assessment tasks that conceptualize the engagement with knowledge as intricately linked with the lives of our fellow citizens, including those without power, voice or position. I suggest that for the links between work and assessment to be meaningful in a social justice sense, they must involve a critical rethinking of work relationships and practices and position students and graduates as active social beings, able to determine their own destiny. Critical thinking should not be tamed as another tick-box trait but should be unleashed to challenge the inequities and injustices perpetuated by the dominant organization of labour.

Work is the site of our interactions with others in society, not simply co-workers but a host of people we do not know. Work practices bring us into close contact with people who are not friends or relatives but actually strangers to whom we owe care. We cannot move towards greater social justice unless the commitment to the social good informs all our working practices. The responsiveness with the world of work must be understood as working in both directions. It is not simply that the work imposes requirements and expectations on what students do, and on what they are assessed in higher education. Equally, we need to be nurturing graduates who will have a positive social influence on that world of work. This point follows very much from that in the previous section, outlining the problems, from our critical theory/social justice perspective, of overly determining in advance the nature of student achievement. We need powerful graduates if we are to deal with real social problems.

A common dilemma for students revolves around who they should direct or write their assessments towards. There is evidence that students misunderstand the task of writing an essay, for example, and think in terms of just one lecturer (Sambell et al., 2013) but what they really need is a sense of a much broader communication across the social plain, and of their ideas in dialogue with fellow citizens. Genuine critical engagement should cast one's gaze beyond the textbooks and lecturer's PowerPoint slides. It should do exactly what the economics student Pauline first thought to do when explaining opportunity cost – to relate it to real problems and issues in the social world around her. That she felt compelled by assessment experiences to forgo this link with her own world, and to draw instead on the textbook example, is terribly sad.

To summarize my argument in this section, I contend that genuine responsiveness to the social world necessitates that we think in terms of embodied practices and not decontextualized attributes. Second, these cannot simply be lists of things desired by employers, but must more robustly and assertively be about the ways in which graduates bring their knowledge to bear in the social realm. Thus, it requires a radical rethinking of the world of work as a nexus of complex social practices and not a one-way relationship between employer and employed.

Conclusion

Assessment practices that are shaped by a general understanding of responsiveness reinforce the interconnection between the public and private, between the social world and education, which is at the heart of critical pedagogy. To try to educate, or assess, within a vacuum is folly. All disciplinary areas of knowledge lead back to the social. So too should our forms of assessment. Both the movement towards predetermining learning outcomes and that of stipulating graduate attributes risk privileging certain forms of assessment that meet the qualities favoured by an audit culture. To truly position the knowledge we assess within its social context is to accept that some things simply cannot be measured. But the powerful, socially conditioned urge to measure is very strong. As witnessed by the graduate attributes movement which, arguably, began by trying to capture important things not measured by traditional forms of assessment, it can gradually be taken over by this drive to measure in order to demonstrate an auditable 'effectiveness'. A procedural instinct to systematize what was intended as breaching the divide between higher education and wider society takes hold. This, I suggest, is why we need to have a strong sense of what we mean by social justice when we reconsider the nature of assessment practices, for the prevailing accepted wisdom, the status quo and the mainstream make powerful opponents. They have a lot on their side, embedded in institutions, practices and values. And yet, I do not believe they stand the scrutiny that comes from thinking outside of predetermined ends or lists of employer-friendly virtues. A genuine connection with the social world reveals its sadnesses and tragedies. We should not shy away from these when we consider our assessments because they, in the end, are what give meaning to the roles that graduates can go on to play. This is meaning embedded in social justice as mutual recognition; thus our own possession of traits or abilities is necessarily linked with the fates of those around us.

10

Conclusion

Reflections on Assessment
for Social Justice

We send our graduates out into a world of great injustice. Assessment cannot be blind to this. The actions of these graduates, born of their educational experiences, can make a difference in an unjust world. Assessment matters because it shapes those educational experiences in a myriad of ways. Scholarship on assessment for learning has persuasively positioned assessment and feedback in terms of their profound impacts on what and how students learn. I have sought to combine these insights with a critical theory perspective. Recall the inspiring words from one of the founders of critical theory, Horkheimer, when he asserted 'it need not be so' (Horkheimer, 1995, p. 227). The possibilities for doing things differently exist through our capacities to question and challenge prevailing practices. Such practices include the relationships we build with students. Commitments such as honesty and trust *do* lie partly within our control, even when broader institutional practices (such as the use of plagiarism software or the workload allocation model) seem remote and less amenable to reform.

I wrote in the Introduction to this book that it is not intended as a book about assessment. This may seem strange as over the previous five chapters I have written a lot about assessment. But the discussion is never about assessment as an end in itself. Few of the examples I have given are themselves new or unknown. On their own, these examples are not necessarily radical. But always, the purpose in this book has been the dialectic between these examples of different assessment practices and the broader understandings that can shape social justice within and through higher education. What is new, I believe, is the explicit connection of assessment to the social justice aims of higher education, including a complex and nuanced understanding of those aims. This is the essence of critical pedagogy, to bring the insights of critical theory to the practices of education. Understood through this social justice lens, seemingly familiar tasks become potentially transformative experiences. Or practices that were followed without question are reframed as potentially unjust and damaging. The lenses of social justice cast long and vibrant shadows. I am, therefore, driven to challenge the assumption that because assessment is really important, it lies outside the field of radical change. Critical pedagogy too often goes quiet when it comes to assessment because it is deemed too difficult to rethink the clear relations of power inherent in assessment regimes. But this is exactly why we must focus on assessment as part of any commitment to genuine, profound change in the social arrangements within our universities and in the society in which those universities are situated, and in whose interests they serve.

I also said in the Introduction to this book that my aim was to be neither too naive nor too world-weary. To take the example of trust, I am not arguing that we pretend academic wrongdoing does not occur. What I have sought to do, instead, is to demonstrate that trusting and not trusting both have consequences for the nature of educational practices and for the relationships that develop through those practices. In appreciating these consequences, we understand that there are, nearly always, choices to be made. The use of plagiarism detective software is not 'the only show in town' as I have heard it referred to. There are alternatives and, at the very least, a commitment to social justice requires that we explore and consider these alternatives. Instrumentalized forms of distrust change the nature of the practices to which they relate. We cannot pretend to ignore this. Academics cannot argue that they have no choice, nor that issues of academic misconduct have only emerged in the internet age. There are many potential pressures on the decisions academics make when they assess students – and I believe we need to challenge the idea that prevailing practices always make sense or are reasonable, while a social justice motivation is considered idealistic or impractical.

Adopting a critical pedagogy perspective casts established and mainstream practices in higher education in a very different light. Issues of power come to the fore, and the damage wrought by unseen and unacknowledged factors becomes paramount. Thus, where once it seemed *only common sense* to put all student essays through a bit of commercial software, the very same practice is revealed as one loaded with issues of instrumentalism and misrecognition. It is all a matter, I believe, of genuine reflection on what we do – and robust interrogation of whether our decisions really do make sense. Similarly, predetermining learning outcomes just *makes good sense*, because otherwise how do we know if they have been achieved, how do we stay accountable? But this practice looks less benign if we consider the power relations inherent in decisions about what forms of learning to approve as desirable and what forms of thinking are disbarred. It is not just individual tasks that are predetermined, but a sense of what is acceptable and socially useful knowledge. Recall the economics student Pauline from the previous chapter. She chose her example of the cotton industry because that was what was expected: to offer anything else would be to trespass into undesirable territory. Critical pedagogy demands that we consider all interactions within higher education as political, and explore and challenge the ways in which entrenched understandings of power permeate pedagogical relationships.

Critical pedagogy challenges the divide between inside the university and a social world outside. It champions educational spaces as public spaces, as civic arenas in which the challenges and responsibilities of the social realm are just as important as outside, and thereby require approaches to education fundamentally enmeshed in that social world. This requires a radical rethinking of the practices that constitute higher education and familiar practices that might seem perfectly logical to come to be regarded as constraining and limiting. What this means for assessment in particular is that our gaze, when considering assessment practices, also extends beyond the university itself. This, in itself, is not a new idea either. Falchikov and Boud (2007) have led scholarship in this area, arguing for the importance of assessment shaping students' future learning. In addition, Boud's (2000) work on sustainable assessment makes this link between present and future activity clear, as does his later work with Soler (Boud & Soler, 2016).

Assessment for social justice builds on these important pieces of scholarship by a more explicit consideration of social justice. Running through this book is the argument that an implicit procedural notion of social justice – or fairness – simply does not attend to all the complex issues that make up social well-being. So much of the lived realities of assessment, and students' future lives, are lost if we just consider due process. But how do we transcend social justice just being a catch phrase, or so nebulous and indistinct to be either an easy buzzword or simply overlooked? The considerable attention paid to the conceptual foundations in Part 1 has, I hoped, demonstrated that we need to theorize robustly claims to social justice. We must think through the meanings of this otherwise trite and overused term so as to analytically work towards its genuine realization.

On one level, my message may seem deceptively simple. If students only recognized that their own self-worth was tied up in their assessed work, they would never want to cheat, engage superficially just for marks or make spurious claims for extenuating circumstances. But I do want to defend the apparent simplicity, for I think that is quite important. The idea of a tangible connection between our labour (as students or academics) and our self-worth and place in society is the bedrock of any critical conception of social justice. On one level, it is that simple. What Honneth then adds is the nuance, the starting to tease away the elements of this otherwise simple proposition. We see threads working in two ways. Downwards go the warp pulling together the two ends of individual and society, ensuring they are ever bound as mutually reinforcing. Across goes the weft, threading through the elements of care, respect and esteem recognition. Social justice requires the satisfaction of all three elements of Honneth's tripartite conceptualization. We must have the particularity of love recognition from family and those closest to us, we must have the universality of respect recognition, understanding and using the rights which are ours, and we must have the individuality of esteem recognition, being seen for the contributions, abilities and qualities we bring to the social whole.

At the heart of Honneth's theory is that we must change the prevailing regimes of recognition in order to move towards greater social justice. Such social justice is then enacted in genuine relationships of mutual recognition. The considerable detail Honneth goes into, the careful elucidation of the three realms of mutual recognition, gives his work its analytical power. The clearest link between Honneth's theory and assessment lies in the notion of esteem recognition, but I would like to take a moment to outline why I have also sought to connect with the other two realms of love and respect recognition. The connection with love recognition is where I clearly move furthest from Honneth's original meaning, but I do so because I believe that we need greater, genuine personalization in higher education. One of the dangers of an overly reductionist, audit-driven approach is a depersonalization of essentially personal actions and relationships. To instrumentalize academic conduct is only possible when one depersonalizes the relationship. And such instrumentalism works both ways. Thus while academics may defend their behaviour as simply good practice to ensure the robustness of assessment systems, they may criticize students who adopt similar instrumental tendencies, such as obsessing over what will be on the exam or taking shortcuts when writing an essay. I also suspect that students who do choose to plagiarize or cheat in any other way often do not realize the genuine hurt experienced by academics when this is discovered.

I have also sought to weave in respect recognition because I believe it is essential to the notion of responsibility and to informed participation in assessment practices. It seems strange to me, and very worrying, that many students are not better informed about how assessment works and what assessment may be for. And we cannot simply blame students for this oversight. Struggling within a crowded curriculum and an unforgiving timetable for learning, students are not offered sufficient opportunities to learn about assessment other than simply by doing an assessment. While learning through doing is actually consistent with social practice theory, this requires genuine time for apprenticeship, for learning along the way such as being able to work with and implement feedback as it is given. A packed curriculum and rigid assessment tasks offer none of this. But students need to be informed actors within the assessment arena in order to experience the respect recognition inherent in having, understanding and using one's rights.

Esteem recognition is clearly at the heart of the assessment for social justice project. This is also the clearest and most easily grasped link between Honneth's critical theory and assessment practices. Esteem recognition encapsulates the interwoven nature of who we are as individuals and our social belonging. It allows for the recognition of personal achievements, but always also understood in solidarity with the social whole. We rightly feel recognition for our actions or abilities when these contribute positively to a broader good. But both elements, the social and the individual, are tied together and are mutually important. Quite simply, when we ask ourselves the purposes of assessment in higher education, the answer, I believe, should be to enable positive contributions to society and, through this, a sense of both personal and social achievement.

I have used all three dimensions of Honneth's work because I believe that is necessary to safeguard against the problems he sees in other theories, which focus on the known and obvious. When one's gaze is confined to political movements, student groups or organized labour there is considerable territory for injustice left in the blind spots. All of these more public groups are important too, but we must begin our examination back a stage or else injustice may be overlooked.

It is because assessment is so difficult to radically change that I have employed such a challenging theorist as Honneth to help with this project. It is much easier to talk about learning and teaching generally, but when we get onto matters of assessment the stakes seem to change, it seems unthinkable to think too far outside what is already known and accepted. This dilemma has, I suggest, enmeshed some of the excellent scholarship on assessment for learning. This has led to a confused stance on the formative and summative divide, often wrongly associating one with learning and the other – summative – seen as off limits to closer scrutiny or change. Defence of such a conservative position may make recourse to professional bodies and their requirements, arguing that it is not within the power of universities to substantially alter assessment for accreditation. But these professional bodies are themselves made up of graduates, shaped and nurtured by their own experiences of assessment and the ways in which it seemed to relate to professional practice. We need to bring them into the conversation about assessment reform.

Assessment for social justice takes the radical promise of assessment for learning and applies it to the very foundations of assessment in higher education. Honneth's critical theory is important for the ways in which it forces the analysis to burrow down to the fundamental aspects of human, social being. Thus assessment comes to be seen through the lens of genuine human achievement, which is itself also always a social achievement. Mutual recognition underpins all social justice because it speaks to the foundations of what it means to be human and to be recognized as such in the human world. It might, therefore, seem a pretension to link assessment with such a philosophical understanding. It may seem a step too far – after all, assessment is important, but is it *that* important? The answer I believe is yes. Assessment matters too much to be ignored, as I fear it has been by some of the critical pedagogy literature, where it is side-stepped because the possibilities for change seem just too fraught, the chances of success too remote.

The difficulty of change is the reason I have also woven practice theory into my approach to assessment for social justice. As already described, there is something of a shotgun wedding to bring practice theory and critical theory together; their antecedents are rather different. But practice theory offers a practical framework for considering *how* change can occur, not simply what change *should* occur. Moreover, in Schatzki's notion of general understandings we have a strong sense of how cultural context links change and everyday practices. The five general understandings I use to structure Part 2 of this book are offered up to enable change in the cultural foundations of how we approach assessment – why we assess, and why that matters. What I have aimed to do in this book is to emphasize both the profound importance of a changed orientation to assessment and the ways in which this can be achieved. My suggestions for change are intended as both radical and everyday. Honesty, for example, is a weighty concept on many levels, but it can, and should, also be part of our everyday practices. It can shape such practices and help form the teleoaffectives structures that give meaning to what we do.

I do not mean to underestimate how difficult this can be in the context of entrenched quality and managerial practices that prop up the status quo. Such challenges are exacerbated by the ongoing casualization of the academic labour force, understandably leaving some colleagues wary of dissent lest they are punished. But I do believe that critical theory provides us with a powerful vocabulary in which to critique and argue against mainstream practices, while social practice theories provide rigorous insights into how to effect change. To return to the issue of power, what is at stake here is whether we are prepared to accept the disempowerment that comes with acceptance of how things are. As a workforce are we prepared to have the academic role deskilled and marginalized? My argument is that this has social justice implications for us, for our students and for the social world in which we live.

My aim is achievable radical reform. Hence, I have sought to provide examples of practices that are consistent with the values of assessment for social justice, as well as practices that are not. At the base of this achievable radical reform there are two, interlinked questions – what is higher education for and what is assessment within higher education for? It seems obvious but the second question should be answered in terms of the first. At all times when we think about assessment we need to be considering the broader purposes of the university itself: What *are* we trying to achieve? Our higher education institutions continue to have proud claims to social missions and the benefit of the whole society, yet maintain tame and limiting assessment regimes, often in the name of standards. But standards for what? Standards according to whom?

I believe strongly in the claims of assessment for learning, that assessment shapes how and what students learn. But we need to push this understanding further, and link it to social justice commitments, rather than pull up short because assessment cannot be fiddled with because it matters so much. It is because it matters so much that we need a radical rethink. In the higher education context, assessment goes to the heart of mutual recognition. If we are to prepare graduates able to challenge existing recognition regimes and work towards greater social justice, this must begin with how they experience recognition within higher education.

My aim in the second part of this book has been to highlight the general understandings, to use Schatzki's phrase, which would shift the culture, and thereby also practices, of assessment towards greater social justice. In the context of each of these I have used different examples of assessment practices. The interconnections between these are an important aspect to take away from my analysis. Indeed, it is as a web of general understandings that I really mean to make use of these. They all – trust, honesty, responsibility, forgiveness and responsiveness – reinforce one another, and none can be fully realized without the others. Each one forms a particular part of the greater tapestry of assessment for social justice. That they need to be broken apart for analysis is one of the inevitable shortcomings of the linearity of writing.

The importance of assessment in higher education is fairly universally acknowledged, but the implications of such importance are rather more diverse. On one level there is the old mantra – if it matters, measure it. A theme of this book is, not unsurprisingly, a critique of an audit-driven, technocratic approach to either assessment or higher education more generally. Critical pedagogy stands in complete defiance of any such instrumentalism and any moves to reduce the purposes of higher education to a simple technical matter of supporting the prevailing economic system.

Currently assessment turns university learning into a treadmill that students fear falling off of, and never regaining their footing. The relentlessness of some regimes of continuous assessment – brought in with the best of intentions as part of the assessment for learning movement – takes all the space away from our students' learning opportunities: the space for creativity, risk, challenge and subversion. The end result is too often seen as obtaining the grades that will allow one to continue on another treadmill. This institutionalizes, even habitualizes, a form of deep misrecognition. It should be clear, therefore, that I am not suggesting social justice as some easy window dressing for business as usual. Many universities now put claims to social justice, or the public good, within their mission statements. Such claims are then repeated in strategies such as graduate attributes. For these claims to be at all genuine they must reside in the vanguard of higher education's purposes. They must lead and shape the way. And we need to root out the practices and institutional structures that are inconsistent with social justice.

To do this requires asking a lot of questions, and posing those questions from within an understanding of social justice based on lived realities and not simply procedures. Consider the following questions by way of examples:

- Why is the course assessment an exam and an essay?
- Why is it acceptable to be 10 per cent above or below the word length?
- Why do essays have to be in on time?
- Why can we have an extension only for medical reasons?

It is simply not acceptable that the answer to any of these is based on a notion of that is *how the system is*. This must be challenged. Academics and managers must see that the answer to each of these questions is not a purely technical matter but imbued with a sense of what social justice means. So to be clear, what is at issue is not whether any of these examples are right or wrong, but the process of decision-making. If we make these decisions, implement these policies, without a rigorous consideration of what social justice means, then we are unlikely to move towards it. The above questions are illustrative only; there are hundreds of other possible questions to ask. What matters is that we begin to challenge the established status quo by asking such questions and understanding there is no simple answer – all depends on the lens of social justice through which one considers them, and even whether one is aware of that lens at all. Here we return to the distinction in Part 1 between procedural notions of social justice and more critical approaches, and the dominant proceduralism that currently informs practices and decisions. Assessment conventions should not simply be accepted: they need to be interrogated through a critical and complex lens of social justice.

Moreover, our gaze needs to shift from perceiving assessment to be in 'good shape' when all the processes and procedures are in place, to judging it by the lived realities. This emphasis on outcomes should not be confused with some of the more strict aspects of the movement for predetermined learning outcomes. The latter does not genuinely celebrate open and unexpected results, but leads itself into a cul-de-sac by limiting results to only those that can be determined in advance. The radical potential of a social justice perspective based in critical theory demands a broader horizon and a richer sense of choice.

This book offers a particular insight into assessment procedures and practices, a philosophical recasting, which is not intended to work as a lone voice. Instead, my aim is to propose the ways in which we need to think about our assessment practices in terms of greater social justice – and that this can then be used with other assessment scholarship, and work within critical pedagogy, when developing and implementing assessment reform.

Honneth (2010a) refers to the idea of an ethical life 'as a drawn-out process of education'. We can invert this too, such that education is, or should be, a drawn-out ethical process. As such, this refers as much to what academics do with regard to assessment as what students do. It invokes the idea of challenging accepted practices, learning about alternatives and the possibilities of doing things differently. To conform simply for the sake of conforming is to act without responsibility. My aim, therefore, is to not only begin a conversation but also to provide a robust theoretical vocabulary and justification about how assessment might be done differently in order to contribute to greater social justice within and through higher education.

References

Adorno, T. W. (1973). *Negative Dialectics*. London: Routledge and Kegan Paul.

Adorno, T. W. (1991). *Notes to Literature 1*. New York: Columbia University Press.

Adorno, T. W. (2005a). *Critical Models*. New York: Columbia University Press.

Adorno, T. W. (2005b). *Minima Moralia*. London: Verso.

Alexander, J. C., & Lara, M. P. (1996). Honneth's new critical theory of recognition. *New Left Review, 220*, 126–36.

Anderson, J. (2011). Situating Axel Honneth in the Frankfurt School tradition. In D. Petherbridge (Ed.), *Axel Honneth: Critical Essays* (pp. 31–57). Boston and Leiden, Netherlands: Brill.

Barnes, B. (2001). Practice as collective action. In T. R. Schatzki, C. K. Knorr & E. von Savigne (Eds), *The Practice Turn in Contemporary Theory* (pp. 25–36). London: Routledge.

Barnett, R. (2007). *A Will to Learn: Being a Student in an Age of Uncertainty*. Maidenhead, UK: Open University Press.

Batten, J., Batey, J., Shafe, L., Gubby, L., & Birch, P. (2013). The influence of reputation information on the assessment of undergraduate student work. *Assessment & Evaluation in Higher Education, 38*(4), 417–35.

Baty, P. (2007). Trust eroded by blind marking. *Times Higher Education*. Retrieved from https://www.timeshighereducation.com/news/trust-eroded-by-blind-marking/209075.article.

BBC News. (1999). 'Anonymous marking' could prevent discrimination. Retrieved from http://news.bbc.co.uk/1/hi/education/293481.stm.

Bengsten, S., & Barnett, R. (2017). Confronting the dark side of higher education. *Journal of Philosophy of Education, 51*(1), 114–31.

Biggs, J. (2003). *Teaching for Quality Learning at University* (2nd ed.). Buckingham, UK: Society for Research into Higher Education and Open University Press.

Biggs, J., & Tang, C. (2011). *Teaching for Quality Learning at University*. Maidenhead, UK: Open University Press.

Birch, P., Batten, J., & Batey, J. (2015). The influence of student gender on the assessment of undergraduate student work. *Assessment & Evaluation in Higher Education, 41*(7)1–16.

Bloxham, S. (2009). Marking and moderation in the UK: False assumptions and wasted resources. *Assessment & Evaluation in Higher Education, 34*(2), 209–20.

Bloxham, S. (2012). 'You can see the quality in front of your eyes': Grounding academic standards between rationality and interpretation. *Quality in Higher Education, 18*(2), 185–204.

Bloxham, S., & Boyd, P. (2012). Accountability in grading student work: Securing academic standards in a twenty-first century quality assurance context. *British Educational Research Journal, 38*(4), 615–34.

Bloxham, S., den-Outer, B., Hudson, J., & Price, M. (2016). Let's stop the pretence of consistent marking: Exploring the multiple limitations of assessment criteria. *Assessment & Evaluation in Higher Education, 41*(3), 466–81.

Bok, D. (2005). *Universities in the Marketplace*. Princeton, NJ and Oxford: Princeton University Press.

Bols, A. (2012). Student views on assessment. In L. Clouder, C. Broughan, S. Jewell & G. Steventon (Eds), *Improving Student Engagement and Development through Assessment* (pp. 4–18). London: Routledge.

Boud and Associates, D. (2010). *Assessment 2020: Seven Propositions for Assessment Reform in Higher Education*. Sydney: Australian Learning and Teaching Council.

Boud, D. (1995a). Assessment and learning: Contradictory or complementary? In P. Knight (Ed.), *Assessment for Learning* (pp. 35–48). London: Kogan Page.

Boud, D. (1995b). *Enhancing Learning through Self-Assessment*. London: Kogan Page.

Boud, D. (2000). Sustainable assessment: Rethinking assessment for the learning society. *Studies in Continuing Education, 22*(2), 151–67.

Boud, D. (2007). Reframing assessment as if learning were important. In D. Boud & N. Falchikov (Eds), *Rethinking Assessment in Higher Education* (pp. 14–25). Abingdon, UK: Routledge.

Boud, D. (2014). Shifting views of assessment: From secret teachers' business to sustaining learning. In C. Kreber, C. Anderson, N. Entwistle & J. McArthur (Eds), *Advances and Innovations in University Assessment and Feedback* (pp. 13–31). Edinburgh: Edinburgh University Press.

Boud, D., & Falchikov, N. (2006). Aligning assessment with long-term learning. *Assessment & Evaluation in Higher Education, 31*(4), 399–413.

Boud, D., & Falchikov, N. (2007a). Introduction: Assessment for the longer term. In D. Boud & N. Falchikov (Eds), *Rethinking Assessment in Higher Education: Learning for the Longer Term* (pp. 3–25). Abingdon,UK: Routledge.

Boud, D., & Falchikov, N. (Eds). (2007b). *Rethinking Assessment in Higher Education*. Abingdon, UK: Routledge.

Boud, D., & Soler, R. (2016). Sustainable assessment revisited. *Assessment & Evaluation in Higher Education, 41*(3), 400–13..

Boud, D., Cohen, R., & Sampson, J. (1999). Peer learning and assessment. *Assessment & Evaluation in Higher Education, 24*(4), 413–26.

Bourdieu, P. (1977). *Outline of a Theory of Practice*. Cambridge: Cambridge University Press.

Boyd, L. (2014). Exploring the utility of workload models in academe: A pilot study. *Journal of Higher Education Policy and Management, 36*(3), 315–26.

Bradley, C. (1984). Sex bias in the evaluation of students. *British Journal of Social Psychology, 23*, 147–53.

Bradley, C. (1993). Sex bias in student assessment overlooked? *Assessment & Evaluation in Higher Education, 18*(1), 3–8.

Brennan, D. (2008). University student anonymity in the summative assessment of written work. *Higher Education Research & Development, 27*(1), 43–54.

Broad, B. (2000). Pulling your hair out: Crises of standardisation in communal writing assessment. *Research in the Teaching of English, 35*, 213–60.

Broadfoot, P., & Pollard, A. (2000). The changing discourse of assessment policy: The case of English primary education. In A. Filer (Ed.), *Assessment: Social Practice and Social Product* (pp. 11–26). London and New York: Routledge Falmer.

Brodkey, L. (1996). *Writing Permitted in Designated Areas Only*. Minneapolis and London: University of Minnesota Press.

Brookfield, S. (2005). *The Power of Critical Theory for Adult Learning and Teaching*. Maidenhead, UK: Open University Press.

Broughan, C., & Grantham, D. (2012). Helping them succeed: The staff-student relationship. In L. Clouder, C. Brougham, S. Jewell & G. Steventon (Eds), *Improving Student Engagement and Development through Assessment* (pp. 45–58). London: Routledge.

Brown, S., & Knight, P. (1994). *Assessing Learners in Higher Education*. London: Kogan Page.

Bruton, S., & Childers, D. (2016). The ethics and politics of policing plagiarism: A qualitative study of faculty views on student plagiarism and Turnitin®. *Assessment & Evaluation in Higher Education, 41*(2), 316–30..

Carless, D. (2006). Differing perceptions in the feedback process. *Studies in Higher Education, 31*(2), 219–33.

Carless, D. (2009). Trust, distrust and their impact on assessment reform. *Assessment & Evaluation in Higher Education, 34*(1), 79–89.

Carless, D. (2015). *Excellence in University Assessment*. London and New York: Routledge.

Carvalho, A. (2013). Students' perceptions of fairness in peer assessment: Evidence from a problem-based learning course. *Teaching in Higher Education, 18*(5), 491–505.

Clarkeburn, H., & Kettula, K. (2012). Fairness and using reflective journals in assessment. *Teaching in Higher Education, 17*(4), 439–52.

Cook, A. (2001). Assessing the use of flexible assessment. *Assessment & Evaluation in Higher Education, 26*(6), 539–49.

Crossman, J. (2007). The role of relationships and emotions in student perceptions of learning and assessment. *Higher Education Research and Development, 26*(3), 313–27.

Czerniawski, G. (2012). Repositioning trust: A challenge to inauthentic neoliberal uses of pupil voice. *Management in Education, 26*(3), 130–9.

Davis, A. (2009). Examples as method? My attempts to understand assessment and fairness (in the spirit of the later Wittgenstein). *Journal of Philosophy of Education, 43*(3), 371–89.

DBIS. (2015). *Fulfilling Our Potential: Teaching Excellence, Social Mobility and Student Choice.* Sheffield: Department of Business, Skills and Innovation (DBIS).

Deeley, S. J., & Bovill, C. (2017). Student-staff partnership in assessment: Enhancing assessment literacy through democratic practices. *Assessment & Evaluation in Higher Education, 42*(3), 463–77.

Deneen, C., & Boud, D. (2014). Patterns of resistance in managing assessment change. *Assessment & Evaluation in Higher Education, 39*(5), 577–91.

Earl-Novell, S. (2001). 'Gendered' styles of writing and the 'inequality in assessment' hypothesis: An explanation for gender differentiation in first class academic achievement at university. *The International Journal of Sociology and Social Policy, 21*(1/2), 160–72.

Ecclestone, K. (1999). Empowring or ensnaring?: The implications of outcome-based assessment in higher education. *Higher Education Quarterly, 53*(1), 29–48.

Ecclestone, K. (2001). 'I know a 2:1 when I see it': Understanding criteria for degree classifications in franchised university programmes. *Journal of Further and Higher Education, 25*(3), 301–13.

Eisner, E. W. (1985). *The Art of Educational Evaluation: A Personal View.* London and Philadelphia: Falmer Press.

Elton, L. (2004a). A challenge to established assessment practice. *Higher Education Quarterly, 58*(1), 43–62.

Elton, L. (2004b). Should classification of the UK honours degree have a future? *Assessment & Evaluation in Higher Education, 29*(4), 415–22.

Entwistle, N. (1991). Approaches to learning and perceptions of the learning environment: Introduction to the special issue. *Higher Education, 22*, 201–4.

Eraut, M. (1997). Curriculum frameworks and assumptions in 14–19 education. *Research in Post-Compulsory Education, 2*(3), 281–98.

Falchikov, N. (1986). Product comparisons and process benefits of collaborative peer group and self assessments. *Assessment & Evaluation in Higher Education, 11*(2), 146–65.

Falchikov, N., & Boud, D. (2007). Assessment and emotion: The impact of being assessed. In D. Boud & N. Falchikov (Eds), *Rethinking Assessment in Higher Education* (pp. 144–55). Abingdon, UK: Routledge.

Flint, N. R., & Johnson, B. (2011). *Towards Fairer University Assessment: Recognising the Concerns of Students.* Abingdon, UK: Routledge.

Flores, M. A., Veiga Simão, A. M., Barros, A., & Pereira, D. (2015). Perceptions of effectiveness, fairness and feedback of assessment methods: A study in higher education. *Studies in Higher Education, 40*(9), 1523–34.

Fraser, N. (2003). Distorted beyond all reconition: A rejoinder to Axel Honneth. In N. Fraser & A. Honneth (Eds), *Redistribution or Recognition?: A Political–Philosophical Exchange* (pp. 198–236). London: Verso.

Fraser, N., & Honneth, A. (2003). *Redistribution or Recognition?: A Political–Philosohical Exchange*. London: Verso.

Freire, P. (1996). *Pedagogy of the Oppressed*. London: Penguin.

Giddens, A. (1984). *The Constitution of Society*. Cambridge: Polity Press.

Goehr, L. (2005). *Reviewing Adorno: Public Opinion and Critique – Introduction to Adorno's Critical Models*. New York: Columbia University Press.

Greene, M. (1995). *Releasing the Imagination: Essay on Education, the Arts, and Social Change*. San Francisco: Jossey-Bass.

Guardian. (20 May 2016). Dear Student, I just don't have time to mark your essay properly. https://www.theguardian.com/higher-education-network/2016/may/20/dear-student-i-just-dont-have-time-to-mark-your-essay-properly. Retrieved from https://www.theguardian.com/higher-education-network/2016/may/20/dear-student-i-just-dont-have-time-to-mark-your-essay-properly.

Haber, S. (2007). Recognition, justice and social pathologies in Axel Honneth's recent writings. *Revista de ciencia política (Santiago), 27*(2).

Hardarson, A. (2017). Aims of education: How to resist the temptation of technocratic models. *Journal of Philosophy of Education, 51*(1), 59–72.

Harland, T., McLean, A., Wass, R., Miller, E., & Sim, K. N. (2015). An assessment arms race and its fallout: High-stakes grading and the case for slow scholarship. *Assessment & Evaluation in Higher Education, 40*(4), 528–41.

Harries, T., & Rettie, R. (2016). Walking as a social practice: Dispersed walking and the organisation of everyday practices. *Sociology of Health and Illness, 38*(6), 874–83.

Hauer, K. E., ten Cate, O., Boscardin, C., Irby, D. M., Iobst, W., & Sullivan, P. S. (2014). Understanding trust as an essential element of trainee supervision and learning in the workplace. *Advances in Health Sciences Education, 19*(3), 435–56.

HEFCE. (2010). National Student Survey: Findings and Trends 2006–2009.

Hemer, S. R. (2014). Finding time for quality teaching: An ethnographic study of academic workloads in the social sciences and their impact on teaching practices. *Higher Education Research and Development, 33*(3), 483–95.

Honneth, A. (1996). *Struggle for Recognition*. Cambridge: Polity Press.

Honneth, A. (2001). Recognition: Invisibility: On the epistemology of 'recognition': Axel Honneth. *Aristotelian Society Supplementary Volume, 75*(1), 111–26.

Honneth, A. (2003a). The point of recognition: A rejoinder to the rejoinder. In N. Fraser & A. Honneth (Eds), *Redistribution or Recognition: A Political–Philosophical Exchange* (pp. 237–67). London: Verso.

Honneth, A. (2003b). Redistribution as recognition: A response to Nancy Fraser. In N. Fraser & A. Honneth (Eds), *Redistribution or Recognition? A Political–Philosophical Exchange* (pp. 110–97). London: Verso.

Honneth, A. (2004a). Organised self-realization: Some paradoxes of individualization. *European Journal of Social Theory, 7*(4), 463–78.

Honneth, A. (2004b). Recognition and justice: Outline of a plural theory of justice. *Acta sociologica [Norway], 47*(4), 351–64.

Honneth, A. (2009). *Pathologies of Reason.* New York: Columbia University Press.

Honneth, A. (2010a). *The Pathologies of Individual Freedom: Hegel's Social Theory.* Princeton and Oxford: Princeton University Press.

Honneth, A. (2010b). The political identity of the green movement in Germany: Social-philosophical reflections. *Critical Horizons, 11*(1), 5–18.

Honneth, A. (2014a). *Freedom's Right: The Social Foundations of Democratic Life.* Cambridge: Polity Press.

Honneth, A. (2014b). *The I in We: Studies in the Theory of Recognition.* Cambridge: Polity Press.

Horkheimer, M. (1995). *Critical Theory: Selected Essays.* New York: Continuum.

Horkheimer, M., & Adorno, T. W. (1997). *The Dialectic of Enlightenment.* London: Continuum.

Hounsell, D. (2003). Student feedback, learning and development. In M. Slowey & D. Watson (Eds), *Higher Education and the Lifecourse* (pp. 67–78). Maidenhead, UK: Society for Research into Higher Education and Open University Press.

Hounsell, D. (2007). Towards more sustainable feedback to students. In D. Boud & N. Falchikov (Eds), *Rethinking Assesment in Higher Education* (pp. 101–13). Abingdon, UK: Routledge.

Hounsell, D., McCune, V., Hounsell, J., & Litjens, J. (2008). The quality of guidance and feedback to students. *Higher Education Research & Development, 27*(1), 55–67.

Howard, R. M. (2007). Understanding 'internet plagiarism'. *Computers and Composition, 24*(1), 3–15.

Hughes, C., & Barrie, S. (2010). Influences on the assessment of graduate attributes in higher education. *Assessment & Evaluation in Higher Education, 35*(3), 325–34.

Hughes, G. (2011). Towards a personal best: A case for introducing ipsative Assessment in higher education. *Studies in Higher Education, 36*(3), 353–67.

Hughes, G. (2014). *Ipsative Assessment: Motivation through Marking Progress.* London: Palgrave Macmillan.

Hughes, G. (2017). Introducing ipsative assessment and personal learning gain. In G. Hughes (Ed.), *Ipsative Assessment and Personal Learning Gain.* London: Palgrave Macmillan.

Hui, A., Schatzki, T. R., & Shove, E. (2017). Introduction. In A. Hui, T. R. Schatzki, & E. Shove (Eds), *The Nexus of Practices: Connections, Constellations, Practitioners* (pp. 1–7). Abingdon, UK: Routledge.

Huttunen, R. (2007). Critical adult education and the political–philosophical debate between Nancy Fraser and Axel Honneth. *Educational Theory, 57*(4), 423–33.

Huxham, M., Hunter, M., McIntyre, A., Shilland, R., & McArthur, J. (2015). Student and teacher co-navigation of a course: Following the natural lines of academic enquiry. *Teaching in Higher Education, 20*(5), 530–41.

Iannone, P., & Simpson, A. (2015). Students' views of oral performance assessment in mathematics: Straddling the 'assessment of' and 'assessment for' learning divide. *Assessment & Evaluation in Higher Education, 40*(7), 971–87.

Ikäheimo, H., & Laitinen, A. (2010). Analyzing recognition: Identification, acknowledgement, and recognitive attitudes towards persons. In B. Van den Brink (Ed.), *Recognition and Power: Axel Honneth and the Tradition of Critical Social Theory* (pp. 33–56). Cambridge: Cambridge University Press.

Iorio, G., Campello, F., & Honneth, A. (2013). Love, society and agape: An interview with Axel Honneth. *European Journal of Social Theory, 16*(2), 246–58.

Jackson, C. (2006). *Lads and Ladettes in School: Gender and a Fear of Failure*. Maidenhead, UK: Open University Press.

Jackson, C. (2010). Fear in education. *Educational Review, 62*(1), 39–52.

James, D. (2000). Making the graduate: Perspectives on student experience of assessment in higher education. In A. Filer (Ed.), *Assessment: Social Practice and Social Product* (pp. 151–67). London and New York: Routledge Falmer.

Jay, M. (1996). *The Dialectical Imagination*. Berkeley and Los Angeles: University of California Press.

Jones, A. (2009). Generic attributes as espoused theory: The importance of context. *Higher Education, 58*(2), 175–91.

Jones, A. (2013). There is nothing generic about graduate attributes: Unpacking the scope of context. *Journal of Further and Higher Education, 37*(5), 591–605.

Kelly, E. (2001). Editor's Foreword. In J. Rawls (Ed.), *Justice as Fairness: A Restatement* (pp. xi–xiii). Cambridge, MA: Belknap Press of Harvard University Press.

Kelly, P. (1998). Contractarian social justice: An overview of some contemporary debates. In D. Boucher & P. Kelly (Eds), *Social Justice: From Hume to Walzer* (pp. 181–99). London and New York: Routledge.

Kenny, J. D. J., & Fluck, A. E. (2014). The effectiveness of academic workload models in an institution: A staff perspective. *Journal of Higher Education Policy and Management, 36*(6), 585–602.

Knight, P. (1995). Introduction. In P. Knight (Ed.), *Assessment for Learning in Higher Education* (pp. 13–23). London: Kogan Page.

Knight, P. (2000). The value of a programme-wide approach to assessment. *Assessment & Evaluation in Higher Education, 25*(3), 237–51.

Knight, P. (2002). Summative assessment in higher education: Practices in disarray. *Studies in Higher Education, 27*(3), 275–86.

Knight, P. (2006). The local practices of assessment. *Assessment & Evaluation in Higher Education, 31*(4), 435–52.

Lave, J., & Wenger, E. (1991). *Situated Learning*. Cambridge: Cambridge University Press.

Leathwood, C. (2005). Assessment policy and practice in higher education: Purpose, standards and equity. *Assessment & Evaluation in Higher Education, 30*(3), 307–24.

Lovett, F. (2011). *Rawls's 'A Theory of Justice'*. London: Bloomsbury.

Lum, G. (2012). Two concepts of assessment. *Journal of Philosophy of Education, 46*(4), 589–602.

Maclellan, E. (2001). Assessment for learning: The differing perceptions of tutors and students. *Assessment & Evaluation in Higher Education, 26*(4), 307–18.

Malcolm, J., & Zukas, M. (2009). Making a mess of academic work: Experience, purpose and identity. *Teaching in Higher Education, 14*(5), 495–506.

Malouff, J. M., Stein, S. J., Bothma, L. N., Coulter, K., & Emmerton, A. J. (2014). Preventing halo bias in grading the work of university students. *Cogent Psychology, 1*(1).

Marcelo, G. (2013). Recognition and critical theory today: An interview with Axel Honneth. *Philosophy and Social Criticism, 39*(2), 209–21.

Maringe, F., & Gibbs, P. (2009). *Marketing Higher Education: Theory and Practice.* Maidenhead, UK: Open University Press.

Marsh, B. (2004). Turnitin.com and the scriptural enterprise of plagiarism detection. *Computers and Composition, 21*(4), 427–38.

McArthur, J. (2010). Achieving social justice within and through higher education: The challenge for critical pedagogy. *Teaching in Higher Education, 15*(5), 493–504.

McArthur, J. (2011). Reconsidering the social and economic purposes of higher education. *Higher Education Research & Development, 30*(6), 737–49.

McArthur, J. (2012). Against standardised experience: Leaving our marks on the palimpsests of disciplinary knowledge. *Teaching in Higher Education, 17*(4), 485– 96.

McArthur, J. (2013). *Rethinking Knowledge in Higher Education: Adorno and Social Justice.* London: Bloomsbury.

McArthur, J. (2014). The learning-feedback-assessment Triumvirate: Reconsidering failure in pursuit of social justice. In C. Kreber, C. Anderson, N. Entwistle & J. McArthur (Eds), *Advances and Innovations in University Assessment and Feedback* (pp. 173–94). Edinburgh: Edinburgh University Press.

McArthur, J., & Huxham, M. (2011). Sharing control: A partnership approach to curriculum design and delivery, ESCalate, Higher Education Academy Education Subject Centre. Retrieved from http://www-new1.heacademy.ac.uk/assets/documents/studentengagement/Edinburgh-2011-student-engagement2.doc. York, UK: Higher Education Academy.

McArthur, J., & Huxham, M. (2013). Feedback unbound: From master to usher. In S. Merry, D. Carless, M. Price, & M. Taras (Eds), *Reconceptualising Feedback in Higher Education.* London: Routledge.

McArthur, J., Huxham, M., Hounsell, J., & Warsop, C. (2011). Tipping out the boot grit: The use of on-going feedback devices to enhance feedback dialogue, ESCalate, Higher Education Academy Education Subject Centre. Retrieved from http://escalate.ac.uk/7686.

McConlogue, T. (2012). But is it fair? Developing students' understanding of grading complex written work through peer assessment. *Assessment & Evaluation in Higher Education, 37*(1), 113–23.

McKeever, L. (2006). Online plagiarism detection services – saviour or scourge? *Assessment & Evaluation in Higher Education, 31*(2), 155–65.

McLean, M. (2006). *Pedagogy and the University*. London and New York: Continuum.

McLean, M., Abbas, A., & Ashwin, P. (2013). A Bernsteinian view of learning and teaching undergraduate sociology-based social science. *Enhancing Learning in the Social Sciences, 5*(2), 32–44.

Morgan, A. (2014). The happiness turn: Axel Honneth, self-reification and 'sickness unto health'. *Subjectivity, 7*(3), 219–33.

Nesbit, P. L., & Burton, S. (2006). Student justice perceptions following assignment feedback. *Assessment & Evaluation in Higher Education, 31*(6), 655–70.

Nicolini, D. (2012). *Practice Theory, Work, & Organization*. Oxford: Oxford University Press.

Nordberg, D. (2008). Group projects: more learning? Less fair? A conundrum in assessing postgraduate business education. *Assessment & Evaluation in Higher Education, 33*(5), 481–92.

Norton, L. (2004). Using assessment criteria as learning criteria: A case study in psychology. *Assessment & Evaluation in Higher Education, 29*(6), 687–702.

NUS. (2008). Mark my words, not my name. Retrieved from http://www.nus.org.uk/en/news/mark-my-words-not-my-name/.

Nussbaum, M. C. (2006). *Frontiers of Justice*. Cambridge, MA: Belknap Press of Harvard University Press.

Nussbaum, M. C. (2011). *Creating Capabilities*. Cambridge, MA: Belknap Press of Harvard University Press.

O'Neill, M., & Williamson, T. (2012). Introduction. In M. O'Neill & T. Williamson (Eds), *Property-Owning Democracy: Rawls and beyond* (pp. 1–14). Chichester: Wiley-Blackwell.

Orr, S. (2010). Collaborating or fight for the marks? Students' experiences of group work assessment in the creative arts. *Assessment & Evaluation in Higher Education, 35*(3), 301–13.

Owen, C., Stefaniak, J., & Corrigan, G. (2010). Marking identifiable scripts: Following up student concerns. *Assessment & Evaluation in Higher Education, 35*(1), 33–40.

Pabian, P. (2015). Why 'cheating' research is wrong: New departures for the study of student copying in higher education. *Higher Education, 69*, 809–21.

Parker, J. (2005). A Mise-en-Scène for the Theatrical University. In R. Barnett (Ed.), *Reshaping the University* (pp. 151–64). Maidenhead, UK: Open University Press.

Penketh, C., & Beaumont, C. (2014). 'Turnitin said it wasn't happy': Can the regulatory discourse of plagiarism detection operate as a change artefact for writing development? *Innovations in Education and Teaching International, 51*(1), 95.

Petersen, A., & Willig, R. (2002). An interview with Axel Honneth: The role of sociology in the Theory of Recognition. *European Journal of Social Theory, 5*(2), 265–77.

Proud, S. (2015). Resits in higher education: Merely a bar to jump over, or do they give a pedagogical 'e.g. up'? *Assessment & Evaluation in Higher Education, 40*(5), 681–97.

Proust, M. (2006). *Remembrance of Things Past, volume 2*. Ware, UK: Wordsworth Editions, I first found this quote through Rowland, S. (2006). *The Enquiring University*, Maidenhead, UK: Society for Research into Higher Education and Open University Press.

QAA. (2016). Assessment of students and the recognition of prior learning. In *UK Quality Code for Higher Education*. Gloucester: Quality Assurance Agency for Higher Education.

Rawls, J. (1971). *A Theory of Justice*. Cambridge, MA: Belknap Press of Harvard University Press.

Rawls, J. (2001). *Justice as Fairness: A Restatement*. Cambridge, MA: Belknap Press of Harvard University Press.

Reckwitz, A. (2002). Toward a theory of social practices: A development in culturalist theorizing. *European Journal of Social Theory, 5*(2), 243–63.

Richardson, P. W. (2004). Reading and writing from textbooks in higher education: A case study from economics. *Studies in Higher Education, 29*(4), 505–21.

Rose, N. (1997). Assembling the modern self. In R. Porter (Ed.), *Rewriting the Self: Histories from the Renaissance to the Present* (pp. 224–48). London and New York: Routledge.

Rossler, B. (2010). Work, recognition, emancipation. In B. van den Brink & D. Owen (Eds), *Recognition and Power: Axel Honneth and the Tradition of Critical Social Theory* (pp. 135–63). Cambridge: Cambridge University Press.

Rowland, S. (2000). *The Enquiring University Teacher*. Buckingham, UK: Society for Research into Higher Education and Open University Press.

Rust, C., Price, M., & O'Donovan, B. (2003). Improving students' learning by developing their understanding of assessment criteria and processes. *Assessment & Evaluation in Higher Education, 28*(2), 147–64.

Sadler, D. R. (1987). Specifying and promulgating achievement standards. *Oxford Review of Education, 13*, 191–209.

Sadler, D. R. (1989). Formative assessment and the design of instructional systems. *Instructional Science, 18*(2), 119–44.

Sadler, D. R. (2002). Ah! … So that's 'quality'. In P. Schwartz & G. Webb (Eds), *Assessment: Case Studies, Experience and Practice from Higher Education* (pp. 130–6). London: Kogan Page.

Sadler, D. R. (2005). Interpretations of criteria-based assessment and grading in higher education. *Assessment & Evaluation in Higher Education, 30*(2), 175–94.

Sadler, D. R. (2007). Perils in the meticulous specification of goals and assessment criteria. *Assessment in Education: Principles, Policy & Practice, 14*(3), 387–92.

Sadler, D. R. (2009). Indeterminacy in the use of preset criteria for assessment and grading. *Assessment & Evaluation in Higher Education, 34*(2), 159–79.

Sadler, D. R. (2010a). Beyond feedback: Developing student capability in complex appraisal. *Assessment & Evaluation in Higher Education, 35*(5), 535–50.

Sadler, D. R. (2010b). Fidelity as a precondition for integrity in grading academic achievement. *Assessment & Evaluation in Higher Education, 35*(6), 727–43.

Sadler, D. R. (2011). Academic freedom, achievement standards and professional identity. *Quality in Higher Education, 17*(1), 85–100.

Sadler, D. R. (2014a). The futility of attempting to codify academic achievement standards. *Higher education: The International Journal of Higher Education and Educational Planning, 67*(3), 273–88.

Sadler, D. R. (2014b). Learning from assessment events: The role of goal knowledge. In C. Kreber, C. Anderson, N. Entwistle & J. McArthur (Eds), *Advances and Innovations in University Assessment and Feedback* (pp. 152–72). Edinburgh: Edinburgh University Press.

Sambell, K., & McDowell, L. (1998). The construction of the hidden curriculum: Messages and meanings in the assessment of student learning. *Assessment & Evaluation in Higher Education, 23*(4), 391–402.

Sambell, K., McDowell, L., & Brown, S. (1997). "But is it fair?": An exploratory study of student perceptions of the consequential validity of assessment. *Studies in Educational Evaluation, 23*(4), 349–71.

Sambell, K., McDowell, L., & Montgomery, C. (2013). *Assessment for Learning in Higher Education*. London and New York: Routledge.

Sandberg, F., & Kubiak, C. (2013). Recognition of prior learning, self-realisation and identity within Axel Honneth's theory of recognition. *Studies in Continuing Education, 35*(3), 351–65.

Schatzki, T. R. (1996). *Social Practices: A Wittgensteinian Approach to Human Activity and the Social*. Cambridge: Cambridge University Press.

Schatzki, T. R. (2001a). Introduction: Practice theory. In T. R. Schatzki, K. Knorr Cetina & E. von Savigny (Eds), *The Practice Turn in Contemporary Theory* (pp. 1–14). Abingdon, UK: Routledge.

Schatzki, T. R. (2001b). Practice mind-ed orders. In T. R. Schatzki, K. Knorr Cetina & E. von Savigny (Eds), *The Practice Turn in Contemporary Theory* (pp. 42–55). Abingdon, UK: Routledge.

Schatzki, T. R. (2002). *The Site of the Social: A Philosophical Account of the Constitution of Social Life and Change*: University Park: Pennsylvania State University Press.

Schatzki, T. R. (2005). The sites of organisations. *Organization Studies, 26*(3), 465–84.

Schatzki, T. R. (2010). *The Timespace of Human Activity: On performance, Society, and History as Intermediate Teleological Events*. Lanham, MD: Lexington Books.

Schatzki, T. R. (2013). A primer on practices. In J. Higgs, R. Barnett, S. Billett, M. Hutchings & F. Trede (Eds), *Practice-Based Education: Perspectives and Strategies* (pp. 13–26). Rotterdam: Sense Publishers.

Sen, A. (2007). *Identity and Violence*. London: Penguin.

Sen, A. (2010). *The Idea of Justice*. London: Penguin.

Sharp, K., & Earle, S. (2000). Assessment, disability and the problem of compensation. *Assessment & Evaluation in Higher Education, 25*(2), 191–9.

Shay, S. (2004). The assessment of complex performance: A socially situated interpretive act. *Harvard Educational Review, 74*(3), 307–29.

Shay, S. (2008). Beyond social constructivist perspectives on assessment: The centring of knowledge. *Teaching in Higher Education, 13*(5), 595–605.

Shore, C., & Wright, S. (2000). Coercive accountability: The rise of audit culture in higher education. In M. Strathern (Ed.), *Audit Cultures: Anthropological Studies in Accountability, Ethics and the Academy* (pp. 57–89). Abingdon, UK: Routledge.

Shove, E., Pantzar, M., & Watson, M. (2012). *The Dynamics of Social Practice: Everyday Life and How It Changes*. London: Sage.

Simonite, V. (2003). The impact of coursework on degree classifications and the performance of individual students. *Assessment & Evaluation in Higher Education, 28*(5), 459–70.

Smithers, R. (1999). NUS claims racial bias in exams. Retrieved from http://www.theguardian.com/uk/1999/mar/10/rebeccasmithers.

Stefani, L. J. (1998). Assessment in Partnership with Learners. *Assessment & Evaluation in Higher Education, 23*(4), 339–50.

Stowell, M. (2004). Equity, justice and standards: Assessment decision making in higher education. *Assessment & Evaluation in Higher Education, 29*(4), 495–510.

Stowell, M., Falahee, M., & Woolf, H. (2016). Academic standards and regulatory frameworks: Necessary compromises? *Assessment & Evaluation in Higher Education, 41*(4), 515–31.

Strathern, M. (2000). New accountabilities: Anthropological studies in audit, ethics and the academy. In M. Strathern (Ed.), *Audit Cultures: Anthropological Studies in Accountability, Ethics and the Academy* (pp. 1–18). Abingdon, UK: Routledge.

Swann, J. (1997). How can we make better plans? *Higher Education Review, 30*(1), 37–53.

Taras, M. (2002). Using assessment for learning and learning from assessment. *Assessment & Evaluation in Higher Education, 27*(6), 501–10.

Taras, M. (2008). Assessment for learning: Sectarian divisions of terminology and concepts. *Journal of Further and Higher Education, 32*(4), 389–97.

Tau, B. (2010). Turnitin.com turns profit on students' work. *The Georgetown Voice*. Retrieved from http://georgetownvoice.com/2010/03/25/turnitin-com-turns-profit-on-students%E2%80%99-work/.

Toniolatti, E. (2009). From critique to reconstruction: On Axel Honneth's Theory of Recognition and its critical potential. *Critical Horizons, 10*(3), 371–90.

Trowler, P. (2008). *Cultures and Change in Higher Education*. Basingstoke and New York: Palgrave Macmillan.

Trowler, P., Saunders, M., & Bamber, V. (2009). Enhancement theories. In V. Bamber, P. Trowler, M. Saunders & P. Knight (Eds), *Enhancing Learning, Teaching,*

Assessment and Curriculum in Higher Education: Theory, Cases, Practices (pp. 7–15). Maidenhead, UK: Society for Research into Higher Education and Open University Press.

Turnitin®. (2014). iParadigms acquires Ephorus to support international expansion. Retrieved from http://turnitin.com/en_us/about-us/media-center/press/item/iparadigms-acquires-ephorus-to-support-international-expansion.

Turnitin®. (2015a). Global study by Turnitin shows 30 percent drop in unoriginal writing in higher education; Digital feedback tools grow by triple digits. Retrieved from http://turnitin.com/en_us/about-us/media-center/press/item/global-study-by-turnitin-shows-30-percent-drop-in-unoriginal-writing-in-higher-education.

Turnitin®. (2015b). Turnitin makes two executirve appointments to support product expansion and global growth. Retrieved from http://turnitin.com/en_us/about-us/media-center/press/item/turnitin-makes-two-executive-appointments-to-support-product-expansion-and-global-growth.

University of Toronto Students' Union. (n.d.). Turnitin.com. Retrieved from http://www.utsu.ca/turnitin/.

Voice, P. (2011). *Rawls Explained: From Fairness to Utopia*. Chicago and La Salle, IL: Open Court.

Vy, T. T., & Dall'Alba, G. (2014). Authentic assessment for student learning: An ontological conception. *Educational Philosophy and Theory, 46*(7), 778–91.

Warin, J. (2010). *Stories of Self: Tracking Children's Identity and Wellbeing through the School Years*. Stoke-on-Trent, UK and Sterling, USA: Trentham Books.

Welch, D., & Warde, A. (2017). How should we understand general understandings? In A. Hui, T. R. Schatzki & E. Shove (Eds), *The Nexus of Practices* (pp. 183–96). Abingdon, UK: Routledge.

Wenger, E. (1998). *Communities of Practice*. Cambridge: Cambridge University Press.

Willig, R. (2012). Grammatology of modern recognition orders: An interview with Axel Honneth. *Distinktion: Scandinavian Journal of Social Theory, 13*(1), 145–9.

Wilson, M. J., Diao, M. M., & Huang, L. (2015). 'I'm not here to learn how to mark someone else's stuff': An investigation of an online peer-to-peer review workshop tool. *Assessment & Evaluation in Higher Education, 40*(1), 15–32.

Winch, C. (2002). Work, well-being and vocational education: The ethical significance of work and preparation for work. *Journal of Applied Philosophy, 19*(3), 261–71.

Woelert, P., & Yates, L. (2015). Too little and too much trust: Performance measurement in Australian higher education. *Critical Studies in Education, 56*(2), 175–89.

Worth, N. (2014). Student-focused assessment criteria: Thinking through best practice. *Journal of Geography in Higher Education, 38*(3), 361–72.

Yorke, M. (2008). *Grading Student Achievement in Higher Education: Signals and Shortcomings*. New York: Routledge.

Yorke, M., Woolf, H., Stowell, M., Allen, R., Haines, C., Redding, M., Scurry, D., Taylor-Russel, G., Turnbull, W., & Walker, L. (2008). Enigmatic variations: Honours degree assessment regulations in the UK. *Higher Education Quarterly, 62*(3), 157–80.

Young, M. (2008). *Bringing Knowledge Back in*. London and New York: Routledge.

Zaher, R. (2012). Democracy in the Israeli education system: The case of the English matriculation exam. *Intercultural Education, 23*(6), 527–40.

Zurn, C. (2015). *Axel Honneth*. Cambridge: Polity Press.

Index